INTRODUCTION TO CLASSICAL LEGAL RHETORIC

To my wife, Barbara, for her love, support, insights and patience

Introduction to Classical Legal Rhetoric:
A Lost Heritage

MICHAEL H. FROST
Southwestern University School of Law, USA

Routledge
Taylor & Francis Group

LONDON AND NEW YORK

First published 2005 by Ashgate Publishing

Published 2016 by Routledge
2 Park Square, Milton Park, Abingdon, Oxfordshire OX14 4RN
711 Third Avenue, New York, NY 10017, USA

First issued in paperback 2016

Routledge is an imprint of the Taylor & Francis Group, an informa business

British Library Cataloguing in Publication Data
Frost, Michael H., 1941-
    Introduction to classical legal rhetoric : a lost heritage.
    - (Applied legal philosophy)
    1. Law - Language 2. Rhetoric, Ancient
    I. Title
    340.1'4

Library of Congress Cataloging-in-Publication Data
Frost, Michael H., 1941-
    Introduction to classical legal rhetoric : a lost heritage / by Michael H. Frost.
       p. cm. -- (Applied legal philosophy)
    Includes bibliographical references and index.
    ISBN 0-7546-2413-7
  1. Law--Language. 2. Rhetoric, Ancient. I. Title. II. Series.

    K213.F76 2005
    340'.14--dc22

2004021464

ISBN 13: 978-1-138-24901-1 (pbk)
ISBN 13: 978-0-7546-2413-4 (hbk)

Contents

Preface

Greco-Roman legal rhetoric is once again taking center stage in the study of legal discourse. As the original art of persuasion, classical legal rhetoric has attracted the attention of prominent thinkers, advocates, and teachers throughout its checkered history. Early in that history, influential figures like Aristotle, Cicero and Quintilian all wrote voluminously on the topic because they saw the need for a systematic, comprehensive introduction to the art of public discourse.

Until recently, however, the study of Greco-Roman legal rhetoric had been largely neglected or altogether forgotten by legal scholars, attorneys and law students. This is unfortunate because it is the original source and a historical reference point for modern analyses of legal reasoning, methods and strategy. Anyone who studies the classical treatises soon discovers that, with some adaptations for modern taste and modern legal practice, the classical rhetorical principles are as applicable today as they were 2500 years ago. Moreover, the classical authors provide what modern lawyers frequently lack: a clear, experience-based, theoretical framework for analyzing and creating legal arguments. They also provide an exhaustive analysis of the roles that emotion and lawyer credibility play in legal argument.

The classical treatises offer detailed, practical advice on almost every aspect of legal discourse and the practice of law, covering everything from lawyer-client relationships to the smallest details of trial lore. They explain how to educate a lawyer, identify a legal issue, prepare a case for trial, and present legal arguments. In short, they are unequaled sources of wisdom on advocacy in all its various forms.

They are especially useful to anyone interested in the long-standing links between the law and other intellectual disciplines. Historically, classical rhetoric has always been closely associated with philosophy, history, and linguistics, but it has an especially close association with the law.

This book describes a rich tradition that began with Greek and Roman rhetoricians of the classical period and shows how that tradition is connected to modern legal rhetoric. For beginning law students, it provides a historically-based, wide-ranging introduction to legal analysis and argument. For experienced attorneys, teachers and judges, it provides new insights into familiar material.

Chapter One traces the creation and evolution of legal rhetoric from its Greco-Roman beginnings to the present day. Chapter Two compares classical and modern methods of analyzing legal problems. Chapter Three describes the classically-approved, five-part structure for legal arguments and applies its principles to modern appellate briefs. Chapter Four examines the complex relationships between legal argument, lawyer credibility and emotion from both classical and modern perspectives. Chapters Five and Six use classical stylistic criteria to analyze the impact that sentence-level writing style has on legal argument. Chapter Six also applies selected classical principles of style to appellate briefs. Chapter Seven applies all the previously described rhetorical principles to a judicial opinion from the U.S. Supreme Court.

Acknowledgments

I wish to thank the editors of several journals for permission to reprint parts of previously published articles. Under the following titles, portions of this book first appeared in the following journals: '*Justice Scalia's Rhetoric of Dissent: A Greco-Roman Analysis of Scalia's Advocacy in the VMI Case*,' 91 Kentucky Law Journal 167 (2002-2003); '*Introduction to Classical Legal Rhetoric: A Lost Heritage*,' 8 Southern California Interdisciplinary Law Journal 613 (1999); '*Greco-Roman Analysis of Metaphoric Reasoning*,' 2 Journal of Legal Writing: The Journal of the Legal Writing Institute 113 (1996); '*Ethos, Pathos*, and Legal Audience,' 99 Dickinson Law Review 85 (1994); '*Greco-Roman Legal Analysis: The Topics of Invention*,' 66 St. John's Law Review 107 (1992) and '*Brief Rhetoric: A Note of Classical and Modern Theories of Forensic Discourse*,' 38 University of Kansas Law Review 411 (1990).

Unless otherwise indicated, quotations from Aristotle's *Rhetoric* are from Cooper, L., translator, *The Rhetoric of Aristotle* © 1960. Reprinted by permission of Pearson Education, Inc., Upper Saddle River, New Jersey.

Quotations from the multi-volume works of Cicero are reprinted by permission of the publishers and the Trustees of the Loeb Classical Library from Cicero: II, *De Inventione*, Loeb Classical Library, Vol. 386, translated by H.M. Hubbell, Cambridge, Mass.: Harvard University Press, 1949; Cicero: II, *De Optimo Genere Oratorum*, Loeb Classical Library Vol. 386, translated by H.M. Hubbell, Cambridge, Mass.: Harvard University Press, 1949; Cicero: II, *Topica*, Loeb Classical Library Vol. 386, translated by H.M. Hubbell, Cambridge, Mass.: Harvard University Press, 1949; Cicero: III, *De Oratore*, Loeb Classical Library Vol. 348, translated by E.W. Sutton and H.M. Hubbell, Cambridge, Mass.: Harvard University Press, 1942; Cicero: IV, *De Partitiones Oratoriae and De Oratore*, Loeb Classical Library Vol. 349, translated by H. Rackham, Cambridge, Mass.: Harvard University Press, 1921 and Cicero: V, *Orator*, Loeb Classical Library Vol. 342 translated by G.L. Hendrickson and H.M. Hubbell, Cambridge, Mass.: Harvard University Press, 1939. The Loeb Classical Library ® is a registered trademark of the President and fellows of Harvard College.

Quotations from the anonymous *Ad C. Herennium* are reprinted by permission of the publishers and the Trustees of the Loeb Classical Library from [Cicero]: I, *Ad C. Herennium*, Loeb Classical Library, Vol. 403, translated by H. Caplan, Cambridge, Mass.: Harvard University Press, 1954. The Loeb Classical Library ® is a registered trademark of the President and fellows of Harvard College.

Quotations from Quintilian's four volume *Institutio Oratoria* are reprinted by permission of the publishers and the Trustees of the Loeb Classical Library from Quintilian: I-IV, *The Institutio Oratoria of Quintilian*, Loeb Classical Library Vols. 124-127, translated by H.E. Butler, Cambridge, Mass.: Harvard University Press,

1921. The Loeb Classical Library ® is a registered trademark of the President and fellows of Harvard College.

Multi-volume works by Cicero and Quintilian are cited first by Loeb Classical Library volume number, then by author, then by title and finally by page number. Thus, citation to the first book of Cicero's *De Oratore* becomes: 3 Cicero, *De Oratore* at 131. Citation to the first book of Quintilian's *Institutio Oratoria* becomes: 1 Quintilian, *Institutio Oratoria* at 61.

Books and essays that are repeatedly referenced in endnotes include the author's full name and title the first time they are used. Thereafter, the author's name and a short title are used. The bibliography contains the names of all authors cited.

Finally, I wish to thank Professor Scott Wood of Loyola Law School, Los Angeles, for reading the book in manuscript form and for his enthusiastic encouragement. I am also grateful to those members of the faculty at Southwestern University School of Law who made insightful suggestions and corrections during the drafting stages of the book. My thanks go to Professors Warren Grimes, James Kushner, Christine Metteer Lorillard, Myrna Raeder and Richard Solomon.

Chapter 1

Greco-Roman Rhetoric:
The Canon and its History

*A subject, which has exhausted the genius of Aristotle, Cicero, and Quinctilian [sic],
can neither require nor admit much additional illustration. To select, combine, and
apply their precepts, is the only duty left for their followers of all succeeding times,
and to obtain a perfect familiarity with their instructions is to arrive at the mastery of
the art.*[1]

John Quincy Adams, Boylston Professor of Rhetoric and Oratory,
Harvard University

In 400 B.C. if an ordinary Greek citizen of the educated class had a legal dispute with
another citizen, he usually appeared and argued his own case before other Greek
citizens and did so without the advice or help of a lawyer. Even so, he analyzed and
argued his case with a near-professional competence and thoroughness. In preparing
his case, he first determined the proper forum for his argument and identified the
applicable law. He then determined which facts were most important, which legal
arguments were meritorious, and which arguments his adversary might use against
him. When choosing his strategies for the trial, he also decided how he would start,
how he would tell the story of the case, organize his arguments, rebut his opponent,
and close his case. Before actually presenting his arguments, he would carefully
evaluate the emotional content of the case and the reputation of the judges. And,
finally, he would assess how his own character and credibility might affect the judges'
responses to his legal arguments. In effect, he was analyzing and preparing his case in
a lawyer-like fashion.

    In making these preparations, he was not depending solely on native
intelligence or good instincts. If he was insecure about his ability to create effective
arguments or if the case was a particularly important one, he might seek help from a
logographoi, or 'forensic ghost-writers.'[2] These were professional writers who
composed speeches for litigants to deliver before the court.[3] A litigant might also be
assisted in court by a *synegoros*, or 'with-speaker,' who could offer help, substantive
or otherwise, during the proceedings.[4]

    With or without assistance, almost anyone preparing a legal case during this
period was probably relying on a lengthy, highly structured, formal education in the
classical art of rhetoric. Rhetoric, which was central to the classical curriculum,
featured the most comprehensive, adaptable, and practical analysis of legal discourse

ever created. In fact, the art of rhetoric was originally created as a flexible technique for training advocates to present cases in Greek and Roman law courts.[5] Moreover, for nearly 1,000 years, the study of rhetoric was at the core of both Greek and Roman education and, in one form or another, has been part of most formal education since that time.

However, in the years since its creation in 450 B.C., classical rhetoric has continuously transformed itself in response to dozens of social, political, educational, religious, and philosophical forces. In the course of these transformations, rhetoric has lost its close identification with legal discourse. Instead of being regarded as the most coherent and experience-based discussion of legal reasoning, analytical methods, and argumentative strategy ever devised, the term rhetoric is now usually associated with meaningless political exaggeration or mere stylistic embellishment. Although this association is unfair and reductive, it is predictable. Throughout its history rhetoric has always suffered from misunderstandings concerning its meaning, value, scope, and purpose.

But because classical rhetoric is an adaptable and, above all, a practical discipline, it always manages to survive and reestablish its original identity as an extremely effective tool for analyzing and creating legal discourse. In fact, with some adaptations for modern stylistic taste and legal procedures, Greco-Roman rhetorical principles can be applied to modern legal discourse as readily as they have been to legal discourse in any other period.

However, to understand how classical principles apply to modern legal discourse, it is first necessary to understand their original principles and how, by virtue of several important historical transformations, these principles are connected to modern rhetorical theories and practice. Fortunately, for the past three decades, interest in classical rhetoric has been growing, and with it an interest in its application to contemporary legal discourse.[6]

A. The Rhetoricians

While countless Greek and Roman rhetoricians studied and wrote about legal rhetoric,[7] the most important ones are Aristotle, Marcus Tullius Cicero, Marcus Fabius Quintilianus and the anonymous author of the *Rhetorica ad Herennium*.[8] A few others made substantial contributions on specialized topics, most notably the rhetorician Hermagoras of Temnos, who is widely credited with creating a technique for classifying various kinds of legal arguments. But the treatises of Aristotle, Cicero and Quintilian form the intellectual core of classical forensic rhetoric and it is their work that is most often relied on when discussing the topic.

Of the three, Aristotle (384-322 B.C.) is the most famous and the most influential. In addition to being a philosopher, scientist, metaphysician, logician and teacher, he also wrote *Rhetoric*, a rhetoric manual that heavily influenced all those who followed him.[9] Cicero and Quintilian are his Roman successors.

Marcus Tullius Cicero (109-43 B.C.) was a politician, legal orator, scholar, Roman consul and author, whose collection of rhetorical works includes *De Inventione* (On Invention), *Brutus*, *De Optimum Genere Oratore* (The Best Kind of Orator),

Orator, *De Partitione Oratoria* (Of the Classification of Rhetoric), *Topica* and, most famously, *De Oratore* (On the Orator).[10] *De Oratore* is a multi-volume comprehensive examination of rhetoric and its place in the world of practical affairs.

Marcus Fabius Quintilianus (35-95 A.D.), a great admirer of both Aristotle and Cicero, was a legal orator but, above all, he was a teacher. In his twelve-book *Institutio Oratoria* (Training of an Orator) he describes not only Roman educational principles, but also principles of legal rhetoric.[11]

B. Origins and Early Development

Much of the historical and current interest in classical rhetoric springs from its origins as a pedagogical tool. The Roman rhetorical education system, which survived in substantially the same form for more than 400 years, was based on an art of rhetoric first formulated in the fifth century B.C. by Corax of Syracuse and developed more fully by Aristotle, Cicero, and Quintilian.[12] The study of rhetoric was central to the Roman education system from the first century B.C. until the fall of the Empire in 410 A.D.[13] Before that, rhetorical education had also been a key component in Greek education from at least 450 B.C.[14] Thus, the formal study of rhetoric, especially as reflected in Aristotle's *Rhetoric*,[15] Cicero's *De Oratore*,[16] and Quintilian's *Institutio Oratoria*,[17] had a virtually continuous 1,000 year history in the Greco-Roman world.

Although all Roman citizens did not complete the full course of study, many completed a substantial part of the ten-to twelve-year rhetoric course which 'carried boys from beginning alphabet exercises at six or seven through a dozen years of interactive classroom activities designed to produce an adult capable of public improvisation under any circumstances.'[18] Designed for use by all members of the educated classes, the rhetoric course included, among other things, detailed instructions for discovering and presenting legal arguments in almost any context and to almost any audience. A student's rhetorical education prepared him to meet all his public speaking obligations, especially his legal obligations.[19]

From its very inception in ancient Syracuse, forensic or judicial discourse has been one of the primary rhetorical topics:

> Certain political and social changes taking place at the time prompted [Corax] to establish some system of rhetoric. When Thrasybulus, the tyrant of Syracuse, was deposed and a form of democracy established, the newly enfranchised citizens flooded the courts with *litigations to recover property* that had been confiscated during the reign of the despot. The 'art' that Corax formulated was designed to help *ordinary men plead their claims in court*. Since, understandably enough, no documentary evidence was available to prove their claims they had to rely on inferential reasoning and on the general topic of probability ... to establish their proprietary rights. Perhaps the chief contribution that Corax made to the art of rhetoric was the formula he proposed for the parts of a judicial speech – proem, narration, arguments (both confirmation and refutation), and peroration – the arrangement that becomes a staple of all later rhetorical theory.[20]

PRINCIPLES OF GRECO-ROMAN FORENSIC RHETORIC: THE CANON

While their analysis of the controlling principles of legal discourse was not absolutely uniform, even a brief (and necessarily simplified) summary reveals that most Greek and Roman rhetoricians nevertheless agreed about legal rhetoric's fundamental features. They divided legal rhetoric into five parts: invention, arrangement, style, memory, and delivery.[21] Memory and delivery are primarily useful in oral, as opposed to written, advocacy.

Understandably, classical rhetoricians focused first on systematic methods for discovering or 'inventing' all the available legal arguments in a given case.[22] To aid in the factual analysis of the case, they compiled detailed checklists and inventories of common types of legally significant facts.[23] Following this they listed and analyzed dozens of commonly used lines of argument called *topoi* or topics of invention. Their classification system was based on the 'characteristic ways in which the human mind reasons or thinks. ... [They were a] codification of the various ways in which the human mind probes a subject to discover something significant or cogent that can be said about that subject.'[24] As they discussed arguments from definition, precedent, ambiguity, legislative intent, etc., they provided numerous illustrations drawn from real and hypothetical cases. They also described rebuttal techniques, logical fallacies, common refutations, and weaknesses frequently associated with particular types of argument.

At the invention stage of the rhetorical process, they simply wanted to ensure that important facts and arguments were not overlooked. Nevertheless, comprehensive as their analysis was, Greco-Roman rhetoricians never regarded their suggestions as anything more than starting points for discovering the available arguments in a given case. Based on their own practical experience, they were acutely aware, and repeatedly reminded their readers, that advocates must be creative, resourceful, and flexible in devising arguments.[25]

The second stage of the rhetorical process concerned the arrangement or organization of arguments.[26] Building on Corax's teachings regarding the standard organization of legal argument and their own observations regarding the practice of experienced advocates, they divided legal arguments into five parts: introduction (*exordium*), statement of the case (*narratio*), argument summary (*partitio*), argument (*confirmatio*), and conclusion (*peroratio).* Their treatises offered detailed explanations regarding the function of each part and the relationships among the parts. They also provided examples drawn from their own and others' experience and discussed strategies for effective presentation.

Classical rhetoricians devoted as much, if not more, attention to rhetorical style as they did to the discovery and organization of arguments. Their conviction that style is inseparable from the substance of argument is epitomized by Cicero's observation that distinction of style is impossible to achieve without worthy ideas. Conversely, ideas remain lifeless without stylistic distinction.[27] They distinguished three different levels of style – the plain style, the middle style, and the grand style – and identified where each was appropriate.[28] They frequently treated figures of speech and figures of thought as almost interchangeable. In their view, style was a technical means of reinforcing or embellishing important argumentative points. They even singled out specific rhetorical devices, such as antithesis and parallelism, as especially suitable to legal discourse when emotional as well as logical impact is desirable. They had a special regard for metaphors because of their subtle, natural emotional impact. They thought that metaphors were not only emotionally engaging, but that they also offered a unique wholeness to intellectual insights without any loss of logical integrity.

Although their analysis was systematic and in some ways dogmatic regarding which types of arguments, organization, and style were suitable to legal discourse, they were also aware of the emotive, nonrational and sometimes imponderable factors at play in a given case. To accommodate for these factors, they analyzed legal arguments from three points of view: arguments based on logic (*logos*), arguments based on emotion (*pathos*), and arguments based on the credibility of the advocate (*ethos*).[29] Using numerous examples drawn from their own and others' experience, they discussed the principal features and effects of each type of argument. Even though they discussed these types of argument under separate heads, they stressed that all three types were closely interconnected with one another. They agreed that any well-framed and successful argument depended on its internal logic, the emotional content of the case, and the credibility of the advocate.

With characteristic thoroughness they analyzed judicial audiences as systematically as they did all other parts of the rhetorical process. Underlying all their observations regarding effective argumentation was their consistent emphasis on the importance of evaluating and playing on the sympathies of the judicial audience. Grounded as it was in basic human psychology, their assessment included advice on which types of arguments would have the greatest impact on a judge, how to avoid boring or confusing a judge, and how to appeal to a judge's sense of justice, self-interest, class, or emotions. Above all, they stressed that advocates must be flexible and sensitive to changes in the judge's moods or needs.

In effect, an advocate must 'understand both the principles of argument and the basis of character and emotion: this, of course, is to say that he must be both a logician and a psychologist.'[30] As Quintilian observed, an advocate has three aims: '[H]e must instruct, move, and charm. ...'[31]

As even this brief summary shows, the classical approach to legal rhetoric is both deep and wide-ranging. Mastery or even extended exposure to this approach enabled ordinary Greek and Roman citizens to competently represent themselves in a legal dispute.

For nearly 1,000 years, Greek and Roman rhetoricians refined and extended their examination of legal discourse. The analytical techniques, classification systems, psychological assumptions, stylistic concerns, terminology, and purposes they described or created are both comprehensive and coherent. They are also the starting point of all subsequent approaches to analysis and creation of legal discourse.[32]

Despite these many virtues, however, classical rhetoric has undergone numerous changes throughout its history. At times, its authors have been forgotten and its precepts distorted. Sometimes its very future has been in doubt.

MEDIEVAL RHETORIC

The virtually unbroken 1,000-year continuity of the Greco-Roman rhetorical tradition began to disintegrate with the collapse of the Roman empire in 410 A.D. Even though classical rhetoric remained an important component in educational systems throughout the medieval period (426-1416 A.D.), analysis and production of legal discourse played a much less important role than it had under the Greek or Roman legal systems:[33]

> [Classical rhetoric] ... almost succumbed to the collapse of its native environment as the cities of the [Roman] empire were destroyed or abandoned in the face of barbarian attack beginning in the early fifth century. With the end of orderly civic life there disappeared not only state support of education but most of the reasons for rhetorical education in its traditional form.[34]

Suffering from the same fragmentation and loss of coherence experienced by other Roman institutions and disciplines, classical rhetoric lost its intimate connections with the law and with other civic entities.[35] It began to undergo a series of transformations caused in part by the loss or only partial survival of the major rhetorical texts:

> Medieval rhetoric is fragmented, first, in the obvious sense that many of the major rhetorical texts either disappeared or survived only in damaged form. Cicero's *Orator* and *Brutus* vanished altogether, and ... *De Oratore* was known [only] to a few scholars ... Quintilian's *Institutes* came down to the Middle Ages in a badly mutilated version. ...[36]

From the viewpoint of legal rhetoric, the greatest loss during this period was the loss of a coherent and all-encompassing approach to legal discourse. In addition, the conceptual framework and terminology of legal rhetoric acquired new meanings as it was transformed or modified by strong religious, ideological, linguistic, geographical, and technological forces.

Naturally enough, because the Church was the main repository of medieval learning, all rhetoric, including legal or forensic rhetoric, acquired ecclesiastical overtones and lost many of its original secular and civic uses: '[Medieval] [r]hetoric informed methods for resolving conflicting assertions in canon law, theology, and philosophy. This facet of its medieval development is seen in the shift of rhetorical terms and concepts from questions of law to questions of faith.'[37] Despite this shift of emphasis, there is still a persistent but highly selective interest in legal rhetoric throughout the period. In fact, only 'in the early twelfth century did law cease to be a subdivision of rhetoric: then the study of law became a subject in its own right, and we witness the rise of law schools ... as part of universities.'[38]

Most medieval writers focus more on logic and argument than on other aspects of rhetoric because in hearings before an 'ecclesiastical official, ... both the official and the petitioner needed some knowledge of law ... and of argumentation.'[39] Although medieval writers occasionally mention other Greco-Roman rhetorical works, classical rhetoric survived mainly in two basic but imminently practical and teachable texts: Cicero's *De Inventione* and the anonymous *Rhetorica ad Herennium.*[40] Because both of these texts focus primarily on legal rhetoric, medieval encyclopedists, preachers, poets, manual writers, and other leading literary figures unavoidably, and perhaps unconsciously, preserved the analytical and organizational principles of legal argument even while they put them to new uses in ecclesiastical courts.

In the works of fifth-century encyclopedists like Cassiodorus[41] and Isidore of Seville,[42] some parts of classical legal rhetoric survived, especially those concerning issue identification and analysis (commonly referred to as *stasis* theory) and rhetorical argument. Cassiodorus' *Institutiones Divinarum et Humanarum Lectionum*, or Introduction to Divine and Human Readings, was a 'basic reference work and educational handbook for centuries and was to be found in almost every medieval library.'[43] Citing Cicero's *De Inventione* and *De Oratore*, Cassiodorus' discussion of rhetoric is 'chiefly devoted to summaries of *stasis* theory and rhetorical argumentation. Thus its logical side is emphasized.'[44]

Another encyclopedist, Isidore of Seville:

> was the author of a vast work entitled *Origines* or *Etymologiae*, which served as an encyclopedia throughout the following centuries. ... [Its] longer chapters are on stasis theory, the syllogism, and the figures of speech and thought. A chapter on law ... is inserted between the discussion of the syllogism and that of style and is important in suggesting that rhetorical invention was useful in the courts of the time.[45]

Not only did medieval rhetoricians regard legal rhetoric as useful in the ecclesiastical courtroom, they also thought it was important in the classroom, especially as an analytical tool. Rulers such as Charlemagne saw the value of rhetorical education. In fact, Charlemagne invited prominent rhetoricians to help effect his mandate on verbal education, *De Litteris Colendis*, by providing 'instruction in grammar and rhetoric so that each individual in the realm could attain his own full capacity of verbal skills and thus be able to read the holy writ with full understanding.'[46] Thus, analytical techniques that were once used to identify and create legal arguments were adapted for use in the reading of religious texts.

Legal rhetoric's practical applications are also evident in the medieval disciplines of letter-writing and sermon-writing. In twelfth-century Italy, for example, the rhetorical art of letter-writing was a university-taught and highly conventionalized discipline. Most diplomatic and legal correspondence was modeled after the *exordium, narratio, partitio, confirmatio,* and *peroratio* structure of classical legal argument:

> In the twelfth century, dictamen, like law, was taught in the University of Bologna. Dictamen (from Latin *dictare*, to write a letter) is a derivative of classical rhetoric, reflecting especially the figures of speech and the parts of the oration, which were adapted into a standard five-part epistolary structure: the *salutatio*, or greeting, the *captatio benevolentiae*, or exordium, which secured the good will of the recipient; the narratio; the petitio, or specific request, demand, or announcement; and a relatively simple conclusio. The dictamen was strongly influenced by the conventions of diplomatic and *legal correspondence*, both civil and ecclesiastical, in medieval courts.[47]

And, in thirteenth-century England, legal rhetoric was adapted to suit the needs of preachers who, like the Italian letter-writers, modified the format and terminology of legal rhetoric as they became more logical and systematic in writing their sermons:

> In the early thirteenth century handbooks of thematic preaching began to appear, perhaps first in England with the manuals of Alexander of Ashby and Thomas Chabham of Salisbury. These works adapt the parts of the [judicial] oration as described in the *Rhetorica ad Herennium* to the needs of preachers. They reflect an interest in form and technique of sermons, rather than just the contents, and foreshadow the 'thematic' preaching which became popular at the University of Paris and elsewhere in a few years. By 'thematic preaching' ... is meant a systematic, logical form of preaching, as opposed to the informality and lack of structure of the homily or of the simple preaching of Saint Francis.[48]

Both of these adaptations also signal a change in rhetorical emphasis from oral to written eloquence. Although both Cicero and Quintilian recognized the importance of writing as an essential first step in the creation of effective argument, their ultimate goal was always face-to-face oral presentation of their points to a judicial (or legislative or ceremonial) audience.[49] However, as the written word began to assume more and more importance, the sense of audience changed: 'Rhetoric was reduced from a two-way to a one-way system. The energies that would otherwise go to elaborating a reciprocal relationship turns inwards, away from a concern with a living context, individuals or institutions susceptible to change, to an intellectual structure.'[50]

As these examples illustrate, legal rhetoric survived throughout the medieval period because it provided a flexible, teachable, and useful analytical framework and because of its many practical applications. Even so, it was removed from its moorings in a larger rhetorical scheme and from widespread use in secular and civic life.[51] Selected parts of legal rhetorical conventions are emphasized, but its sense of wholeness was eroded. This pattern of selectivity and fragmentation pervades the medieval period and continues, with variations, into the Renaissance and the modern periods.

RENAISSANCE RHETORIC

Sparked by the rediscovery of the complete rhetorical treatises of Quintilian, Cicero, and Aristotle, classical rhetoric had a substantial resurgence in the Renaissance.[52] The recovery of these works, especially those of Cicero and Quintilian, liberated legal rhetoric from the narrow and compartmentalized forms that evolved in the medieval period, and reintroduced it into the broad and creative context of civic life.[53] Once again rhetoric 'occupied a privileged position in the school curriculum, being reserved to the higher classes, forming the climax of a pupil's education.'[54] Its ascendance is exemplified by the practice in English grammar schools and universities, where rhetoric became one of the primary academic disciplines in a widespread and standardized educational system.[55] At the university level, '[w]here logic [had] held the main place [in medieval educational systems], rhetoric and grammar ... now shared it with logic. ...'[56] Even kings took the standard rhetoric course. Like any ordinary schoolboy or university student of the period, King Edward VI wrote Latin compositions using the classical approach: 'First he collected all his main arguments (*inventio*), also listing similes and examples which he intended to use; then he divided the material up in the form of the five parts of speech (*dispositio*); lastly he wrote the whole thing out, neatly using up all his quotations.'[57]

Not only were the classical texts recovered and used in schools, but rhetoric was reintegrated into civic life, albeit with more emphasis on its practical uses in civic and social matters than on the forensic or judicial uses that were emphasized during the Greco-Roman or medieval period.[58] In fact, the stress on practicality is perhaps the most distinctive feature of the Renaissance rediscovery of classical rhetoric. In Italy, George of Trebizond cited the trad-itional definition of rhetoric as 'the civil science by which we speak in civil questions with the assent, as much as possible, of the listeners' – a mosaic of passages from *Rhetorica ad Herennium, De Inventione*, and later texts – the concept of civil questions, which survives in medieval rhetoric without any real understanding of its meaning, is now interpreted as referring to rhetoric's role in society and especially the *vita activa*.[59]

And, in England, Francis Bacon[60] noted that 'profoundness of wisdom will help a man to name or admiration, ... [but] it is eloquence that prevaileth in an active life.'[61] As an experienced advocate and legislator, Bacon was both a theoretician and practitioner of rhetorical eloquence. In his *De Augmentis Scientiarum* (an analysis and criticism of both Aristotle and Cicero), Bacon echoed classical observations regarding legal argument when he expounded on (among other rhetorical matters) the classic conflict between the letter and the intent of the law and listed forty-seven different arguments on the subject.

Throughout England, classical rhetoric was frequently linked with both the study and the practice of law:

> [S]ixteenth-century lawyers learned some rhetoric at the universities (which increasing numbers of them attended before beginning their legal studies at an Inn of Chancery or Inn of Court), and some seem likely to have begun some kind of study of rhetoric first in an Inn of Chancery and then in an Inn of Court; others, we know, deepened their command of rhetoric by private study.[62]

Sir Edward Coke, one of England's most famous jurists and the author of *Institutes of the Laws of England*, 'had in his library Aristotle's and Quintilian's rhetorics ... some Cicero, and a book of elocution ...'[63] Thomas Wilson, an eminent sixteenth-century scholar, wrote *Arte of Rhetorique* which was an 'extremely influential' synthesis of law and rhetoric 'for young noblemen who did not have time and patience to master rhetoric from the Latin textbooks.'[64] George Puttenham, a lawyer himself and from a family of lawyers, frequently refers to Cicero and to Quintilian in his *The Arte of English Poesie* which contains numerous 'anecdotes relating to the law courts and lawyers ... The legal anecdotes, perhaps a dozen in number, in general illustrate the effects of rhetoric ...'[65]

Even though rhetoric had a large sphere of influence during the Renaissance period, much of that influence was turned in the direction of literature, not the law.

Most importantly for later perceptions of rhetoric, the expressive function of rhetoric received much greater attention than it had in the medieval period: 'The writings of the ancients were read in the original Greek and Latin and were appreciated first of all for their beauty of expression and then for their relevance to contemporary life.'[66] Renaissance rhetoricians regarded the classical canon as a source of both eloquence and wisdom.[67] Consequently, while rhetoric's practical applications in civic life were always recognized, its analysis and suggestions regarding stylistic excellence received greater and greater attention. In its most extreme forms, 'Renaissance rhetoricians in reasserting the human role in judging all things retained the stylistic machinery of earlier eras, [but] found courtliness an adequate replacement for assured [religious or philosophical] Truth.'[68]

Their concern with style reflected an increased interest in how the emotional effects of style and eloquence persuade audiences to the writer's point of view. They also concentrated on the aesthetic and poetic dimensions of classical figures and tropes because they were convinced that 'the ultimate power of rhetoric in written communication [resided] in the figures and tropes, the last stage of elaboration of persuasive composition.'[69] Drawing heavily on the legal rhetoric techniques of Quintilian and of the *Rhetorica ad Herennium*, Renaissance rhetoricians analyzed the persuasive value of figures and tropes.[70] They were convinced that rhetorical figures represented 'not just forms of language but states of feeling ...'[71] In fact, they regarded rhetorical figures as 'deriving originally from life.'[72] For example, they observed that '[i]n anger human beings will cry out, appeal to some stander-by, to God, or to part of the scenery to bear witness to their sufferings: this gesture came to be known as *apostrophe* or *exclamatio*.'[73] Like classical rhetoricians, they knew that the 'effectiveness of rhetoric derived ... from its power over the emotions.'[74] And, like all rhetoricians, they 'offer a classification of verbal devices. Particular structures are identified, named, their function discussed, and rules given concerning their use and abuse.'[75]

Unfortunately, subsequent critics and commentators, including modern commentators, have misunderstood the purpose and underlying rationale for Renaissance interest in verbal devices. Instead of focusing on their persuasive powers, these commentators focused on how the rhetorical figures and devices were abused and characterized them as frivolous, tedious, and mechanistic.[76] These misunderstandings, as much as any other criticisms of rhetoric, account for rhetoric's present-day associations with florid, stilted exaggerations in language.

ENGLISH NEOCLASSICAL RHETORIC

Rhetorical style was also important to seventeenth and eighteenth-century English rhetoricians, but they focused as much of their attention on oral delivery style and 'elocution' as they did on written style. Rhetorical training in grammar schools still focused on studying Latin and writing theses based on Greco-Roman rhetoric, thereby fostering a receptive climate for the works of Cicero and Quintilian. But, at the university level, the focus turned to the oral delivery of rhetorical compositions because a 'major function of British universities ... was the training of the clergy.

Attention to preaching was thus very appropriate in courses on rhetoric.'[77] In effect, this emphasis on oral delivery reestablished an important part of classical rhetorical training. But instead of concentrating on civic, legislative, or legal rhetoric, the Neoclassical focus was on religious rhetoric.

In addition, with the advent of a growing interest in empirical science and in formal logic, rhetorical reasoning, dependent as it is on emotional arguments and probabilities rather than on objective, scientific, or mathematical certainties, caused neoclassical critics to question its intellectual validity. John Locke, a one-time lecturer on rhetoric at Oxford, criticized traditional rhetoric in *An Essay Concerning Human Understanding* as 'an art of deceit and errour' and 'wanted to exclude figures of speech and other rhetorical devices from serious discourse.'[78]

The topics of invention, a staple of Greco-Roman legal analysis, were dismissed by other critics as useless in discovering the 'truth or in demonstrating it, and the five traditional parts of [legal] rhetoric are a form of deception.'[79] Legal rhetoric was also neglected because changes in the legal system and in law practice limited the opportunities for legal oratory. In his essay, *Of Eloquence*, the Scottish philosopher David Hume claimed that legal rhetoric's diminished relevance was due to modern legal procedures and rules of evidence which restricted opportunities for legal oratory.[80]

Two eighteenth-century rhetoricians, George Campbell and Hugh Blair, wrote influential and widely read rhetorical treatises in which the authors acknowledged their indebtedness to classical rhetoric but which, in fact, departed significantly from classical precepts. Campbell's *The Philosophy of Rhetoric* was an attempt to 'think out a new theory of rhetoric on the basis of the work of the British Empiricist philosophers, and especially the work of David Hume.'[81] He wanted to 'explore human nature and find therein the principles which underlie and explain the art of rhetoric.'[82] While acknowledging classical rhetoric's importance and conceding that the rhetorical principles of 'Aristotle, Cicero, and Quintilian have been for the most part only translated by later critics, or put into a modish dress and new arrangement,' Campbell nevertheless thought that Hume's philosophical and psychological works provided critical insights into the art of persuasion that were unknown to and therefore unexamined by the classical authors.[83] He concentrated much of his attention on these insights to supplement his classical sources.

Hugh Blair, a contemporary of Campbell's and a professor of Rhetoric and Belles Lettres at the University of Edinburgh, focused his attention on rhetorical style rather than on philosophy or psychology. He has been described as the British Quintilian and it is his work, more than Campbell's, that has affected modern perceptions of rhetoric. He too based his work on classical rhetoric. Although he discusses all the classical principles in *The Lectures on Rhetoric and Belles Lettres*, he is most influential for his observations on rhetorical taste, criticism, sublimity, and beauty, that is, on style.[84] Because of his belief that close examination of great literature is essential to understanding and producing oratorical excellence, much of his work is devoted to comparing the literary merits of various classical and modern works. He provided a very influential model 'for using literature to teach writing.'[85] Despite both men's indebtedness to classical sources, neither Campbell nor Blair devotes substantial attention to legal rhetoric. In this, they typify the Neoclassical neglect of the subject.

CLASSICAL RHETORIC IN NINETEENTH-CENTURY AMERICA

Initially, seventeenth and eighteenth-century Americans' interests in rhetoric simply reflected the British interests.[86] The empiricist-inspired works of George Campbell and the belletristic works of Hugh Blair were as popular and widespread in America as they were in Britain. But, like a few of their English counterparts, some American educators focused their attention on traditional classical rhetoric. For example:

> John Quincy Adams, the first holder of the Boylston Professorship of Rhetoric and Oratory at Harvard [observed], 'A subject which has exhausted the genius of Aristotle, Cicero, and Quintilian, ... can neither require nor admit much additional illustration. To select, combine, and apply their precepts, is the only duty left for their followers of all succeeding times, and to obtain a perfect familiarity with their instructions is to arrive at the mastery of the art.'[87]

Grounded as it was in the classical tradition, Adams' *Lectures on Rhetoric and Oratory* offered a unique opportunity in America's formative years for a legal rhetoric based in a civic and legislative context resembling that of the classical period. But 'Adams' rhetoric had little impact even in his own time. Initially published in 1810, it did not see another printing for 150 years ... [primarily because it] was associated with an [Aristotelian] epistemology that was being assaulted on all fronts in America and abroad in the nineteenth century.'[88]

So, instead of using Adams' Greco-Roman model, American rhetoricians and educators modelled themselves after Campbell or Blair. They divided themselves into two camps: 'One group emphasized Campbell, presenting rhetoric as a scientific body of principles, grounded in human nature. The other saw rhetoric as an art, deriving its impulse from Blair's belletristic position.'[89]

Even while these principles were being taught, classical rhetoric was losing its central place in the curriculum of American colleges and was being relegated to speech departments, rhetoric departments, and English departments: '[R]hetorical theory became an aspect of belles lettres and English composition. In the course of the century the Boylston Professorship, despite the founder's intention, was converted first into a chair in belles lettres and ultimately into a professorship of poetry.'[90]

These changes at Harvard and at most nineteenth-century American colleges and universities were linked not only to changes in rhetorical philosophy but also to a rapid growth in college populations. As the student populations increased, colleges adopted curricular and classroom strategies (most notably the system by which students select or elect certain specialized courses) to accommodate the increased numbers.[91] Educators gravitated toward more efficient teaching methods and away from the time-consuming approaches that characterized traditional rhetorical training. The fragmentation that periodically overwhelmed classical rhetoric once again divided what was originally a comprehensive and coherent whole into a number of discrete and essentially unconnected departments and disciplines.

Another significant and related change at the university level was an increased emphasis, based on Hugh Blair's work, on written, as opposed to oral, discourse.[92] At Harvard, for instance, 'the composition class [was] the sole course required of all students in an otherwise elective curriculum.'[93] Legal rhetoric was likewise affected by this increased emphasis on writing:

> [T]he forensic system [at Harvard] continued the old tradition of debate in the final years of the curriculum, but it was a written adaptation of the oral debate. During the 1870s, students attended lectures and recitation on rhetoric in the last three years (freshmen took elocution), but the catalogue also specifically prescribed 'themes once every four weeks' for sophomores, 'once every three weeks' for juniors, and 'four forensics' for seniors ... At least at their inception, the requirements were thus a kind of *written* continuation of the ancient tradition of rhetoricals.[94]

While there was an increased interest in written rhetoric, this new approach did not retain close connections with those classical principles that provide a clear sense of audience, a clear method for discovering what to say, and a clear sense of how emotion, style, and personal credibility contribute to effective argument. Instead, it was based in part on George Campbell's empiricist theories and in part on the demands of the business and scientific communities who were interested in efficient ways to manage or organize pre-existing technological or scientific information.[95] This rhetoric, commonly referred to as 'Current-Traditional' rhetoric, emerged during the last two decades of the nineteenth century.[96] Under this quasi-scientific system:

> the writer's duty is to rid himself of the trappings of culture that distort his perceptions. He is to be objective, detached, in observing experience. The purpose of writing is to report, not to interpret, what is inductively discovered ... Invention (discovery of arguments or subject matter) is not necessary: after all, the scientist does not invent meaning, he discovers it through the correct use of his method.[97]

Current-traditional rhetoric is also characterized by an emphasis on the forms of discourse, discussions of usage, grammar and style as reflected in concepts of unity, coherence, and emphasis. Coupled with this focus on 'superficial correctness'[98] was an almost exclusive emphasis on expository writing.[99] Consequently, very little attention was given to argument generally or to legal argument in particular.

CLASSICAL RHETORIC IN TWENTIETH-CENTURY AMERICA

Current-traditional rhetoric predominated in the American educational system until the late 1930s and the early 1940s. Then, prompted by student demand for practical training for business purposes, Speech and English departments began combining speaking, writing, listening, and reading skills in ways that restored 'basic rhetorical principles into composition classrooms.'[100] In effect, they were restoring classical coherence and completeness to the teaching of rhetoric. Soon, they returned to the classical texts for inspiration and guidance.

Despite this return to the classical texts, most modern rhetoricians concentrate on a single topic like 'invention' or the discovery of arguments.[101] Sometimes they attempt to apply all the classical principles to modern topics. Occasionally, classical rhetoric is used as a starting point for a 'new' rhetorical theory loosely based on classical principles.

Kenneth Burke, for example, seeks to discover a 'generating principle' for discovering the available arguments using a method that differs from but echoes the classical topics of invention. Burke's 'dramatistic' principle uses five 'master terms': Act, Scene, Agent, Agency, Purpose. By systematically employing these terms, a writer or advocate will discover 'what is being done (the Act); under what circumstances or in what situation (Scene) the act takes place; what sort of person (Agent) does it; by what means (Agency) he does it, and for what end or Purpose.'[102] Burke's 'master terms' are fewer in number, but serve a similar purpose to Cicero's list in *De Inventione* which examines a topic in terms of name, nature, manner of life, fortune, habit, feeling, interests, purposes, achievements, accidents, and speeches made.[103]

In almost all cases, modern rhetoricians are primarily interested in applying classical rhetorical techniques to meet the many practical requirements of modern discourse. Their applications depend on their theoretical point of view or purpose. Thus:

> [t]o the composition [or law] teacher, rhetoric is an 'art' of writing which focuses the student's attention on the strategic nature of communication. To the literary [or legal] scholar, it is a critical 'apparatus' that covers all the techniques by which a writer establishes rapport with the reader. To the philosopher of language [or the law], it is a 'study' of misunderstanding and its remedies. To the self-described rhetorician [or legal advocate], it is a 'method' of argumentation which looks to an
> audience to discover the means of persuasion.[104]

Only rarely, however, do modern rhetoricians or scholars devote much attention to how classical rhetoric applies to modern judicial or legal discourse. One exception is Chaim Perelman, a widely respected, legally trained Belgian philosopher, whose *The Idea of Justice and the Problem of Argument* analyzes judicial uses of legal precedent in order to illuminate connections between classical and modern methods of legal argument.[105] Perelman's *The Idea of Justice* and his *The New Rhetoric: A Treatise on Argumentation*[106] emphasize, in ways that are reminiscent of the classical techniques of legal argument, modes of 'nonformal logic which [can] "induce or increase the mind's adherence to theses presented for its assent."'[107] Perelman's work, however, is a notable departure from a widespread disregard for the links between classical rhetoric and modern legal discourse.

Despite this neglect, a growing number of modern lawyers, judges, and legal academics have begun employing classical rhetorical principles in their analyses of legal discourse. For example, Robert F. Hanley refers to the classical concepts of *ethos* (an advocate's credibility) and *pathos* (the emotional aspects of a legal argument) when recommending various courtroom argumentative strategies.[108] In his treatise on legal logic, Judge Ruggero Aldisert examines modern legal arguments using the classical rhetorical concept of enthymetic proofs (an enthymeme is a syllogism in which the major premise is only probable, or in which one term is omitted).[109] Judge Richard Posner's book on law and literature contains a section on judicial 'style as persuasion' in which he states that 'it is an open question whether the style of judicial opinions is better studied from the standpoint of linguistics and rhetoric or from that of literary criticism. ...'[110] Anthony G. Amsterdam and Randy Hertz' analysis of the rhetorical structure of closing arguments includes quotes from Aristotle, Cicero, and Quintilian.[111] More recently, Steven Jamar shows how Aristotle's principles of 'enthymematic' proof applies to modern legal discourse and also briefly discusses the topics of invention.[112] Most ambitious of all is Michael R. Smith's *Advanced Legal Writing: Theories and Strategies in Persuasive Writing*.[113] Throughout his book, Smith relies on the classical concepts of *logos*, *ethos*, and *pathos* to analyze various persuasion techniques and matters of style. In doing so, he repeatedly cites his classical sources.

Most of these commentators are interested in how classical rhetoric can help advocates discover or explain the internal logic and persuasive value of legal argument. Understandably, given their limited purposes, they rarely call much attention to the larger context from which these classical principles were drawn. That is, they apply the classical principles without referring to the overall classical system, in part because such references are unnecessary. As seasoned lawyers and judges, they can rely on their own experience for much of the information and advice that is contained in the classical sources.

But inexperienced lawyers and law students do not have that background to draw on and can certainly benefit from a greater familiarity with the comprehensive, coherent, and experience-tested classical system, which offers detailed advice for handling a legal case from the initial issue and fact determinations to the final courtroom techniques and strategies. As this chapter demonstrates, rhetoric has always been an educational tool geared to meet the practical demands of the legal profession. For 2,500 years it has survived and adapted to those demands and can certainly do so again.

Notes

1. 1 John Quincy Adams, *Lectures on Rhetoric and Oratory* 28-29 (Russell and Russell, Inc. 1962) (1810).
2. J.A. Crook, *Legal Advocacy in the Roman World* 30-31 (1995) Crook notes that at 'Athens the litigant in principle appears and argues in person. What we find the Athenian doing, in fact, is delivering by heart a speech written for him, for a fee, by a rhetorical expert.' Dennis Peter Maio, on the other hand, is skeptical about how frequently speech writers were employed: 'The conventional view, that "it was a common practice [for a litigant] in the fourth century to get a speech written by a speech writer [for delivery at trial]" hardly seems sound ... Although speech writing was evidently well-paid, we are therefore, not surprised to note that it was not widely-practiced ... the speech writer played a part only in extraordinary litigation.' Dennis Peter Maio, '*Politeia* and Adjudication in Fourth-Century B.C. Athens,' 28 American Journal of Jurisprudence 16 (1983).

3.   Aristotle, *The Art of Rhetoric* 5 (H.C. Lawson-Tancred trans. 1991) In his discussion of the rise in professionalism in rhetorical theory, Lawson-Tancred notes the new-found prominence of *logographoi*: 'The emergence around this time of the *logographoi* is of great significance ... Now for the first time there was a class of men whose primary occupation ... was the production of effective speeches ... [F]rom this time onwards a secondary industry develops which seeks to supply professional and amateur speakers with the technical underpinning essential for consistent success.'

4.   Crook, *Legal Advocacy in the Roman World* at 32-33, 'The litigant was obliged ... to appear in person, but there was nothing to prevent him being supported and assisted by a cloud of friends and well-wishers, to cheer, testify or plead on his behalf. ...'

5.   Corax of Syracuse is generally credited with inventing rhetoric in the fifth century B.C. None of Corax's handbooks on rhetoric have survived although '[t]here are references in Plato, Aristotle, Cicero and Quintilian to the part that Corax ... played in formulating rhetorical theory.' Edward P.J. Corbett, *Classical Rhetoric for the Modern Student* 595 (2d ed. 1971). See also George A. Kennedy, *Classical Rhetoric and its Christian and Secular Tradition from Ancient to Modern Times* 8 (1980) (observing that 'Corax and Tisias ... are traditionally described as "inventors" of rhetoric').

6.   'During the 1960s, enthusiasm mounted for a reexamination of the full rhetorical tradition of classical times for what it could offer to the teaching of English composition.' Jean Dietz Moss, 'The Revival of Practical Reasoning,' in *Rhetoric and Praxis: The Contribution of Classical Rhetoric to Practical Reasoning* 1, 8 (Jean Dietz Moss ed., 1986). Most generalizations about 'recent' developments in a 2450-year-old intellectual discipline are necessarily broad. The resurgence of interest in classical rhetoric in the 1960s must be viewed in terms of dozens if not hundreds of similar resurgences that dot rhetoric's history. Moreover, previous resurgences often spanned centuries, not mere decades.

7.   Marcus Tullius Cicero, *Brutus* (G.L. Hendrickson, trans. 2001 ed.) For a contemporary account, see Cicero's *Brutus*, which contains an exhaustive description of rhetoricians and orators of the Greco-Roman period . Also see generally George Kennedy, *A New History of Classical Rhetoric* (1994).

8.   Anonymous, *Rhetorica ad Herennium* (H. Caplan trans. 1954).

9.   Aristotle, *The Rhetoric of Aristotle* (Lane Cooper trans. 1932).

10. Marcus Tullius Cicero, *De Inventione* (H.M. Hubbell trans. 1949), *De Optimo Genere Oratorum* (H.M. Hubbell trans. 1949), *Orator* (H.M. Hubbell trans. 1939), *De Partitione Oratoria* H. Rackham trans. 1921), *Topica* (H.M. Hubbell trans. 1949), *De Oratore* (E.W. Sutton and H. Rackham trans. 1942).

11. Marcus Fabius Quintilianus, *Institutio Oratoria* (H.E. Butler trans. 1954).

12. 5 Cicero, *Brutus* at 49 (G.L. Hendrickson and H.M. Hubbell trans. 1939). 'Thus Aristotle says that in Sicily, after the expulsion of tyrants, when after a long interval restitution of private property was sought by legal means, Corax and Tisias the Sicilians ... first put together some theoretical precepts; that before them, while many had taken pains to speak with care and with order arrangement, no one had followed a definite method or art.' Also see Corbett, at 595.

13. See James J. Murphy, 'Roman Writing Instruction as Described by Quintilian,' in *A Short History of Writing Instruction from Ancient Greece to Twentieth-Century America* 19, 20 (James J. Murphy ed. 1990).

14. See Edward P.J. Corbett, *Classical Rhetoric for the Modern Student* 596 (1971 2nd ed.) *See generally* Murphy, 'Roman Writing Instruction' at 38.

15. Aristotle, *The Rhetoric of Aristotle* (Lane Cooper trans. 1932).

16. Marcus Tullius Cicero, *De Oratore* (E.W. Sutton and H. Rackham trans. 1942).
17. Marius Fabius Quintilianus, *Institutio Oratoria* (H.E. Butler trans. 1954).
18. Murphy, 'Roman Writing Instruction' at 19-20.
19. 'The ancients taught all voting citizens, who, without lawyers or federal forms to complete, had to argue for the restoration of their property in open court. Both new democracy and a new technology – writing – made the individual responsible for mastering the rhetorical habits we now so sorely miss, from "thinking on your feet" to "good delivery". Citizens in Greece also had to be critical thinkers, ready for service on juries that numbered five hundred or as members of the executive council, elected monthly.' Susan Miller, 'Classical Practice and Contemporary Basics,' in *The Rhetorical Tradition and Modern Writing* 52-53 (James J. Murphy ed. 1982).
20. Corbett, *Classical Rhetoric for the Modern Student* at 595 (emphasis added).
21. See Cicero, *Rhetorica ad Herennium* 9 (H. Caplan trans. 1954). See also Corbett, *Classical Rhetoric for the Modern Student* at 600 (noting that authorship of the *Rhetorica ad Herennium* is questionable). '[W]ritten probably between 86 and 82 B.C., ... [it is] the earliest extant Latin work on rhetoric and the earliest treatment of prose style in Latin. ... Although virtually unknown in the ancient world, the *Ad Herennium* enjoyed wide currency in the Middle Ages and the Renaissance.'
22. See Chapter Two for an extended discussion of how classical analytical techniques apply to modern legal discourse.
23. See 2 Cicero, *De Inventione* at 71 (H.M. Hubbell trans. 1949). 'All propositions are supported in argument by attributes of persons or of actions. We hold the following to be the attributes of persons: name, nature, manner of life, fortune, habit, feeling, interests, purposes, achievements, accidents, speeches made.'
24. Kathleen E. Welch, *The Contemporary Reception of Classical Rhetoric: Appropriations of Ancient Discourse* 60-61 (1990) (quoting Edward P.J. Corbett, 'The *Topoi* Revisted,' in *Rhetoric and Praxis: The Contribution of Classical Rhetoric to Practical Reasoning* 43, 47 Jean Dietz Moss ed. 1986).
25. For an extended discussion of the topics of invention see Chapter Two.
26. For an extended discussion of how classical organizational strategies apply to modern legal discourse, see Chapter Three.
27. See 4 Cicero, *De Oratore* at 21(E.W. Sutton and H. Rackham trans. 1942); S. Michael Halloran and Merrill D. Whitburn, 'Ciceronian Rhetoric and the Rise of Science: The Plain Style Reconsidered,' in *The Rhetorical Tradition and Modern Writing* 61 (James J. Murphy ed., 1982).
28. For a fuller discussion of the range of emotions classical rhetoricians considered, see S. Michael Halloran and Merrill D. Whitburn, 'Ciceronian Rhetoric and the Rise of Science: The Plain Style Reconsidered,' in *The Rhetorical Tradition and Modern Writing* at 61:
    In Aristotle's view style is simply a *matter of genre*; distinguishable styles are appropriate for different speaking situations. ... [By contrast] Cicero associates the three styles with three *effects* a speaker must work on the audience: the plain style instructs, the middle style delights, and the grand style moves to belief or action. A well-wrought speech will use all three to orchestrate the audience's response according to the speaker's aim. Plain, middle, and grand styles are levels *of embellishment* and *emotional concentration* rather than generically distinct modes of language. (Emphasis added).
29. For an extended discussion of how the classical concepts of *pathos* and *ethos* apply to modern legal discourse, see Chapter Four.
30. Aristotle, *The Art of Rhetoric* 17 (H.C. Lawson-Tancred trans. 1991).

31. 1 Quintilian, *Institutio Oratoria* at 397.
32. Some commentators reject or de-emphasize the notion of a classical 'canon.' For example, Thomas P. Miller questions the existence of a unified rhetorical canon:

   We have succeeded in making the [classical] rhetorical tradition something to be studied, taught, and tested. Perhaps we ought to ask if it actually exists, or at least if it is the only story we need to be telling ourselves about our past. If we can set aside the idea of a *unified* rhetorical tradition of canonical texts, we may be able to take a broader perspective that makes rhetorical processes like canonization the object of historical study. (emphasis added). Thomas P. Miller, 'Reinventing Rhetorical Traditions,' in *Learning from the Histories of Rhetoric: Essays in Honor of Winifred Bryan Horner* 26, 27 (Theresa Enos ed. 1993).

33. 'If I can risk a grand cultural generalization, I would define two great breakdowns in the rhetorical tradition: the first, in the Middle Ages, was followed by the long process of rebuilding and rediscovery in the Renaissance. The second ... started in the early nineteenth century. ...' Brian Vickers, *In Defence of Rhetoric* 215 (1988).
34. George Kennedy, *Classical Rhetoric and its Christian and Secular Tradition from Ancient to Modern Times* 173-174 (1980).
35. George Kennedy, *Classical Rhetoric and its Christian and Secular Tradition from Ancient to Modern Times* 173-174 (1980).
36. Vickers, *In Defence of Rhetoric* at 215.
37. Mark Backman, 'Richard McKeon and the Renaissance of Rhetoric,' in *Rhetoric: Essays in Invention and Discovery* xvi (Mark Backman ed. 1987).
38. Richard J. Schoeck, 'Lawyers and Rhetoric in Sixteenth-Century England,' in *Renaissance Eloquence: Studies in the Theory and Practice of Renaissance Rhetoric* 274 (James J. Murphy ed. 1983). But see J. A. Crook who dates the creation of law schools to fourth or fifth century Rome: '[T]hough it remains uncertain how and when [law schools] began, they were flourishing in the fourth and fifth centuries AD, the famous one being that of Berytus. They were "Technical Universities" with a fixed curriculum, and by Justinian's time entry to a Bar depended on the presentation of certificates.' Crook at 45.
39. George Kennedy, *Classical Rhetoric and its Christian and Secular Tradition from Ancient to Modern Times* 180 (1980).
40. 'In [any] event, the medieval rhetorician's knowledge of classical rhetoric texts was largely confined to those introductory and extremely practical school texts, Cicero's *De Inventione* and the anonymous *Rhetorica ad Herennium*, often found combined in manuscripts, of which John Ward estimates that "between 1,000 and 2,000 copies" survive, "making them the major works of Latin antiquity for the Middle Ages" and "arguably the most widely used classical Latin writings of all time".' Vickers, *In Defence of Rhetoric* at 216.
41. Flavius Magnus Aurelius Cassiodorus (circa 490-585) was a Roman historian. He founded the monastery of Vivarium in Apulia, Italy for the purpose of translating and preserving both ancient and Christian manuscripts.
42. Isidore of Seville (circa 560-636) was a Spanish theologian and archbishop. In his *Etymologiae*, Isidore of Seville attempted to compile all secular and religious knowledge. The *Etymologiae* was a standard reference and textbook throughout the medieval period.
43. George Kennedy, *Classical Rhetoric and its Christian and Secular Tradition from Ancient to Modern Times* 177 (1980).
44. Kennedy, *Classical Rhetoric* at 178 (emphasis added).
45. Kennedy, *Classical Rhetoric* at 180 (emphasis added).
46. Kennedy, *Classical Rhetoric* at 182.

47. Kennedy, *Classical Rhetoric* at 186 (emphasis added).
48. Kennedy, *Classical Rhetoric* at 191.
49. 'In *writing* are the roots, in writing are the foundations of *eloquence*.' This judgment, written in A.D. 95 by Marcus Fabius Quintilianus in his *Institutio Oratoria*, was not unique to him. It was an idea pervasive in Roman culture over many centuries. Quintilian himself quotes Cicero as saying a century and a half earlier that the pen is 'the best modeler and teacher of eloquence.' Murphy, 'Roman Writing Instruction as Described by Quintilian' at 19 (emphasis added).
50. Vickers, *In Defence of Rhetoric* at 227.
51. A few commentators reject the preceding generalizations about the medieval period. For instance, Marjorie Curry Woods finds an 'extraordinary coherence in the school texts on which literacy was based during the Middle Ages. The books that formed the basis of rhetorical education in composition at the beginning of the Middle Ages continued to be taught more than a thousand years later.' In 'The Teaching of Writing in Medieval Europe,' in *A Short History of Writing Instruction from Ancient Greece to Twentieth-Century America* 77, 81 (James J. Murphy ed. 1990).
52. Vickers, *In Defence of Rhetoric* at 254-255. 'Poggio, hunting through the abbey of St. Gall in 1416, found a complete Quintilian "safe and unharmed, though covered with mould and filthy with dust" in a cell at the foot of a tower, together with a manuscript of Asconius' commentaries on Cicero's speeches. ... [I]n 1421, Gerardo Landriani, bishop of Lodi, found a complete manuscript of Cicero's *De Oratore, Orator*, and *Brutus*, the last totally unknown, the other two known only from mutilated versions.'
53. Kennedy, *Classical Rhetoric* at 196-197. '[Renaissance scholars learned] that rhetoric was the discipline which had created the forms, disposed the contents, and ornamented the pages which they admired and sought to imitate. Rhetoric proved to be not the arid study of the medieval trivium or the technical teachings of *De Inventione* and the *Rhetorica ad Herennium*, but a noble and creative art, characteristic of man at his best.'
54. Vickers, *In Defence of Rhetoric*, at 256.
55. Vickers, *In Defence of Rhetoric* at 257.
56. Vickers, *In Defence of Rhetoric* at 265.
57. Vickers, *In Defence of Rhetoric* at 263.
58. Vickers, *In Defence of Rhetoric* at 285: 'The decline of forensic and deliberative eloquence, the continuing shift from primary rhetoric (spoken, often in face-to-face confrontation) to secondary (written, at a distance), left more space for epideictic [or ceremonial rhetoric]. ...' (emphasis added).
59. Vickers, *In Defence of Rhetoric* at 270-71. See also Kennedy, *Classical Rhetoric* at 199 (noting that '[o]f the Greek emigrants to Italy, the most important for the history of rhetoric is George Trebizond (1395-1472), who introduced Hermogenes and the Byzantine Greek rhetorical tradition to the West'). George of Trebizond's greatest work is *Rhetoricorum Libri V.* or Five Books of Rhetoric, published in 1433 or 1434.
60. 'Francis Bacon (1565-1621), lord chancellor of England ... was a distinguished orator in the House of Commons and the lawcourts.' In his *De Augmentis Scientiarum*, he discusses Aristotle's rhetoric. Kennedy, *Classical Rhetoric* at 215.
61. Vickers, *In Defence of Rhetoric* at 276.
62. Richard Schoeck, 'Lawyers and Rhetoric in Sixteenth-Century England,' in *Renaissance Eloquence: Studies in the Theory and Practice of Renaissance Rhetoric* (James J. Murphy ed. 1983) at 275.
63. Richard Schoeck, 'Lawyers and Rhetoric' at 278.
64. Richard Schoeck, 'Lawyers and Rhetoric' at 284-86.

65. Richard Schoeck, 'Lawyers and Rhetoric' at 288.
66. Jean Dietz Moss, 'Revival of Practical Reasoning,' at 5.
67. Kennedy, *Classical Rhetoric* at 196: '[Renaissance scholars] were intoxicated with the language and literature of antiquity and sought to recover all possible knowledge of it and to make that knowledge the basis of the twin ideals of wisdom and eloquence in the culture of the times ...'
68. Richard Lloyd-Jones, 'Using the History of Rhetoric,' in *Learning from the Histories of Rhetoric: Essays in Honor of Winifred Bryan Horner* 20 (Theresa Enos ed. 1993).
69. Vickers, *In Defence of Rhetoric* at 294.
70. Vickers, *In Defence of Rhetoric* at 316. Quintilian lists dozens of figures of *thought* such as the rhetorical question, apostrophe, insinuation, and dissimulation, and divides figures of *speech* into four types: variations of syntax, modes of iteration, word-play, and balance and antithesis.
71. Vickers, *In Defence of Rhetoric* at 239.
72. Vickers, *In Defence of Rhetoric* at 296.
73. Vickers, *In Defence of Rhetoric* at 296.
74. Vickers, *In Defence of Rhetoric* at 276.
75. Vickers, *In Defence of Rhetoric* at 295.
76. Vickers, *In Defence of Rhetoric* at 295.
77. Kennedy, *Classical Rhetoric* at 228.
78. Kennedy, *Classical Rhetoric* at 227.
79. Kennedy, *Classical Rhetoric* at 222.
80. Kennedy, *Classical Rhetoric* at 230.
81. Kennedy, *Classical Rhetoric* at 232.
82. George Campbell, *The Philosophy of Rhetoric* xxviii (Lloyd F. Bitzer ed. 1963).
83. Campbell, *The Philosophy of Rhetoric* at li.
84. Kennedy, *Classical Rhetoric* at 235.
85. James A. Berlin, *Writing Instruction in Nineteenth-Century American Colleges* 27 (1984).
86. Nan Johnson, 'Three Nineteenth-Century Rhetoricians: The Humanist Alternative to Rhetoric as Skills Management,' in *The Rhetorical Tradition and Modern Writing* 106 (James J. Murphy ed. 1982). 'Before the publication of Theremin's *Eloquence a Virtue* (1844), Day's *Elements of the Art of Rhetoric* (1850), and Hope's *Princeton Textbook in Rhetoric* (1854), rhetorical education in American colleges was generally dominated by the extremely popular English rhetorics of Hugh Blair, George Campbell, and Richard Whately.'
87. Kennedy, *Classical Rhetoric* at 240. In addition, Berlin states that:
    > Nicholas Boylston had provided 1,500 pounds for a chair of rhetoric at Harvard in 1771, but the endowment was not used until 1806, when John Quincy Adams was appointed the first Boylston Professor of Rhetoric. The statute of the endowment specifically stipulated that the instructor in rhetoric was to follow the classical model in theory and in classroom practice. ... Instruction was to focus on invention, disposition (arrangement), elocution (style), and pronunciation. Berlin, *Writing Instruction in Nineteenth-Century American Colleges* at 14.
88. Berlin, *Writing Instruction in Nineteenth-Century American Colleges* at 17.
89. Berlin, *Writing Instruction in Nineteenth-Century American Colleges* at 35.
90. Kennedy, *Classical Rhetoric* at 240.
91. Berlin, *Writing Instruction in Nineteenth-Century American Colleges* at 9: 'In the eighties and nineties, the elective system at the new American university ... divided the entire academic community into discrete parts, leading to an assembly-line conception of

education. As far as rhetoric is concerned, this meant that persuasive discourse – the appeal to the emotions and the will was now seen to be possible only in oratory, and concern for it was thus relegated to the speech department. Discourse dealing with imagination was made the concern of the newly developed literature department. The writing course was left to attend to the understanding and reason, deprived of all but the barest emotional content.'

92. Berlin, *Writing Instruction in Nineteenth-Century American Colleges* at 34: 'As the nineteenth century progressed, college rhetorics increasingly came to focus on written language ... America was changing from an oral culture to a print culture ... The ability to write effectively was becoming more important than the ability to speak at public gatherings.'

93. Berlin, *Writing Instruction in Nineteenth-Century American Colleges* at 60.

94. David R. Russell, *Writing in the Academic Disciplines* 52 (1991) (emphasis added).

95. See Berlin, *Writing Instruction in Nineteenth-Century American Colleges* at 29. Richard Whately's *Elements of Rhetoric* provided 'a new inventio of management to replace the classical inventio of discovery. Whately provides specific advice on how material appropriated elsewhere is to be managed in composition ...' See generally Susan Miller, 'Classical Practice and Contemporary Basics,' in *The Rhetorical Tradition and Modern Writing* 46 (James J. Murphy ed. 1982) (stating that in current-traditional textbooks '[w]e teach "patterns of organization" for "material" somehow already discovered rather than the original inventive *topoi* that find and recall content pertinent to a writer's purpose. For example, instead of suggesting that students may find something to say by comparing one thing to another, we teach them how to organize the details of comparisons they have derived from prior observations and good luck.')

96. Ross Winterowd, *A Teacher's Introduction to Composition in the Rhetorical Tradition* 31 (1994).

97. Berlin, *Writing Instruction in Nineteenth-Century American Colleges* at 63.

98. Berlin, *Writing Instruction in Nineteenth-Century American Colleges* at 73.

99. Winterowd, *A Teacher's Introduction* at 34.

100. Robert J. Connors et al., 'The Revival of Rhetoric in America,' in *Essays In Classical Rhetoric and Modern Discourse* 8 (Robert Connors, Lisa Ede and Andrea Lunsford eds. 1984).

101. See *Landmark Essays on Rhetorical Invention in Writing* (Richard Young and Yameng Liu eds. 1994) (containing a series of essays by various authors, beginning in 1943 and ending in 1986, which surveys the classical topic of 'invention' or discovery of arguments from different modern philosophical, ethical, epistemological, aesthetic, and organizational perspectives).

102. Kenneth Burke, 'The Five Master Terms: Their Place in a "Dramatistic" Grammar of Motives,' in *Landmark Essays on Rhetorical Invention in Writing* 1 (Richard Young and Yameng Liu eds., 1994).

103. See 2 Cicero, *De Inventione* at 71. 'All propositions are supported in argument by attributes of persons or of actions. We hold the following to be the attributes of persons: name, nature, manner of life, fortune, habit, feeling, interests, purposes, achievements, accidents, speeches made.'

104. Mark Backman, 'Richard McKeon and the Renaissance of Rhetoric,' in *Rhetoric: Essays in Invention and Discovery* vii (Mark Backman ed. 1987). See also Jean Dietz Moss, 'Prologomenon: The Revival of Practical Reasoning,' in *Rhetoric and Praxis: The Contribution of Classical Rhetoric to Practical Reasoning* (Jean Dietz Moss ed. 1986) 'The essays in this volume were composed with one common aim: to retrieve from the

classical age of rhetoric some methods of practical reasoning – methods of stimulating and ordering thought about matters of common concern – that might inform our teaching of writing today.'

105. Chaim Perelman, *The Idea of Justice and The Problem of Argument* (John Petrie trans. 1963).

106. Chaim Perelman and L. Olbrechts-Tyteca, *The New Rhetoric: A Treatise on Argumentation* (John Wilkinson and Purcell Weaver trans. 1969).

107. Corbett, *Classical Rhetoric for the Modern Student* at 629.

108. Robert F. Hanley, 'Brush Up Your Aristotle,' 12 Litigation 39, No. 2 (Winter 1986).

109. Ruggero J. Aldisert, *Logic for Lawyers: A Guide to Clear Legal Thinking* 54 (1989).

110. Richard A. Posner, *Law and Literature: A Misunderstood Relation* 270-71 (1988). Posner explains that '[a]s used by Aristotle and his successors, "rhetoric" ran the gamut of persuasive devices in communication, excluding formal logic. It thus embraced not only style but much of reasoning. Since the Middle Ages the word has come more and more to mean just the eloquent or effective use of language, and that is the approximate sense in which I shall use the word "style". The broader signification of "rhetoric" has its adherents, though.'

111. Anthony G. Amsterdam and Randy Hertz, 'An Analysis of Closing Arguments to a Jury,' 37 New York Law School Law Review 55 (1992).

112. Steven D. Jamar, 'Aristotle Teaches Persuasion: The Psychic Connection,' 8 Scribes Journal of Legal Writing 61 (2001-2002).

113. Michael R. Smith, *Advanced Legal Writing: Theories and Strategies in Persuasive Writing* (2002).

Chapter 2

Greco-Roman Legal Analysis: The Topics of Invention

Despite a wealth of commentary on legal reasoning, modern writers on the subject demonstrate a curious and regrettable disregard for the close connections between classical Greco-Roman theories of legal discourse and modern theories of legal reasoning and analysis. A few books on logic and legal reasoning, including Judge Ruggero Aldisert's *Logic for Lawyers* and Steven Burton's *An Introduction to Law and Legal Reasoning* are exceptions to this rule.[1] Their books fall within the 2,500-year-old tradition of rhetorical analysis and discourse created by Aristotle, Cicero, and Quintilian. They, like countless rhetoricians, philosophers, linguists and lawyers before them, have attempted to build on that classical tradition.

Judge Aldisert implicitly acknowledges his indebtedness to the classical tradition with an epigraph drawn from Cicero's *De Republic*, with his choice of subject matter, and with his use of centuries-old rhetorical terminology.[2] Steven Burton's approach to legal analysis and argument can also be traced back to ancient rhetorical treatises especially written for the instruction of beginning advocates. Their reliance on these ancient traditions is understandable because, from its inception down to the present day, effective legal discourse has always depended on the same time-honored argumentative topics and rhetorical techniques.

Even experienced lawyers have discovered that, in most important ways, thinking about legal problems has not changed very much in 2,500 years. As Karl Keating demonstrates in *Winning with Aristotle: The Four Kinds of Arguments*, a good understanding of classical logical and analytical principles can save time and make modern lawyers even more persuasive.[3] Writing from a practitioner's perspective, Keating asserts that modern lawyers rely primarily on four types of argument. In most cases, he says, they make arguments from definition (deduction) and similitude (induction) and support them with policy arguments drawn from circumstance and consequence.

The *locus classicus* for Keating's four types of argument, and for almost every other form of formal or informal argument, is Aristotle's *Organon*, a collection of treatises on logic. Two of those treatises, *Prior Analytics* and *Posterior Analytics*, focus on general approaches to deductive and inductive reasoning. Both were adapted for use in legal argument, first by Aristotle and later by Roman orators like Cicero and Quintilian.[4] In their own treatises on legal argument, Cicero and Quintilian described the rhetorical techniques of famous Greek and Roman orators. What they discovered was an analytical technique that is as applicable today as it was then.

DIALECTICAL 'PROOF' AND RHETORICAL 'PROBABILITY'

The Roman rhetorical treatises were written for inexperienced advocates or for anyone who might sometime argue a case in court.[5] The treatises were not directed solely at students but were intended for use by all members of the educated classes.[6] In effect, they were practice manuals replete with examples drawn from famous cases. They described the analytical techniques and practice of experienced advocates and were descriptive, rather than prescriptive, in force. With varying degrees of success, these treatises systematized legal analysis and suggested ways of effectively organizing the available arguments. These books treated 'rhetoric' in its Aristotelian sense of being the 'faculty [power] of discovering in the particular case what are the available means of persuasion.'[7]

Most Roman rhetoricians were directly or indirectly indebted to Aristotle's *Rhetoric* for their basic assumptions about reasoning in general and legal reasoning in particular. Aristotle divided reasoning into two categories – induction and deduction.[8] Using special technical terms, Aristotle explained how induction and deduction function in rhetorical discourse: '[I]n Dialectic [logic] we have, on the one hand, induction, and, on the other, the syllogism and apparent syllogism, so in Rhetoric: the example is a form of induction; while the enthymeme is a syllogism, the apparent enthymeme an apparent syllogism.'[9]

Centuries later, Aristotle's two categories were adapted for use by Roman rhetoricians like Cicero, who relied on them and even employed Aristotle's terminology. In his *De Inventione*, for example, Cicero observes that:

> [a]ll argumentation, then, is to be carried on either by induction or by deduction. *Induction* is a form of argument which leads the person with whom one is arguing to give assent to certain undisputed facts; through this assent it wins his approval of a doubtful proposition because this resembles the facts to which he has assented.[10]

When creating *deductive* arguments, Cicero and other Roman rhetoricians 'used an adaptation of the logical syllogism ... in the form of the enthymeme, a syllogism in which the major premise is only probable, or one in which one term is omitted.'[11]

Aristotle carefully distinguished between the discipline of formal logic, or dialectic, as it appears in his *Prior and Posterior Analytics*, and the discipline of rhetoric.[12] According to him, dialectic is designed to produce irrefutable proofs. Rhetoric, on the other hand, deals with probabilities, not 'proof' and was created for use before deliberative bodies and judges.[13] In both those contexts, the 'rhetorical' arguments are designed to demonstrate probabilities, not irrefutable proofs.

Aristotle and other rhetoricians recognized and emphasized that formal logic had limited usefulness as a tool of persuasion and were careful to describe those limits. They also emphasized that their books were written to introduce readers to traditional forms of legal analysis and to teach a systematic method of devising and organizing arguments.[14] Using numerous examples drawn from famous cases and their own experience, they recommend a multifaceted and recursive analytical process under which advocates examine and re-examine the procedural, factual, and legal issues of a case before choosing the most effective lines of argument.

Status Theory and Issue Identification

Within the large categories of deductive and inductive argument, classical rhetoricians approached argument-creation or 'invention' very methodically, gradually narrowing and particularizing their search. First, they began by categorizing legal arguments according to their *status*. The term *status* means 'position' or 'answer to an action.'[15] For Quintilian a cause of action arises 'from the fact that it is on [the case's *status*] that the first collision between the parties to the dispute takes place, or that [the parties' position] forms the *basis* or *standing* of the whole case.'[16] Roughly speaking, this 'collision between the parties' creates the 'issue' in the case.

Quintilian, along with many others, attributed 'status' theory to Hermagoras, a second-century B.C. rhetorician.[17] Hermagoras' approach to invention divides arguments into four kinds: those based on facts, those based on definition, those based on justification or 'quality,' and those based on procedural issues or 'processes.'

Drawing on Hermagoras' categories, Cicero begins his discussion of invention with the assertion that '[e]very subject which contains in itself a controversy ... involves a question about a fact, or about a definition or about the nature of an act, or about legal processes.'[18] He explains that '[w]hen the dispute is about a fact, the issue is said to be conjectural ... because the plea is supported about conjectures or inferences [about what has been done].'[19] A question about a definition arises when 'the deed appears differently to different people and for that reason different people describe it in different terms.'[20] A qualitative issue arises in two categories: the equitable and the legal: 'The equitable is that in which there is a question about the nature of justice and right or the reasonableness of reward or punishment. The legal is that in which we examine what the law is according to the custom of the community and according to justice ...'[21]

Cicero devotes most of his attention to the first three categories, but does insist that advocates also examine their cases from a 'process' or procedural point of view, especially:

> when the case depends on the circumstance that it appears that the right person does not bring the suit, or that he brings it against the wrong person, or before the wrong tribunal, or at a wrong time, under the wrong statute, or the wrong charge, or with a wrong penalty, [In those cases,] the issue ... seems to require a transfer to another court or alteration in the form of pleading.[22]

Quintilian, using a somewhat different vocabulary, elaborates on Cicero's categories, adding distinctions of his own and providing numerous examples of how this approach enables advocates to discover which arguments to make. In the end, however, he concedes that 'there are three things on which enquiry is made in every case: we ask *whether a thing is, what it is* and *of what kind it is.*' For both Cicero and Quintilian, the question of a case's *status* was critical to their analysis of available arguments.

FACTUAL ANALYSIS

Under classical theory, factual analysis is closely connected to the question of a case's *status*. Before advocates can choose arguments or an argumentative strategy, they must have a thorough understanding of the facts of their case and the applicable law.

According to Aristotle, 'in forensic speaking[,] prosecution and defence alike must be based upon a study of the facts ... The more facts he has at his command, the more easily will he make his point; and the more closely they touch the case, the more germane will they be to his purpose, and the less like sheer commonplace.'[23] They regarded factual analysis a key step in *inventio* (to come upon or find arguments).[24] To insure that this factual analysis was conducted effectively, they inventoried and illustrated the kinds of facts that are most likely to be legally significant. These inventories functioned as informal checklists to insure that no significant facts were overlooked.

Cicero, like many other rhetoricians, assumed that '[a]ll propositions are supported in argument by attributes *of persons or of actions*. We hold the following to be the attributes of persons: name, nature, manner of life, fortune, habit, feeling, interests, purposes, achievements, accidents, speeches made.'[25] Quintilian provided a slightly different list when he observed that 'all arguments fall into two classes, those concerned with things and those concerned with persons.'[26] According to Quintilian, most arguments from *person* focus on birth, nationality, country, sex, age, training, bodily constitution, fortune, occupation, past life, and previous utterances.[27] Quintilian's checklist and others like it were designed to comb the record for legally significant information regarding the personality and background of those involved in the case and to focus the advocate's attention on all legally significant facts.

In addition to analyzing the personal attributes of litigants and witnesses, advocates must also analyze the circumstances within which the events in question took place. For Cicero, this meant classifying facts according to kind, nature, meaning, importance, time, and place.[28] For Quintilian, it meant taking into account 'time, place, occasion, instruments, means.'[29] Quintilian also noted that a thorough analysis focuses on why, where, and how the conduct transpired.[30] The *Rhetorica ad Herennium* suggested examining the place where the events took place, the time they took place, the duration of events, the special circumstances surrounding events, the person's hope of success, and the person's hope of escaping detection.[31] Each rhetorician's checklist differs somewhat from the others, but the purpose of each is the same – to ensure an exhaustive examination of the facts giving rise to a legal dispute.

Aristotle understood, of course, that arguments depend on the particular facts of the case and that factual analysis must, therefore, be focused as well as thorough. Stressing the need for selectivity, he noted that arguments 'do not start out from any and every fact, but from the *characteristic* facts belonging to their *particular* subject.'[32] But he also noted that the 'more facts he [the advocate] has at his command, the more easily will he make his point; and the more closely they touch the case, the more germane will they be to his purpose, and the less like sheer commonplace (generic facts).'[33]

TOPOI OR COMMON LINES OF ARGUMENT

A preliminary, but focused, factual analysis helps advocates identify which arguments they should make. But it is in the creation of *topoi* – the identification and description of argumentative premises – that Aristotle made one of his most significant and enduring contributions. Aristotle listed, described, and illustrated dozens of *topoi*, or commonly used lines of argument.[34] Like the checklists for insuring that no important facts are overlooked, the *topoi* insure that no line of argument is overlooked.

For Aristotle, *topos* is a live metaphor, a place where arguments of different kinds may be found:

> [They] are the commonplaces in which are found the universal forms of argument used by all men, and in every science. And, again, [they] are *special places* [like judicial or forensic *topoi*] where you naturally seek a particular argument, or an argument on some point in a more special branch of knowledge ... *Topos*, then, may be regarded as a place or region in the whole realm of science, or as a pigeon-hole in the mind of the speaker.[35]

These *topoi* provide invaluable shortcuts to discovering available arguments and issues. When coupled with factual analysis, they provide advocates with a comprehensive 'investigative research methodology.'[36]

Although the *topoi* are important, they are not infallible, as Quintilian observed when he stated that the 'places' may be an obstacle to progress 'unless a certain innate penetration and a power of rapid divination seconded by study lead us straight to the arguments which suit our case.'[37] As Quintilian and the other rhetoricians compiled their *topoi*, they understood that 'the discovery of arguments was not the result of the publication of text-books, but every kind of argument was put forward before any rules were laid down, and it was only later that writers of rhetoric noted them and collected them for publication.'[38] Thus, the handbooks and manuals written by Greco-Roman rhetoricians described and memorialized the most effective *topoi* and the most successful techniques of their colleagues, but did not attempt to create or recommend untested arguments or techniques.

A. Confirmatio or Affirmative Arguments

Classical rhetoricians divided forensic argument into two broad categories – *confirmatio*, or affirmative arguments, and *refutatio*, or refutations.[39] Cicero described *confirmatio* as that part of the argument 'which by marshalling arguments lends credit, authority, and support to our case.'[40] *Refutatio* is that part 'in which arguments are used to impair, disprove, or weaken the confirmation or proof in our opponents' [argument].'[41] Within these broad categories, advocates place the 'proofs' of their case.

Although some of Aristotle's *topoi* are inapplicable in a modern legal context, most of them still apply. Aristotle identified several *topoi* as being particularly suitable in forensic discourse: arguments based on induction, existing decisions (precedents), definition, time, ambiguity, division (status and enumeration), consequence, motivation, conflicting facts, and cause and effect.[42]

In compiling their own lists of argumentative *topoi*, Cicero, Quintilian, and the author of the *Rhetorica ad Herennium* discussed and illustrated almost all of Aristotle's *topoi*, and, in the process, identified the most distinctive qualities of forensic arguments. The complexity and depth of their analysis of each *topos* is exemplified by the attention they gave to *topoi* such as 'previous decisions' (precedents), examples (either historical or hypothetical), and definition.

In discussing various inductive arguments, for example, Roman rhetoricians thoroughly analyzed and illustrated even the comparatively unimportant *topos* of 'existing decisions' (precedents).[43] Unlike Anglo-American lawyers who rely heavily on 'existing decisions' or precedents to support their arguments, Greco-Roman rhetoricians regarded the use of precedents as a stylistic embellishment, not a substantive requirement.[44] Moreover, since the Greeks and Romans had code-based rather than common-law legal systems, the precedential value of 'existing decisions' was limited.[45] Notwithstanding the limited applicability of precedent-based arguments in the classical context, these rhetoricians nevertheless compiled a nearly comprehensive catalogue of all the points that advocates must consider when making arguments based on precedent.

Beginning with Aristotle's rather broad discussion of 'existing decisions,' they emphasized that the precedent must be on point factually and widely accepted as authoritative:

> Another *topos* is from an existing decision. The decision may be on the point at issue, or on a point like it, or on the opposite point – preferably a decision that has been accepted by all men at all times; but if not that, then a decision accepted by the majority of mankind; or by wise or good men, all or most of them; or by the actual judges of our question; or by men whose authority these judges accept.[46]

The *Rhetorica ad Herennium* offers a similarly broad description of precedent-based arguments, but takes a different tack by focusing on the logical flaws commonly associated with them:

> The citing of a Previous Judgment will be faulty if the judgement applies to an unlike matter, or one not in dispute, or if it is discreditable, or is of such a kind that previous decisions either in greater number or of greater appropriateness can be offered by our adversaries.[47]

Cicero elaborated on these same points, but focused most of his attention onprecedent-based argumentative strategies:

> In case a decision or judgement is offered as an argument, it should ... be attacked by using the same topics (lines of argument) by which it is supported, viz. by praising those who have made the decision, by the similarity between the matter under discussion and the matter about which judgement has been given; by stating that not only has the judgement not been attacked but that it has received universal approval; and by demonstrating that the case cited was more difficult or more important to

decide than the present case. ... One ought also to notice if a unique or extraordinary case has been cited when many decisions have been made in the opposite tenor.[48]

Quintilian, a great admirer of Cicero, built on Cicero's list and suggested additional techniques for dealing with adverse precedents:

[W]e must complain of the negligence shown in the conduct of the previous case or of the weakness of the parties condemned, or of undue influence employed to corrupt the witnesses, or again of popular prejudice or ignorance which reacted unfavourably against our client ... If none of these courses can be adopted, it will still be possible to point out that the peculiar circumstances of many trials have led to unjust decisions. ... We must also ask the judges to consider the facts of the case on their merits rather than make their verdict the inevitable consequence of a verdict given by others.[49]

Taken together, these writers' advice regarding the use of precedents is nearly comprehensive; they identify most of the available precedent-based arguments. As even this limited sampling shows, they clearly understood the basic principles of precedent-based arguments.

The preceding passages also reveal a number of critical differences between classical and modern inductive methods and use of authority. The most important difference is that Greco-Roman rhetoricians, unconstrained by the principle of *stare decisis*, had greater flexibility than do modern lawyers in choosing precedents or other authorities to support their arguments. In a common-law system, for instance, modern lawyers reason inductively to synthesize a general rule based on the holdings of numerous precedents. These precedents provide 'examples' of how previous courts have solved legal disputes and control the ways in which a case may be used. The persuasive value of cases is, in some instances, dispositive of the dispute.

By contrast, under the Greek and Roman code-based systems, precedents were not sources of law.[50] Moreover, advocates were free to reason inductively from numerous historical and hypothetical, or 'invented,' examples instead of relying on judicial 'examples' (precedents). Despite these differences, classical rhetoricians used examples in much the same way that modern advocates use judicial precedents – to support and illustrate their arguments.

For classical rhetoricians, 'existing decisions' were a special type of 'example' that advocates could use to embellish or strengthen an argument. When Aristotle said that '[e]xamples serve the end of logical proofs,'[51] he had two types of 'examples' in mind – historical and hypothetical.[52] Aristotle also emphasized that the function, quality, and placement of these examples determines their strategic value. To make his point, Aristotle compared examples with witnesses:

If however he (the advocate) has Enthymemes, he must use Examples for the ends of confirmation, subsequent and complementary to the Enthymemes. The *Examples* should not precede [the enthymemes] ... When they *follow* the Enthymemes, Examples function like witnesses – and there is always a tendency to believe a witness. Accordingly, when the speaker puts the Examples *before* [the enthymeme], he must use a good many of them; if he puts them *after*, one may suffice – on the principle that a single witness, if you have a good one, will serve the purpose.[53]

In some respects, modern lawyers analyze the relationship between enacted law and cases interpreting that law in the same way that Aristotle analyzes the relationship between the major premise of an enthymeme and examples that support it. When, for instance, a modern advocate applies a statute to the facts of a case and then supports his argument with a case (example), one 'good' case will 'serve the purpose.'

'Examples' are also included in Cicero's list of comparison-based arguments:

> Lastly, probability (proof) which depends on comparison involves a certain principle of similarity running through diverse material. It has three subdivisions, similitude, parallel, example. A similitude is a passage setting forth a likeness of individuals or characters. A parallel is a passage putting one thing beside another on the basis of their resemblances. An *example* supports or weakens a case by *appeal to precedent* or experience, citing some person or historical event.[54]

Like Cicero, Quintilian included example-based arguments in his class of inductive arguments. And, like Cicero, he emphasized that the choice of examples depends on factual parallels between the example and the client's case: 'We must therefore consider whether the parallel is complete or only partial, that we may know whether to use it in its entirety or merely to select those portions which are serviceable.'[55]

As the preceding analysis demonstrates, classical rhetoricians supported and illustrated their arguments in much the same way as modern advocates. The principal difference between them is that classical rhetoricians relied heavily on historical or hypothetical 'examples,' whereas modern lawyers rely on judicial precedents. Notwithstanding these differences, the analytical techniques and argumentative strategies that classical rhetoricians developed for working with 'examples' apply equally well to modern judicial precedents. That is, both classical and modern advocates use the same types of argument to support their interpretation of the law.

B. Deductive 'Proofs' and Statutory Interpretation

Given the code-based system within which they worked, Greek and Roman rhetoricians understandably devoted much of their analysis to what Aristotle termed 'particular' (enacted) laws, that is, laws 'which an individual community lays down for itself,' as opposed to the 'universal' law or the law of nature, which is a 'natural and universal notion of right and wrong, one that all men instinctively apprehend ...'[56] They used this 'particular' or enacted law as a starting point for syllogistic arguments in support of their case.

In their search for a strong major premise, they again used standardized arguments, or *topoi*, to analyze the language and intent of the law. Once they established their major premise, they formed their minor premise from the facts of the case. Then, based on the relationship between these two premises, they drew their conclusions.

Aristotle's principal contributions to this subject were his suggestions about which kinds of arguments to look for and his insistence on examining and defining the premises of those arguments.[57] Classical rhetoricians' selection of deductive *topoi* was governed in part by their understanding that, given the imperfect nature of the legislative process and the inherent ambiguities of language, enacted laws are very often imprecise or incomplete:

> [Imprecision] is unintentional when a point escapes their (the legislators') notice. It is intentional when they find themselves unable to make the law precise, and are forced to lay down a sweeping rule, but only one that is applicable to the majority of cases; also when the endless number of possible cases makes it hard to frame specific laws – hard, for example, [when making a law regarding] 'wounding with an iron instrument' to specify sizes and kinds. Life would be too short to enumerate them.[58]

Given the imprecision and limits of language and the inevitable question of legislative intent, Aristotle described several commonplace arguments, beginning with those that are useful when the law is adverse to an advocate's case. He suggested that, when faced with an adverse law, an advocate can argue that the statute is inequitable, ineffective, self-contradictory, ambiguous, outdated or in conflict with another law:

> [I]f the written law is adverse to [the advocate's] case, he must appeal to the universal law, and to the principles of equity as representing a higher order of justice ... equity is permanent and unchanging, and the universal law likewise ... whereas the written laws are subject to frequent change ... [or he can contend that] the written law is a sham, since it does not produce the effect of true law ... [or that] a given law ... conflicts with another, approved, law, or even contradicts itself ... [or that] a law is ambiguous ... [or that] the circumstances for which the law was made no longer exist, while the law remains in force.[59]

Like Aristotle, Cicero was acutely aware that legislative draftsmen and those who draft contracts must work with imprecise language and do not always clearly express their intent. His analysis of enacted laws and written contracts focused on five common problems:

> In one case it seems that there is a variance between the actual words and the intent of the author; in another, that two or more laws disagree; again, that what is written has two or more meanings; again, that from what has been written something is discovered which has not been written; finally, that there is a question about the meaning of a word ... [T]he first class is said to be concerned with the letter and the intent, the second with the conflict of laws, the third with ambiguity, the fourth with reasoning by analogy, and the fifth with definition.[60]

Quintilian compiled a similar list and, in addition, suggested several techniques for resolving problems and creating arguments. If, for instance, an issue is raised by a conflict between the letter and the spirit of a law, advocates can show that obeying the letter of the law is impossible ('[c]hildren shall support their parents under penalty of imprisonment' does not apply to infants, indigents, incompetents, imbeciles, etc.')[61] Advocates may also 'find something in the actual words of the law which enables [them] to prove that the intention of the legislator was different.'[62] If the issue is raised by a conflict of laws, the advocate must determine which law is most 'stringent,' which is the oldest, which will suffer most by its contravention, and consider whether the laws concern the state or private individuals, rewards or punishments.[63] Issues based on ambiguity should be settled by reference to what is most natural and equitable and which most reflects the intent of the author.[64]

These lists of argument topics show that classical rhetoricians had a clear understanding of the most common and effective argumentative strategies when dealing with an enacted law or written contract. In an effort to find the best possible premise from which to argue a case, they classified these arguments in various ways. Moreover, their frequent emphasis on precision, on the letter and spirit of laws, and on ambiguity reveals their understanding that definition is a quintessential starting point for syllogistic or enthymematic arguments.

According to Aristotle, an argument from definition explicates important terms, 'gets at [their] essential meaning, and then proceeds to reason from it on the point at issue.'[65] In one way or another, the rhetoricians' *topoi* help advocates define critical terms and focus on the important issues. Sometimes, as the *Rhetorica ad Herennium* notes, an argument from definition requires refuting contradictory definitions:

> When we deal with the Issue of Definition, we shall first briefly define the term in question ... then we shall connect our conduct with the explanation of the term; finally, the principle underlying the contrary definition will be refuted, as being false, inexpedient, disgraceful, or harmful.[66]

Quintilian provided the most complete discussion of definition-based arguments. He stated that the 'most effective method of establishing and refuting definition is derived from the examination of properties and differences, and sometimes even from consideration of etymology ...'[67] Elsewhere, he stated that definition 'consists mainly in the statement of *genus, species, difference* and *property.*'[68] He cautioned, however, against definitions that are superfluous, irrelevant, ambiguous, inconsistent, or too narrow.[69] Important as they are, he also observed that over-reliance on arguments from definition 'is a most dangerous practice, since, if we make a mistake in a single word, we are like to lose our whole case.'[70]

C. Enthymemes

Quintilian's reservations about the dangers surrounding arguments from definition reflect his awareness that advocates seldom argue solely on the basis of a narrow definition or a formally correct syllogism. Instead of using formal syllogisms, Greco-Roman rhetoricians used a modified form of syllogism called an enthymeme to compose their rhetorical 'proofs.' Like a syllogism, an enthymeme comprises a major premise, a minor premise, and a conclusion. However, in an enthymeme, the major premise is left unstated or is understood.[71] For Quintilian, an enthymeme is a 'rhetorical syllogism ... an incomplete syllogism, because its parts are not so clearly defined or of the same number as those of the regular syllogism.'[72]

According to Aristotle, enthymemes are a 'kind of syllogism which almost entirely deals with [human life and action]'[73] and are divided into two classes:

(1) Demonstrative Enthymemes, which prove that a thing is, or is not, so and so; and (2) Refutative Enthymemes [which controvert the Demonstrative]. The difference between the two kinds is the same as that between syllogistic proof and disproof in dialectic. By the demonstrative enthymeme we draw a conclusion from *consistent* propositions; by the refutative we draw a conclusion from *inconsistent* propositions.[74]

Unlike the complex, formal proof achieved with a traditional syllogism, enthymematic 'proofs' or arguments are comparatively simple, informal arguments which, like all rhetorical arguments, draw only 'a *probable* conclusion from the *facts* under consideration.'[75] Aristotle emphasized both this informality and simplicity and the importance of facts when he admonished advocates not to:

> begin the chain of reasoning too far back, or its length will render the [enthymematic] argument obscure; and you must not put in every single link, or the statement of what is obvious will render it *prolix*. These are the reasons why uneducated men are more effective than the educated in speaking to the masses ... Educated men lay down *abstract principles* and draw general conclusions; the uneducated argue from their *everyday knowledge*, and base their conclusions upon immediate *facts*.[76]

Thus, enthymematic arguments, like other syllogistic arguments, depend on the advocate's clear, precise presentation, his complete grasp of the relevant facts, and his ability to detect and deal with any unstated premises.

D. Refutatio or Refutation

Although the *topoi* help advocates discover the 'available means of persuasion' and devise affirmative arguments for their case, they can also help advocates discover ways to refute their opponents' arguments. Some of these standard refutations have already been discussed in connection with inductive and deductive arguments.[77] As that discussion showed, classical rhetoricians were very resourceful in finding faults and logical flaws in their opponents' arguments.

Cicero said that to detect these flaws, advocates must use 'the same sources of invention that *confirmation* (affirmative argument) does, because any proposition can be attacked by the same methods of reasoning by which it can be supported.'[78] Quintilian concurred, observing that the 'principles of argument in refutation can only be drawn from the same sources as those used in proof, while topics and thoughts, words and figures will all be on the same lines.'[79]

To illustrate this point, many rhetoricians discussed refutative enthymemes which are refutations based on the *form* of the argument and which focus on the enthymeme's premises and conclusion. Aristotle, for example, listed four common techniques: attack your opponent's own premise, adduce another premise like it, adduce a premise contrary to it, and adduce previous decisions.[80] Quintilian adopted a similar strategy and noted that the form of an enthymematic proof may be 'countered in three ways, that is to say it may be attacked in all its parts. For either the major premise or the minor or the conclusion or occasionally all three are refuted.'[81] Aristotle particularly liked 'refutative enthymemes' because 'the refutative kind brings out, in small compass, two opposing arguments, and the two things, side by side, are plainer to the audience.'[82]

Aristotle listed and described several fallacious or 'spurious enthymemes,' some of which – hasty generalization, *post hoc, ergo propter hoc* – are familiar logical fallacies.[83] The *Rhetorica ad Herennium* and other Roman handbooks also contain extensive lists of these fallacies along with examples of how to detect them. The *Rhetorica ad Herennium* calls these fallacies 'faults'[84] and says they appear, for instance, if 'we misapply a sign designating a variety of things in such a way as to indicate specifically a single thing' or if 'that which is directed against the adversary can as well fit some one else or the speaker himself'[85] or if we 'assume as certain, on the ground that 'it is universally agreed upon,' a thing which is still in dispute.'[86] Cicero's formulation is similar: 'Therefore in the refutation it will be shown ... that it is not a sign, or not an important one, or that it favours one's own side rather than the opponents', or that it is absolutely false, or that it can be shifted so as to create a suspicion in a different quarter.'[87]

Like the affirmative arguments, these refutations deal with probabilities, not irrefutable 'proofs.' Their principal purpose is to enable advocates to point out flaws in their opponent's argument and thereby impair its credibility. Moreover, by directing advocates' attention back to the same *topoi* they used for their affirmative arguments, the rhetoricians help ensure that they engage in a recursive and thorough analysis that characterizes the classical method.

Refutations based on the form of an argument or on its logical fallacies are not, however, the only argumentative tools at an advocate's disposal. Rhetorical treatises also provide extensive descriptions of argumentative strategies designed to ensure that arguments are effectively presented. Classical rhetoricians thought advocates should devote as much attention to organizational and stylistic strategies as to substantive arguments. In fact, according to these rhetoricians, organization and style are integral parts of argument because they strengthen and embellish argumentative 'proof' by drawing on and reinforcing familiar patterns of thought.[88]

Because they recognized the importance of effective presentation, they discussed argumentative strategy on a variety of levels. For example, Aristotle's warning against lengthy chains of reasoning[89] and his assertion that refutations are 'better liked' because they are 'plainer to the audience'[90] reflect his preference for short, clear arguments. He insists that arguments succeed, in part, on the manner of presentation.

Aristotle's focus on presentation techniques is also reflected in the *Rhetorica ad Herennium* which discusses how to organize an argument:

> In the Proof and Refutation of arguments it is appropriate to adopt an Arrangement of the following sort: (1) the strongest arguments should be placed at the beginning and at the end of the pleading; (2) those of medium force, and also those that are neither useless to the discourse nor essential to the proof, which are weak if presented separately and individually ... should be placed in the middle ... (3) when ceasing to speak ... [it is useful] to leave some very strong argument fresh in the hearer's mind.[91]

Cicero, on the other hand, provides insights into his own argumentative strategies and gives advice about how to compensate for weaknesses in his case:

> [M]y own method ... is to take the good points of my case and elaborate these, embellishing and enlarging and lingering and dwelling on and sticking to them, while any bad part or weakness in my case I leave on one side, not in such a manner as to give the appearance of running away from it but so as to disguise it and entirely cover it up by embellishing and amplifying the good point referred to.[92]

Of all the Roman rhetoricians, Quintilian provides the most comprehensive discussion of argumentative strategies. He not only endorses the *Rhetorica ad Herennium's* recommendations on 'Arrangement', but also explains why it is effective:

> In insisting on our strongest arguments we must take them singly, whereas our weaker arguments should be massed together: for it is undesirable that those arguments which are strong in themselves should have their force obscured by the surrounding matter, since it is important to show their true nature: on the other hand arguments which are naturally weak will receive mutual support if grouped together. Consequently arguments which have no individual force on the ground of strength will acquire force in virtue of their number, since all tend to prove the same thing.[93]

Elsewhere, Quintilian noted that various authorities disagree about such matters as whether a strong argument must be placed at the end of the plea, but added that 'in the disposition of our arguments we must lie guided by the interests of the individual case.'[94] He also warned against burdening 'the judge with all the arguments we have discovered, since by so doing we shall at once bore him and render him less inclined to believe us.'[95]

On the topic of refuting an opponent's arguments, Quintilian observed that:

> [w]e must further consider whether we should attack our opponent's arguments *en masse* or dispose of them singly. We shall adopt the former course if the arguments are so weak that they can be overthrown simultaneously, or so embarrassing that it would be inexpedient to grapple with them individually.[96]

Elsewhere, he suggested that those arguments which rely on their cumulative force must be analysed individually ... The cumulative force of these arguments is damaging. But if you refute them singly, the flame which derived its strength from the mass of fuel will die down as soon as the material which fed it is separated.[97]

These and other observations about how audiences respond both to the merits of an argument and to the way it is presented illustrate why classical rhetoricians are sometimes regarded as the first practical psychologists.[98] Their desire to devise arguments that are clear, interesting, memorable, and 'better liked' and to avoid 'embarrassing' themselves or 'boring' their audience shows they thought that argumentative strategy was as important as logical integrity and consistency. Their suggestions are grounded in human psychology, and, in the case of Cicero and Quintilian, are also grounded in their own practical experience in arguing cases.

MODERN APPROACHES TO THE TOPICS OF INVENTION

Classical rhetoricians described the topics of invention in narrowly focused, frequently lengthy, treatises or chapters. Inspired by Aristotle's extensive treatment in his *Rhetoric*, Cicero devotes most of *De Inventione* to the subject.[99] He again addresses the topics of invention in *Topica*[100] and, briefly, in *De Oratore*.[101] In the *Rhetorica ad Herennium*, the special and common topics are identified and linked to fixed sequences of argument.[102] Quintilian's multi-volume *Institutio Oratoria* also contains a lengthy discussion of methods for finding arguments.[103] Argument collections of this kind functioned as critical and convenient sources of information for advocates who would otherwise have to rely on intuition or luck in their search for effective arguments.

Moreover, classical rhetoricians explicitly, and sometimes passionately, interwove lessons in morality, philosophy, history, politics and poetics into their discussion of potential arguments. In their evaluation of various lines of argument, they routinely used the vocabulary of morality and taste. When criticizing the law, they were comfortable discussing 'discreditable' precedents,[104] 'sham' statutes,[105] 'disgraceful' definitions,[106] and 'embarrassing' arguments.[107] Sometimes they even recommended arguments based on personal praise of judges and legislators, a practice that would strike modern advocates as inadvisable if not unethical.[108]

By contrast, none of the modern handbooks on legal analysis and argument address the topics of invention with the breadth, depth or tone of the classical sources. With rare exceptions, most do not acknowledge their classical predecessors at all.[109] Geared primarily toward law students or beginning practitioners, modern advocacy handbooks are usually single-volume, how-to manuals that do not discuss commonplace lines of argument in a focused way, preferring instead to distribute argument-creation advice throughout the text.

Moreover, modern authors usually adopt an impersonal, dispassionate approach to legal analysis. As they catalogue and illustrate various types of legal arguments, their tone is clinical, almost scientific. Except by implication, philosophy, poetics and politics are not included in their analysis. Despite these substantial differences, they nevertheless identify many of the same sources of argument as Aristotle, Cicero, and Quintilian. As the following examples show, some types of legal argument are timeless and have attracted the attention of both ancient and modern authors.

Wilson Huhn, whose *The Five Types of Legal Argument* exemplifies the spare, direct, checklist-type approach to argument identification, asserts that legal arguments are reducible to five: text, intent, precedent, tradition, and policy.[110] 'Text' arguments, for example, include those based on constitutions, statutes, regulations, ordinances, regulations, contracts, wills, deeds, etc. Using cases and statutes to illustrate his point, he explains how to create arguments based on 'text' (plain meaning, canons of construction, 'intra-text' analysis). His analysis of the other four types of argument follows the same pattern of description and illustration.

In the first half of his book, Huhn discusses how to find and make arguments. In the second half, he discusses how to attack them.[111] This argument/counterargument pattern recalls the *confirmatio* (affirmative arguments)/*refutatio* (refutation arguments) pattern used by Cicero and others.[112] Still other similarities with the classical texts emerge from a comparison of Huhn's technique for attacking both text and precedent-based arguments.

Huhn's general approach was foreshadowed by Aristotle who pointed out that advocates can attack 'text-' or 'law-' based arguments by showing that a 'given law ... conflicts with another ... law, or even contradicts itself ... [or that] a law is ambiguous ...'[113] Huhn makes similar recommendations when he suggests, among other tactics, that advocates attack 'text' arguments by asserting that the text is ambiguous, has a different plain meaning, contains conflicting inferences, or conflicts with other 'texts' on the same subject.[114]

On the subject of attacking adverse precedents, classical rhetoricians used a checklist approach like one from the *Rhetorica ad Herennium* that says a 'previous judgment' is faulty if it 'applies to unlike matter, or one not in dispute ... or is of such a kind that previous decisions either in greater number or of greater appropriateness can be offered ...'[115] Huhn also offers a checklist that includes arguments that a case is distinguishable, either factually or for policy reasons, or that it conflicts with other authorities.[116]

Unique in its lengthy and single-minded focus on argument-creation techniques, Huhn's handbook differs from most modern handbooks. Although a few other handbooks also include argument checklists, those checklists are comparatively short. In *Writing and Analysis in the Law*, for example, the authors devote several pages to standard types of argument based on precedent, statute, and policy.[117] They acknowledge that such lists are helpful, but emphasize that their list is not 'exhaustive.'

Similar checklists also appear in *Legal Reasoning and Legal Writing: Structure, Strategy and Style*, which lists eight skills for working with precedent (ranking, analogizing/distinguishing, synthesizing, reconciling, etc.) and ten tools for working with statutes (wording, legislative intent, court interpretation, policy, etc.)[118] A similar statute-based checklist appears in *Legal Reasoning, Writing, and Persuasive Argument*, which also identifies types of arguments based on precedents and on facts.[119] None of these texts, however, cites or relies on the classical topics of invention, despite their near-exhaustive treatment of the subject.

SIMILARITIES AND DIFFERENCES

As even this very limited sampling of modern handbooks shows, modern authors recognize the need to identify and illustrate generic lines of legal argument. They know that students and new practitioners need help in identifying 'commonplaces in which are found the universal forms of argument.'[120] However, unlike the classical authors, who collected them in a single location for ease of reference and accessibility, modern authors spread their argument checklists throughout their books, thereby making them more difficult to find and use.

Moreover, unlike the classical authors, modern authors are scrupulously neutral. When discussing authority or arguments, they avoid emotion-laden adjectives like 'discreditable,' 'sham,' 'disgraceful,' 'embarrassing.' Instead of interweaving lessons on morality or taste, modern authors confine their comments to the 'soundness' of authority or the 'efficiency' of arguments. On those rare occasions when they do discuss morality or ethics, they typically restrict that discussion to a lawyer's obligation of candor to the court.[121] As for matters of taste, the authors' preferences are usually left implicit. Occasionally, they will express a preference for a particular organizational strategy or word choice, usually on the grounds of convention or grammatical correctness.

In sum, while modern authors recognize the need for the topics of invention, they do not treat the subject as thoroughly as the classical sources. Their interests may lie elsewhere, but they could easily supplement their treatment of the topic with some discussion of the classical sources. To take just one example, advocates, like their ancient counterparts, could use enthymematic proofs to examine their own and their opponent's arguments for the underlying, but sometimes unstated, premises.[122] During this examination, they could also consider whether the case or argument depends on what the classical rhetoricians called 'demonstrative' proofs (based on consistent propositions) or 'refutative' proofs (based on inconsistent propositions).

Even though the classical rhetorical treatises thoroughly analyze the subject of argument creation, they were never regarded, even by their authors, as encyclopedic or definitive. Their primary purpose was to give 'technical instruction in the art of rhetoric.'[123] Throughout their works, the classical rhetoricians repeatedly warn against over-reliance on checklists and mechanical approaches to legal analysis. As Quintilian put it:

> [A]ll the forms of argument which I have just set forth cannot be found in every case ... [I]t is no use considering each separate type of argument and knocking at the door of each with a view to discovering whether they may chance to serve to prove our point ... Such a proceeding merely retards the process ... to an incalculable extent ...[124]

According to Quintilian, each of the *topoi* contains 'an infinite number of arguments.'[125] Obviously, all of them cannot be used in every case. Instead, he recommends that advocates treat the *topoi* as a starting point for deeper analysis. Their main purpose is to help ensure that important facts and arguments are not overlooked.[126] Classical rhetoricians also repeatedly insisted that, to be most effective, the *topoi* must be internalized until they are part of an advocate's very thought processes.

Candid as they were about the limitations of their approach to legal analysis, these rhetoricians nonetheless offer timeless and invaluable insights into analytical methods and argumentative strategy. By familiarizing themselves with the classical works, modern lawyers can attain a broader understanding of analytical methods and legal logic. Many of them need to be reminded or, in some cases, informed for the first time about standard analytical techniques, common arguments and refutations, basic logical principles, and the relationships between argument and presentation techniques.

Based on years of experience, most practicing lawyers have acquired this knowledge and use it instinctively. But beginning lawyers do not have the same breadth of experience to draw on, and even experienced lawyers sometimes forget.

The real value of these rhetorical treatises lies more in what they teach about the basic principles of legal reasoning, legal analysis, and rhetorical strategy than it does in any particular example or illustration. They explain what it means to 'think like a lawyer' and how to develop lawyer-like habits of mind. Aristotle, Cicero, and Quintilian know at least as much about 'thinking like a lawyer' as any modern authority on the subject.

Notes

1. Ruggero J. Aldisert, *Logic for Lawyers: A Guide to Clear Legal Thinking* (1989); Steven J. Burton, *An Introduction to Law and Legal Reasoning* (2nd ed. 1995).
2. Aldisert, *Logic for Lawyers*, at 54. Here and elsewhere, Judge Aldisert uses the term 'enthymeme' to describe a rhetorical concept that was analyzed extensively by classical rhetoricians. See Chapter Two for a fuller discussion of the enthymeme.
3. Karl Keating, 'Winning with Aristotle: The Four Kinds of Arguments,' 52 California State Bar Journal 308 (1977).
4. Aristotle, *Aristotle's Prior and Posterior Analytics* (W.D. Ross trans. 1957).
5. In addition to serving these functions, rhetorical treatises also describe a comprehensive educational curriculum and provide instruction on public speaking for ceremonial and political occasions.
6. 1 Marcus Fabius Quintilianus, *Institutio Oratoria* at 5-19 (H.E. Butler trans. 1954); Susan Miller, 'Classical Practice and Contemporary Basics,' in *The Rhetorical Tradition and Modern Writing* 46 (James J. Murphy ed. 1982); Donovan J. Ochs, 'Cicero's Rhetorical Theory,' in *A Synoptic History of Classical Rhetoric* 96 (James J. Murphy ed., 1983).
7. Aristotle, *The Rhetoric of Aristotle* 7 (Lane Cooper trans. 1932).
8. Aristotle, *The Rhetoric of Aristotle* at 7. Also see Cicero's *Topica*, where Cicero credits Aristotle with originating the topics of invention: 'Every systematic treatment of argumentation has two branches, one concerned with invention of arguments and the other with judgement of their validity; Aristotle was the founder of both in my opinion.' 2 Cicero, *Topica* at 387.
9. Aristotle, *Rhetoric* at 10. An enthymeme is a syllogism whose major premise is unstated. See Ruggero J. Aldisert, *Logic for Lawyers: A Guide to Clear Legal Thinking* at 54 and accompanying text; *see also* Edward P.J. Corbett, *Classical Rhetoric for the Modern Student* 73 (2d ed. 1971):

    > In modern times, the enthymeme has come to be regarded as an abbreviated syllogism – that is, an argumentative statement that contains a conclusion and one of the premises, the other premise being implied. A statement like this would be regarded as an enthymeme: 'He must be a socialist because he favors a graduated income-tax.' Here the conclusion (He is a socialist) has been deduced from an expressed premise (He favors a graduated income-tax) and an implied premise (either [a] Anyone who favors a graduated income-tax is a socialist or [b] A socialist is anyone who favors a graduated income-tax).

10. 2 Cicero, *De Inventione* at 93; see also 2 Quintilian, *Institutio Oratoria* at 273 (noting that Cicero divides all arguments into two classes, induction and ratiocination [deduction]).
11. 2 Cicero, *De Inventione* at 104, note (a).
12. Aristotle, *Rhetoric* at 9-10. 'Rhetoric is a branch of Dialectic, and resembles that. Neither ... is a science with a definite subject-matter; both are faculties for providing arguments.'

13. James L. Kinneavy, 'Translating Theory into Practice in Teaching Composition: A Historical View and a Contemporary View,' in *Essays on Classical Rhetoric and Modern Discourse* 70 (Robert J. Connors et al. eds. 1984).

14. Aristotle, *Rhetoric* at 1.

15. *Cassell's New Compact Latin Dictionary* 212 (1971).

16. 1 Quintilian, *Institutio Oratoria*, at 409.

17. 2 Cicero, *De Inventione* at 17 and 1 Quintilian, *Institutio Oratoria*, at 409.

18. 2 Cicero, *De Inventione*,at 21.

19. 2 Cicero, *De Inventione*,at 21.

20. 2 Cicero, *De Inventione*,at 23.

21. 2 Cicero, *De Inventione*, at 31

22. 2 Cicero, *De Inventione* at 23; see also *Rhetorica ad Herennium*, at 89 ('[W]e [must] first examine whether one has the right to institute an action, claim, or prosecution in this matter, or whether it should not rather be instituted at another time, or under another law, or before another examiner.')

23. Aristotle, *Rhetoric* at 157-58.

24. Donovan Ochs 'Cicero's Rhetorical Theory,' in *A Synoptic History of Classical Rhetoric* 93 (James J. Murphy ed. 1983).

25. 2 Cicero, *De Inventione* at 71 (emphasis added).

26. 2 Quintilian, *Institutio Oratoria*, at 213 (emphasis added).

27. 2 Quintilian, *Institutio Oratoria* at 213-15.

28. 2 Cicero, *De Inventione* at 127.

29. 2 Quintilian, *Institutio Oratoria* at 213.

30. 2 Quintilian, *Institutio Oratoria* at 219.

31. *Rhetorica ad Herennium*, at 67.

32. Aristotle, *Rhetoric* at 157 (emphasis added).

33. Aristotle, *Rhetoric* 157-58. This section of Aristotle's *Rhetoric* lists most, but not all, available *topoi*. Aristotle discusses other *topoi* elsewhere in *Rhetoric*. For more discussion see Chapter Two.

34. Aristotle, *Rhetoric* at 159.

35. Aristotle, *Rhetoric* at xxiv.

36. Donovan J. Ochs, 'Cicero's Rhetorical Theory,' in *A Synoptic History of Classical Rhetoric* (James J. Murphy ed. 1983).

37. 2 Quintilian, *Institutio Oratoria* at 271.

38. 2 Quintilian, *Institutio Oratoria* at 269.

39. 2 Cicero, *De Inventione* at 69 and 123.

40. 2 Cicero, *De Inventione* at 69.

41. 2 Cicero, *De Inventione* at 123.

42. Aristotle, *Rhetoric* at 159-72.

43. But see 2 Cicero, *De Inventione* at 209 (noting necessity of *topoi* for discovering all important arguments and of focusing those arguments).

44. *Rhetorica ad Herennium*, at 141. 'Since *Embellishment* consists of similes, examples, amplifications, *previous judgments*, and the other means which serve to expand and enrich the argument, let us consider the faults which attach to these.' *Rhetorica ad Herennium* at 141 (emphasis added).

45. Alan Watson, *The Spirit of Roman Law* 60 (1995) 'There is nothing at all in the legal sources, whether juristic, statutory or rulings of the emperors, and in the literary sources we have only the slightest indications that orators might refer to previous decisions in their speeches.' On the use of precedents in Athenian courts, see Adriaan Lanni, 'Precedent and

Legal Reasoning in Athenian Courts: A Noble Lie?' 43 American Journal of Legal History 27, 46 (1999) 'There was no way to verify a litigant's citation of a precedent ... and although citing a non-existent law in court was punishable by death, no decree outlawed the invention of favorable precedents. The fact that verdicts were not recorded and that the court records which were kept do not seem to have been well-organized or regularly consulted indicates that consistency of verdicts and adherence to precedent ... were not, and indeed could not have been primary goals of the Athenian legal system.'

46. Aristotle, *Rhetoric* at 164-65.
47. *Rhetorica ad Herennium*, at 143.
48. 2 Cicero, *De Inventione*, at 129.
49. 2 Quintilian, *Institutio Oratoria* at 161.
50. Crook, *Legal Advocacy in the Roman World* at 40.
51. Aristotle, *Rhetoric* at 149 (emphasis added).
52. Aristotle, *Rhetoric* at 147.
53. Aristotle, *Rhetoric* at 149 (emphasis added).
54. 2 Cicero, *De Inventione*, at 89-91 (emphasis added) (emphasis removed).
55. 2 Quintilian, *Inventione Oratoria*, at 275.
56. Aristotle, *Rhetoric* at 73.
57. Forbes I. Hill, 'The Rhetoric of Aristotle,' at 54 in *A Synoptic History of Classical Rhetoric* (James J. Murphy ed. 1983).
58. Aristotle, *Rhetoric* at 76-77.
59. Aristotle, *Rhetoric* at 80-81. The *Rhetorica ad Herennium* offers a similar list of suggestions as well as a schematic for organizing an argument:
    When the intention of the framer appears at variance with the letter of a text, speaking in support of the letter we shall employ the following topics: ... a eulogy of the framer ... next the questioning of our adversaries ... After that the interpretation devised and given to the text by our adversaries will be disparaged and weakened ... Then we shall ascertain the writer's intention and present the reason why he had in mind what he wrote, and show that that text is clear, concise, apt, complete, and planned with precision. Thereupon we shall cite examples of judgements rendered in favour of the text ... Finally, we shall show the danger of departing from the letter of the text. *Rhetorica ad Herennium*, at 81.
60. 2 Cicero, *De Inventione*, at 35-37 (emphasis added)(footnote omitted); see also *Rhetorica ad Herennium*, at 81 (discussing framers' intent).
61. 3 Quintilian, *Institutio Oratoria*, at 139.
62. 3 Quintilian, *Institutio Oratoria* at 139.
63. 3 Quintilian, *Institutio Oratoria* at 147; see also *Rhetorica ad Herennium*, at 85. 'When two laws conflict, we must first see whether they have been superseded or restricted, and then whether their disagreement is such that one commands and the other prohibits, or one compels and the other allows.'
64. 3 Quintilian, *Institutio Oratoria* at 161.
65. Aristotle, *Rhetoric* at 163.
66. *Rhetorica ad Herennium*, at 87-89.
67. 3 Quintilian, *Institutio Oratoria* at 97.
68. 3 Quintilian, *Institutio Oratoria* at 85. (Emphasis in original.)
69. 3 Quintilian, *Institutio Oratoria* at 95.
70. 3 Quintilian, *Institutio Oratoria* at 93.

71. 2 Cicero, *De Inventione* at 104-05, note a. 'The rhetorician used an adaptation of the logical syllogism either in the form of the enthymeme, a syllogism in which the major premise is only probable, or one in which one term is omitted ...'
72. 2 Quintilian, *Institutio Oratoria* at 203.
73. Aristotle, *Rhetoric* at 150.
74. Aristotle, *Rhetoric* at 158 (emphasis added).
75. Donovan J. Ochs, 'Cicero's Rhetorical Theory,' in *A Synoptic History of Classical Rhetoric* 101 (James J. Murphy ed. 1983).
76. Aristotle, *Rhetoric* at 155-56.
77. See previous discussion and illustration of logical flaws associated with adverse 'previous judgments,' adverse definitions and enacted laws adverse to a client's interests.
78. 2 Cicero, *De Inventione* at 123.
79. 2 Quintilian, *Institutio Oratoria* at 311.
80. Aristotle, *Rhetoric* at 177.
81. 2 Quintilian, *Institutio Oratoria* at 361 (emphasis removed).
82. Aristotle, *Rhetoric* at 172.
83. Aristotle, *Rhetoric* at 172.
84. *Rhetorica ad Herennium*, at 125.
85. *Rhetorica ad Herennium* at 129; also see 2 Cicero, *De Inventione* at 139 (criticizing argument 'which is no less helpful to the opponents' case than to ours'); 2 Quintilian, *Institutio Oratoria* at 329.
86. *Rhetorica ad Herennium*, at 129; compare 2 Cicero, *De Inventione* at 141 (criticizing use of 'controvertible' arguments in 'which a dubious reason is given to prove a dubious case').
87. 2 Cicero, *De Inventione*, at 127.
88. See Chapter Three on organization.
89. See Aristotle, *Rhetoric* at 155-56.
90. See Aristotle, *Rhetoric* at 172.
91. *Rhetorica ad Herennium*, at 189.
92. 3 Cicero, *De Oratore* 421.
93. 2 Quintilian, *Institutio Oratoria*, 299-300.
94. 2 Quintilian, *Institutio Oratoria* at 305.
95. 2 Quintilian, *Institutio Oratoria* at 303.
96. 2 Quintilian, *Institutio Oratoria* at 317-19.
97. 2 Quintilian, *Institutio Oratoria* at 319.
98. Aristotle, *Rhetoric* at xvii.
99. Aristotle, *Rhetoric* at 154. Cicero credits Aristotle with originating the topics of invention: 'Every systematic treatment of argumentation has two branches, one concerned with invention of arguments and the other with judgement of their validity; Aristotle was the founder of both in my opinion.' Cicero's *Topica*, at 387.
100. Cicero, *Topica* (H.M. Hubbell trans. 1949).
101. 2 Cicero, *De Oratore*, at 315-323.
102. *Rhetorica ad Herennium*, at 81.
103. 2 Quintilian, *Institutio Oratoria* at 157-369.
104. *Rhetorica ad Herennium* at 143.
105. Aristotle, *Rhetoric* at 80-81.
106. Anonymous, *Rhetorica ad Herennium* at 87-89.
107. 2 Quintilian, *Institutio Oratoria* at 319.
108. *Rhetorica ad Herennium* at 81.

109. See Chapter One for a list of those who are expressly indebted to the classical sources. Also see Karl Keating, 'Winning with Aristotle: The Four Kinds of Legal Arguments,' 52 California State Bar Journal 308 (1977) and Ruggero Aldisert, *Logic for Lawyers: A Guide to Clear Legal Thinking* (1989).
110. Wilson Huhn, *The Five Types of Argument* 13 (2002). Huhn's five types may be compared with those appearing in the *Rhetorica ad Herennium*, at 91. 'We can discuss this [legal] question, once a cause is given, when we know the departments of which the Law is constituted. The constituent departments, then, are the following: Nature, Statute, Custom, Previous Judgements, Equity, and [private]Agreement.'
111. Huhn, *The Five Types of Argument* at 92-93. Huhn provides a checklist of 26 different attack strategies.
112. 2 Cicero, *De Inventione* at 41.
113. Aristotle, *Rhetoric* at 80-81.
114. Huhn, *The Five Types of Argument* at 95-103.
115. *Rhetorica ad Herennium* at 143.
116. Huhn, *Five Types of Argument*, at 111-125. Huhn also lists several other lines of argument based on disagreements about the holding, the dissent status of the opinion, the authority of the court, etc.
117. Helene S. Shapo et al, *Writing and Analysis in the Law* 185-202 (4th ed. 1999).
118. Richard K. Neumann, Jr., *Legal Reasoning and Legal Writing: Structure, Strategy and Style*. 135 and 157 (4th ed. 2001).
119. Robin S. Wellford, *Legal Reasoning, Writing and Persuasive Argument* 285 (2002).
120. Aristotle, *Rhetoric* at xxiv.
121. Wellford, *Legal Reasoning, Writing and Persuasive Argument* at 353 (discussing an advocate's obligation to disclose adverse case law). See also Linda Edwards, *Legal Writing: Process, Analysis, and Organization* 169 and 260 (3rd ed. 2002) (listing an advocate's general professional responsibilities and, more particularly, obligations of candor regarding the law); Michael R. Smith, *Advanced Legal Writing: Theories and Strategies in Persuasive Writing* 313 (2002) (providing a chapter entitled 'The Ethics and Morality of Persuasion').
122. See also Steven D. Jamar, 'Aristotle Teaches Persuasion: The Psychic Connection,' 8 Scribes Journal of Legal Writing 61 (2001-2002) (analyzing enthymemes in modern legal discourse and in connection with the topics of invention).
123. *Rhetorica ad Herennium*, at xxiv.
124. 2 Quintilian, *Institutio Oratoria* at 269.
125. 2 Quintilian, *Institutio Oratoria* at 257.
126. 2 Quintilian, *Institutio Oratoria* at 257.

Chapter 3

Brief Rhetoric:
The Organization of Argument

But just as it is not sufficient for those who are erecting a building merely to collect stone and timber and other building materials, but skilled masons are required to arrange and place them, so in [writing], however abundant the matter may be, it will merely form a confused heap unless arrangement be employed to reduce it to order and to give it connection and firmness of structure.[1]

By necessity, instinct, and design, modern lawyers organize and write their arguments according to rhetorical principles that would be familiar to Aristotle, Cicero, and Quintilian. This is particularly true of modern appellate briefs, which must conform to court-imposed format requirements. Except for a few minor differences, these format requirements follow rules for argument that were invented by classical rhetoricians over two thousand years ago.

For example, under U.S. Supreme Court rules 14 and 24, briefs must begin with the legal questions presented for review, state the facts upon which the case is based, summarize the forthcoming argument, provide an argument based on relevant law and facts, and conclude with a description of the remedy sought.[2] Both rules emphasize that substantive sections of the brief must be organized exactly in the order just described.

In all important respects, these organizational requirements are the same as those first formulated in the fifth century B.C. by Corax of Syracuse, who is traditionally credited with creating them. Corax divided forensic discourse into the 'Introduction,' the 'Narration,' the 'Argument,' and the 'Peroration.'[3] These divisions serve some of the same purposes in classical legal arguments as the 'Question Presented,' the 'Statement of the Case,' the 'Argument Summary,' the 'Argument,' and the 'Conclusion' sections serve in a modern appellate brief.

Although modern lawyers instinctively make rhetorical decisions when organizing their arguments, instinct alone does not account for their fidelity to classical rhetorical principles. Those principles are also included in practice manuals and legal writing handbooks. While they seldom cite the classical sources, many of these manuals and handbooks nevertheless employ classical concepts and terminology. They also give formatting advice that is almost identical to that given by classical rhetoricians.

CLASSICAL PRINCIPLES OF ORGANIZATION

Rhetoric has always had strong links to judicial and forensic discourse[4] and has always been particularly concerned with the most effective and persuasive ways of organizing an argument.[5] Corax, a Sicilian whose teachings were admired by Greek rhetoricians, divided argument into 'proem' or 'Introduction,' 'Narration,' 'Argument,' and 'Peroration' or 'Conclusion.'[6]

These divisions, with some additions and modifications by Aristotle, Cicero, and Quintilian, have survived substantially intact for over two millenia. Although Aristotle maintained that an argument actually contains only two essential parts, the 'Statement of the Case' and the 'Proof,' he conceded that in practice orators usually added two more parts, the 'Introduction' and the 'Conclusion.'[7] Aristotle's Roman successors – Cicero, Quintilian, and the anonymous author of the *Rhetorica ad Herennium* – developed and refined the divisions first described by Corax.[8] They also added an argument summary section thus creating a five part division – 'Introduction' (*exordium*), 'Statement of the Case' (*narratio*), 'Argument Summary' (*partitio*), 'Proof of the Case' (*confirmatio*), and 'Conclusion' (*peroratio*) – which survived virtually intact throughout the classical period.[9] This five-part organization of legal arguments is the same as that required by the U.S. Supreme Court Rules 14 and 24.

Based on observation and analysis of the techniques of successful advocates, these divisions of the argument were never followed in a mechanical fashion. Instead, classical rhetoricians expected advocates to use the kind of flexibility that Socrates employed in his famous *Apology*.[10] Although his *Apology* predates the Roman rhetoric manuals, it nevertheless loosely adheres to their organizational strictures.[11]

In his introduction (*exordium*), Socrates first divides the charges against him into old charges (that he makes the worse seem the better cause) and new charges (that he corrupts the youth and that he rejects the old gods in favor of new ones). He then addresses each charge separately, first by briefly summarizing the important facts (*narratio*) and then by refuting the charges point by point (*confirmatio/refutatio*). He concludes each section (*peroratio*) in the same way that he began, by questioning the motives of his accusers.[12]

Despite its organizational integrity, Socrates' speech was not a successful piece of advocacy. As Socrates clearly understood, conforming to an effective format does not guarantee success.

Even so, classical rhetoricians were convinced that good legal arguments followed the same predictable pattern. To support their position, classical rhetoricians analyzed forensic discourse part by part. As they described the function of each part and discussed its connection to the argument as a whole, they developed a comprehensive taxonomy of legal discourse that prefigures the organization of modern legal arguments.

A. Exordium or 'Questions Presented'

> *The questions presented for review, [should be] expressed concisely in relation to circumstances of the case, without unnecessary detail. The questions should be short and concise and should not be argumentative or repetitive. The statement of any question presented is deemed to comprise every subsidiary question fairly included therein.*[13]

Classical conventions required that legal arguments begin with an *exordium* identifying the legal issue(s) before the court. *Exordium*, which means 'the warp of a web,' or 'a beginning,' is an especially apt metaphor that connects nicely in spirit, if not in sense, with the legal maxim that the law is a seamless web.[14] In both cases, the metaphor stresses the integration of the parts with the whole, a point that is important when analyzing the structure of arguments.

The classical *exordium* occasionally consisted solely of questions, a practice used by Cicero, and approved by Quintilian.[15] Usually, however, classical rhetoricians used an *exordium* that was much longer than its modern equivalent and was intended for a listening rather than a reading audience.[16]

In his analysis of forensic discourse, Quintilian identifies the *exordium* as that 'portion of a speech addressed to the judge before he has begun to consider the actual case.'[17] Its purpose is 'to prepare our audience in such a way that they will be disposed to lend a ready ear to the rest of our speech.'[18] This is accomplished by including 'the points which seem most likely to serve our purpose'[19] and by rebutting or lessening the force of points that damage our case.[20]

Cicero's analysis of the *exordium* is similar to Quintilian's, except that he adds that '[t]o secure an intelligent and an attentive hearing, we must start from the actual facts themselves.'[21] The *Rhetorica ad Herennium* also emphasizes that the purpose of the *exordium* is to 'enable us to have hearers who are attentive, receptive, and well-disposed.'[22] Like Cicero, the author of the *Rhetorica ad Herennium* insists that the *exordium* be framed only in terms of the facts of the case being heard, noting that an 'introduction is faulty if it can be applied as well to a number of cases.'[23]

Even allowing for differences between the spoken *exordium* and the written Questions Presented, the classical rules for composing *exordia* apply to modern 'Questions Presented.' They serve the same purpose; they introduce the court to the legal issues to be decided. Most modern textbooks on appellate advocacy provide advice similar to that of Aristotle, Cicero, and Quintilian.

As to the most effective way to introduce a case, Edward Re observes in *Brief Writing and Oral Argument* that:

> The statement of the questions presented is counsel's opportunity to focus the attention of the court on the specific question that counsel considers vital. For this purpose, a simple statement of the issue as an abstract proposition of law is too general to be of value ... The brief writer should frame the question in such a manner as to include the *key* facts of the case on appeal. Inclusion of the facts will give substance and concreteness to an otherwise abstract proposition.[24]

In *Writing in Law Practice*, Frank E. Cooper emphasizes the same point and adds that the 'Question Presented' should be 'phrased in a manner which will arrest the attention of the judges and ... induce an attitude receptive to the argument which the draftsman proposes to make.'[25] As these suggestions demonstrate, the 'Questions Presented' gives modern advocates an opportunity to make an *exordium*-like introduction to their arguments.

Other, more recent, handbooks make the same points. They recommend using the Questions Presented as 'a way of getting the court to see the issues in the case from your client's point of view by framing the question so that it suggests a response in your favor,'[26] or 'us[ing] the Question to persuade by framing it in terms of the facts at the core of your theory,'[27] or 'to begin persuading the judge to decide [the] issue in your client's favor.'[28]

U.S. Supreme Court rules for the submissions of briefs also emphasize the importance of a clear and focused introduction. Those rules require that briefs adhere to a fixed order of march, starting with the questions presented. Supreme Court Rules 14 and 24 require that these questions precede all other parts of the brief.[29] Further, these rules require that the 'questions presented for review, [be] expressed concisely in relation to the circumstances of the case, without unnecessary detail.'[30] This compels advocates to identify and particularize the forthcoming arguments. According to Rule 14, '[t]he statement of any question presented is deemed to comprise every subsidiary question fairly included therein.'[31] Although these instructions are broadly stated, they nonetheless encompass the basic principles for classical *exordia*. That is, the Supreme Court expects the 'Questions Presented' to be comprehensive with regard to the 'questions' (issues) addressed, and specific with regard to the 'circumstances' (facts) of the case.

Classical rhetoric manuals, modern legal writing handbooks, and U.S. Supreme Court rules give remarkably consistent advice about how to organize arguments. The enduring value of that advice is visible in the ways modern lawyers applied it in a high-profile First Amendment/copyright case, *Harper & Row, Publishers v. Nation Enterprises.*[32]

The 'questions presented' in *Harper & Row v. Nation Enterprises* show how modern advocates, using classical principles, create client-favorable issue statements. In this case, Plaintiff Harper & Row, owners of the copyright to former President Gerald Ford's White House memoirs, accused Defendant *Nation* magazine of unlawfully printing portions of Ford's memoirs prior to their authorized publication.[33] In response, *Nation* claimed that its publication of a small portion of Ford's memoirs dealing with former President Richard Nixon's pardon constituted a 'fair use.' They also claimed it was protected by the First Amendment.[34] Each litigant, therefore, had a different legal theory and a differently phrased 'question presented.'

Harper & Row's 'question presented' asked: 'Does the First Amendment prevail over Copyright in a fair use case, where the copyrighted material *allegedly published in the name of harvesting knowledge* was in fact *soon to be published by the copyright owner?*'[35] Using a few key facts ('soon to be published'), the publisher's brief emphasized the imminent publication of the copyrighted material in an attempt to forestall *Nation's* first amendment and 'fair use' claims. By limiting the issue to the fact of the material's imminent publication, the publisher hoped that the Court would accept its principal argument and view the case from its perspective.

By contrast, the 'question presented' in the Defendant *Nation's* brief does not focus on facts at all. Instead, it emphasizes a different set of 'circumstances': traditional principles of copyright law. For the *Nation*, the question was '[w]hether the United States Court of Appeals for the Second Circuit correctly applied long established principles of copyright law to the facts of this case[.]'[36] Broadly phrased as it is, this question aligns the magazine's legal theory with a 'long established' legal principle.

Different theories led the litigants to take different rhetorical approaches. One litigant, Plaintiff Harper & Row, follows Cicero's advice to 'start from the actual facts themselves' and bases its argument on the facts of the case (imminent publication).[37] The other litigant, Defendant *Nation* magazine, follows Quintilian, who recommended that advocates include 'the points which seem most likely to serve [their] purpose,' and bases its argument on the law ('long established principles').[38] Despite their different approaches, both advocates adopt introductory strategies that classical rhetoricians would recognize and approve.

B. Narratio or 'Statement of the Case'

> *A brief submitted to the United States Supreme Court must contain '[a] concise statement of the case containing the facts material to consideration of the questions presented.'[39]*

As with the 'Questions Presented,' when modern-day lawyers write a 'statement of the case' they are conforming to classical teachings on how to tell the story of the case. In classical nomenclature, the second principal part of a legal argument, the *narratio* or 'Statement of the Case,' is based on the truism that *ex facto oritur jus* – the law arises from the fact. For classical and modern advocates the purpose of the *narratio* is essentially the same.

For Aristotle, a forensic speech had two 'indispensible constituents': Statement of the facts and proof.[40] He added that the statement of the facts should not be too long and that advocates could 'narrate whatever tends to your own credit, or to the discredit of the other side ...'[41]

According to Cicero, the *narratio* is an account 'of the facts and ... a base and foundation for the establishment of belief.'[42] Quintilian said that the *narratio* consists of an exposition of 'that which either has been done, or is supposed to have been done ... [It is] a speech instructing the audience as to the nature of the case in dispute.'[43]

This narrative must, however, be more than a bare recitation of the facts. It must be written so that 'the judge knows not merely what has been done, but takes a view of the facts which is favorable to our case. For the purpose of the statement of the facts is not merely to instruct, but rather to persuade the judge.'[44] According to the *Rhetorica ad Herennium* 'when we set forth the facts [we should] turn every detail to our advantage so as to win the victory ...'[45] In addition, the narrative 'will be clear, if we set forth the facts in the precise order in which they occurred, observing their actual ... chronology ... [W]e must see that our language is not confused, involved, or unfamiliar ... [and we must not] omit anything pertinent.'[46]

Even more than the ancient handbooks, modern advocacy handbooks stress the importance of the statement of the facts:

> A good brief can often win a case on its factual statement alone. If the statement is clear and compelling the legal argument to follow approaches the superfluous. As the judges absorb the facts, they will call to mind, without prompting, the principles that should decide the case; all they need is a confirmation in the form of suitable authorities. The facts point directly to the applicable rules of law, and the rules of law decide the case.[47]

Echoing the 'precise order' advice of the *Rhetorica ad Herennium*, modern handbooks insist that the fact statement be logically organized, clearly written, and candid. They suggest that in 'making your statement of facts, always keep in mind the three *c*'s: chronology, candor, and clarity. Begin at the beginning and face the facts as they developed. Be objective lest your adversary point out an obvious omission.'[48] Some even quote Quintilian on the necessity of couching the facts in a way that favors the client's case: 'We must state our facts like advocates, not witnesses.'[49]

As was the case with the 'Questions Presented,' modern handbooks and classical handbooks agree that the Statement of the Case prepares readers for the arguments that follow. In varying ways, they recommend that advocates 'present your client's version of [the] facts so convincingly that a court is ready to rule in your client's favor even before reading the Argument,'[50] '[t]ightly focus the Statement of the Case on facts that advance your theory,'[51] or '[u]se the Statement to set the stage for your argument.'[52] Occasionally, these handbooks also add that it is 'common to include only those emotionally significant facts that favor your client.'[53]

While the U.S. Supreme Court requires advocates to provide a statement of the case before making their arguments, its rules regarding the 'Statement of the Case' are stated even more broadly than those regarding the 'Questions Presented.'[54] The Court rules simply require advocates to provide a 'concise statement of the case setting out the facts material to consideration of the questions presented.'[55]

Modern lawyers interpret this rule very loosely. Experienced advocates instinctively summarize the facts in a light favorable to their clients. In doing so, they frequently provide the court with dramatically contrasting accounts of the same events. For example, opposing briefs in the *Harper & Row Publishers* case use similar techniques to describe how Gerald Ford's unpublished memoirs were acquired and used. Both sides are very selective about which facts they emphasize and very careful with their wording.

The Plaintiff's brief, for example, stresses the Defendant *Nation's* furtive ('secretly'), unsanctioned ('unauthorized'), and hasty ('rushed into print') appropriation of substantial portions of the memoirs:

> In late March 1979, a person, never identified, secretly gave [*Nation's* editor] Navasky a copy of the unpublished manuscript of the memoirs. Navasky knew that his receipt of the manuscript was unauthorized. Over the next 24 hours or weekend, the Nation rushed into print for its April 7, 1979 edition, a 2,250 word cover-featured piece 'The Ford Memoirs-Behind the Nixon Pardon,' derived almost exclusively from the memoirs, 83 percent ... of which was copied ... from the unpublished manuscript.[56]

By contrast, the *Nation's* brief emphasizes the length of the memoirs and the fact that the *Nation* was a passive recipient of an unsolicited manuscript from an anonymous source:

> Early in April, 1979, a copy of the 655 page, 200,000 word manuscript of *A Time to Heal* was provided to Victor Navasky, editor of The Nation ... It is undisputed that the manuscript was not sought; it was not paid for; indeed, The Nation had had no prior connection of any sort with the book.[57]

Juxtaposed in this way, both passages seem patently biased and somewhat heavy-handed. However, in the context of the entire Statement of the Case, the bias is less noticeable. Even short passages like these offer advocates opportunities to use narrative techniques that would be familiar to classical rhetoricians. In the words of the *Rhetorica ad Herennium*, both advocates 'turn every detail to [their] advantage so as to win the victory ...'[58]

C. Partitio or 'Summary of Argument'

> *A brief submitted to the Supreme Court must contain a 'summary of argument, suitably paragraphed. The summary should be a clear and concise condensation of the argument made in the body of the brief; mere repetition of the headings under which the argument is arranged is not sufficient.*[59]

Some classical rhetoricians also recommended placing a short summary of the entire argument immediately after the statement of facts but before the argument proper.[60] Sometimes called an 'exposition,' sometimes a 'partition,' its purpose is to 'set forth, briefly and completely, the points we intend to discuss.'[61] Quintilian says that the summary adds:

> to the lucidity and grace of our speech. For it not only makes our arguments clearer by isolating the points from the crowd in which they would otherwise be lost and placing them before the eyes of the judge, but relieves his attention by assigning a definite limit to certain parts of our speech, just as our fatigue upon a journey is relieved by reading the distances on the milestones which we pass.[62]

According to classical authorities, then, the summary's function is to focus the court's attention on the most important points and to limit the scope of the argument.

Modern handbooks also emphasize that an argument summary is 'required in order that the court may have a bird's-eye view of your argument, in somewhat more elaborate form than that available from the index ...'[63] They stress that the argument summary 'permits the court to see the interrelationship of one point to the other, and to the entire argument. It thereby places each point in its proper perspective.'[64] Echoing Quintilian's praise for its fatigue-relieving function, some handbooks observe that the argument summary 'permits a busy judge to grasp the core of an advocate's position before oral argument if he does not have time to read the brief itself ... It may reach a judge who does not read the whole brief, and it may clarify the argument for the judges who do.'[65] Other handbooks emphasize that it should 'set out [the] theory of the case,'[66] 'stick to the main points,'[67] or 'condense the argument into a few paragraphs.'[68]

Like the classical rules, Supreme Court rules require briefs to contain '[a] summary of argument, suitably paragraphed. The summary should be a clear and concise condensation of the argument made in the body of the brief ...'[69] In meeting this requirement, modern lawyers instinctively follow the rhetorical principles just described.

Argument summaries in the *Harper & Row* case illustrate the persuasive value of a good argument summary. For example, in an *amicus* brief supporting Plaintiff Harper & Row, the writer encapsulates the publisher's argument in a few sentences by repeatedly emphasizing that President Ford's memoirs were 'unpublished':

> Congress intended that the fair use doctrine be 'narrowly limited' in its application to *unpublished* works, and that 'under ordinary circumstances' it should not be applied to privilege the unauthorized reproduction of such works. The Court of Appeals erred in failing to consider this principle.
>
> There are no extraordinary circumstances that would justify the application of fair use to Respondents' unauthorized use of Petitioners' *unpublished* manuscript in this case. The manuscript *had not been disseminated* and was *about to be published* ... in any event.[70]

An amicus brief supporting the Defendant *Nation* magazine adopts an altogether different legal theory, but uses a similar rhetorical approach. Its argument summary ignores the unpublished nature of the manuscript. Instead, it repeatedly emphasizes that ideas and facts are 'not copyrightable':

> In determining whether a newspaper or magazine article constitutes copyright infringement of another work, courts must ask first ... what material taken for the article was copyrightable. In answering that question, courts should apply important statutory doctrines that mediate between First Amendment rights and the interests protected by the Copyright Act: ideas, as opposed to the form of expressing those ideas, are *not copyrightable*; facts, as opposed to the form of expressing those facts, are *not copyrightable*; works of the United States are not copyrightable; and material not original to the author is *not copyrightable*.[71]

Comparison of these argument summaries shows fundamental differences in the advocates' legal theories, but substantial similarities in rhetorical technique. Both advocates use carefully selected facts and points of law to predispose the Court toward their client's point of view. Different facts and law notwithstanding, both advocates meet the Supreme Court's requirement that the argument summary provide a concise summary of complex legal arguments. In subtle and client-friendly ways, both advocates concisely 'set forth, briefly and completely, the points [they] intend to discuss.'[72]

D. Confirmatio or 'Argument'

> *A brief submitted to the Supreme Court must contain an 'argument, exhibiting clearly the points of fact and of law being presented, citing the authorities and statutes relied on.'*[73]

The heart of the brief, the argument itself, follows the argument summary. Both classical and modern analysts emphasize that legal arguments are so dependent on the particular facts of the case and applicable law that advice concerning argumentative methods and organization is necessarily general. As Quintilian observes, the organization of arguments 'is generally dependent on expediency, and ... the same question will not always be discussed first by both parties.'[74]

Classical discussions of legal argument are so grounded in Greek and Roman law that comparison with modern legal arguments is difficult except in the broadest terms. Their general approaches to argument appear in their discussions of the topics of invention.

There and elsewhere they discuss not only which arguments to consider, but also how to organize or present them. For example, when discussing organization, Aristotle suggested that, generally speaking, 'you should first present your own argument, and then meet the opposing argument by direct refutation or by pulling them to pieces in advance.'[75] Quintilian varies Aristotle's strategy by suggesting:

> the first place should be given to some strong argument, but the strongest [argument] should be reserved to the end, while the weaker arguments should be placed in the middle, since the judge has to be moved at the beginning and forcibly impelled to a decision at the end.[76]

Cicero and the author of the *Rhetorica ad Herennium* offer basically the same advice as Aristotle and Quintilian except the *Rhetorica ad Herennium* recommends that arguments of 'medium force, and also those that are neither useless to the discourse nor essential to the proof, which are weak if presented separately and individually, but become strong and plausible when conjoined with the others, should be placed in the middle.'[77]

In *De Oratore* Cicero discloses his own argumentative strategy:

> [M]y own method ... is to take the good points of my case and elaborate these, embellishing and enlarging and lingering and dwelling on and sticking to them, while any bad part or weakness in my case I leave on one side, not in such a manner as to give the appearance of running away from it but so as to disguise it and entirely cover it up by embellishing and amplifying the good point referred to ...[78]

Like Aristotle, Cicero, and Quintilian, most modern authorities insist that advocates begin with strong arguments, group weak arguments so that they gain strength from their numbers and juxtaposition, and directly rebut adverse arguments rather than ignoring them altogether:

> [O]rdinarily counsel for the appellant or petitioner or moving party will place his strongest point first, because he wants to make a powerful impression on the judges from the onset. He has the burden of persuading them and he must get their attention; if he saves his best for the last, their minds may be set against him before they ever reach it.[79]

Other handbooks focus on argument sequence: 'begin with your strongest argument, followed by the next strongest argument.'[80] Or on audience: '[j]udges usually presume that the strongest argument is first, and thus prejudge the subsequent arguments as even weaker.'[81] Or on the advocate's credibility: '[s]tarting with a compelling argument will impress the court with the soundness of your legal position and enhance your credibility.'[82] As for rebutting an adverse case or line of argument, modern handbooks recommend two general approaches: questioning the legal merits of the opposing arguments and authority or deemphasizing opposing arguments by means of organizational and stylistic strategies. When confronted by adverse precedents, for example, advocates should 'distinguish a case on its facts or its reasoning; ... but [they] will not allow it to go unanswered. Nor will [they] ignore an opposing argument that might appeal to a judge. [They] will show it to be unsound or illogical or irrelevant, but [they] will deal with it.'[83] Or they can argue that the 'precedents are not followed universally ... [they] conflict with sound public policy ... [they] are inconsistent with trends in related fields.'[84] Advocates can also 'consider favorable dicta.'[85]

In effect, modern handbooks are adopting Cicero's approach to refutation in which affirmative and responsive arguments are frequently mirror-images of one another. They are relying on 'the same sources of invention that *confirmation* [affirmative argument] does, because any proposition can be attacked by the same methods of reasoning by which it can be supported.'[86]

Stylistically, advocates can use sentence structure to subordinate opposing arguments.[87] Advocates can also deemphasize adverse authority in ways that preempt its effectiveness or devote only minimal space to it.[88] These and other techniques are just variations on Cicero's suggestion that 'any bad part or weakness in my case I leave on one side, not in such a manner as to give the appearance of running away from it but so as to disguise it and entirely cover it up ...'[89]

Beyond stipulating the ways that briefs must be organized, the Supreme Court is scrupulously neutral about acceptable types of argument. Its rules are deliberately open-ended and provide advocates with considerable latitude in selecting and organizing their arguments. Rule 24 simply states that the argument must exhibit 'clearly the points of fact and of law presented and citing the authorities and statutes relied on.'[90] The rule offers no suggestions concerning organization or other matters.

Even so, modern advocates organize their arguments according to Quintilian's precept that 'the same question [is] not ... discussed first by both parties.'[91] As the Argument Summaries in the *Harper & Row* case show, Plaintiff Harper & Row began its brief by arguing that the 'fair use' principle applies narrowly or not at all to President Ford's 'unpublished memoirs,' since their theory depends on the lack of publication. Using a different legal theory, the Defendant *Nation* magazine brief began by arguing that most of the memoirs are 'not copyrightable' at all.[92] Only after their own arguments have been fully developed do these advocates turn to refuting their opponent's arguments.

In keeping with classical principles, both advocates selected their issues carefully, began with their strongest arguments, and then refuted their opponent's arguments. In doing so, they rely in part on common sense and, in part, on time-honored rhetorical conventions.

E. Peroration or 'Conclusion'

Classical and modern practice differ when it comes to the *peroration* or Conclusion of the argument. The classical *peroration* was a dramatic and very often lengthy summary of the argument. By contrast, modern advocates usually conclude written arguments with one or two sentences describing the relief or remedy sought. Because of these pronounced differences, this chapter contains no analysis of the peroration. However, *perorations* are discussed in some detail in Chapter Four, which discusses connections between *perorations* and closing arguments in a trial.

Notes

1. 3 Quintilian, *Institutio Oratoria* 3 (H. Butler trans. 1954).
2. U.S. Supreme Court Rule 14; U.S. Supreme Court Rule 24.
3. Edward P.J. Corbett, *Classical Rhetoric For The Modern Student* 595 (2d ed. 1971). None of Corax's handbooks on rhetoric have survived although 'there are references in Plato, Aristotle, Cicero and Quintilian to the part that Corax played in formulating rhetorical theory.'
4. James L. Kinneavy, 'Translating Theory into Practice in Teaching Composition: A Historical View and a Contemporary View,' in *Essays On Classical Rhetoric And Modern Discourse* 70 (1984).
5. Edward P.J. Corbett, *Classical Rhetoric for the Modern Student* at 595.
6. Edward P.J. Corbett, *Classical Rhetoric for the Modern Student* at 595.
7. Aristotle, *The Rhetoric of Aristotle* at 220.
8. Edward P.J. Corbett, *Classical Rhetoric for the Modern Student* at 36.
9. *Rhetorica ad Herennium* at 9.
10. 3 Quintilian, *Institutio Oratoria* at 7.
11. Edward P.J. Corbett, *Classical Rhetoric for the Modern Student* at 215.
12. Edward P.J. Corbett, *Classical Rhetoric for the Modern Student* at 228.
13. U.S. Supreme Court Rule 14. 1(a).
14. *Cassell's New Compact Latin Dictionary* 85 (1963).
15. 2 Quintilian, *Institutio Oratoria* 63 (H. Butler trans. 1921).
16. Richard Enos, *The Literate Mode of Cicero's Legal Rhetoric* 60 (1988). 'Oral and written expression were so inextricably bound in ancient discourse that its unity was an written unquestioned presumption upon which theories of rhetoric were developed.' This presumption was based on the fact that silent reading was rare (especially for Greeks) and that most writing was intended to be presented orally.
17. 2 Quintilian, *Institutio Oratoria* at 7.
18. 2 Quintilian, *Institutio Oratoria* at 9.
19. 2 Quintilian, *Institutio Oratoria*. at 17.
20. 2 Quintilian, *Institutio Oratoria* at 21.
21. 4 Cicero, *De Partitiones Oratoria* at 335 (H. Rackham trans. 1921).
22. *Rhetorica ad Herennium* at 13.
23. *Rhetorica ad Herennium* at 21.

24. Edward D. Re, *Brief Writing And Oral Argument* 125-34 (6th ed. 1987).
25. Frank Cooper, *Writing In Law Practice* 73 (2nd ed. 1963).
26. Helene S. Shapo et al, *Writing and Analysis in the Law* 305 (4th ed. 1999).
27. Richard K. Neumann, Jr., *Legal Reasoning and Legal Writing: Structure, Strategy, and Style* 355 (4th ed. 2001).
28. Linda Edwards, *Legal Writing: Process, Analysis, and Organization* 340 (3rd ed. 2002).
29. U.S. Supreme Court Rule 14.1(a); Supreme Court Rule 24.1(a).
30. U.S. Supreme Court Rule 14.1(a).
31. U.S. Supreme Court Rule 14.1(a). `
32. Harper & Row Publishers v. Nation Enters., 471 U. S. 539 (1984).
33. Petition for Certiorari at 1, Harper & Row Publishers v. Nation Enters., 471 U.S. 539 (1984) (No. 83-1632).
34. Petition for Certiorari at 1, Harper & Row Publishers v. Nation Enters., 471 U.S. 539 (1984) (No. 83-1632).
35. Petition for Certiorari at 1, Harper & Row Publishers v. Nation Enters., 471 U.S. 539 (1984) (No. 83-1632) (emphasis added). The italicized words reflect Harper & Row's attempt to frame the issue in its favor.
36. Respondent's Brief in Opposition at i, Harper & Row Publishers v. Nation Enters., 471 U.S. 539 (1984) (83-1632).
37. 4 Cicero, *De Partitiones Oratoria* 335. (H. Rackham trans. 1921).
38. 2 Quintilian, *Institutio Oratoria* at 17.
39. U.S. Supreme Court Rule 14.1(8) (emphasis added).
40. Aristotle, *Rhetoric* at 220.
41. Aristotle, *Rhetoric* at 229.
42. 4 Cicero, *De Partitione Oratoria* at 335.
43. 2 Quintilian, *Institutio Oratoria* at 67.
44. 2 Quintilian, *Institutio Oratoria* at 61.
45. *Rhetorica ad Herennium*, at 23.
46. *Rhetorica ad Herennium* at 27.
47. Girvan G. Peck, *Writing Persuasive Briefs* 110 (1984).
48. Edward D. Re, *Brief Writing and Oral Argument* at 136.
49. Frank Cooper, *Writing in Law Practice* at 217.
50. Helene S. Shapo et al, *Writing and Analysis in the Law* at 311.
51. Richard K. Neumann, Jr., *Legal Reasoning and Legal Writing: Structure, Strategy, and Style* at 344.
52. Nancy L. Schultz and Louis J. Sirico, Jr., *Legal Writing and Other Lawyering Skills* 293 (3rd ed. 1998).
53. Laurel Currie Oates and Anne Enquist, *Just Briefs* 102 (2003).
54. U.S. Supreme Court Rule 14.1(g); Supreme Court Rule 24.1(g).
55. U.S. Supreme Court Rule 14.1(g); U.S. Supreme Court Rule 1(g).
56. Brief for Petitioner at 7, Harper & Row Publishers v. Nation Enters., 471 U.S. 539 (1984) (No. 83-1632).
57. Brief for Respondent at 3, Harper & Row Publishers v. Nation Enters., 471 U.S. 539 (1984) (No. 83-1632) (citation omitted).
58. *Rhetorica ad Herennium*, at 23.
59. U.S. Supreme Court Rule 24.1(h).
60. *Rhetorica ad Herennium*, at 29.
61. *Rhetorica ad Herennium*, at 31.
62. 2 Quintilian, *Institutio Oratoria* at 149.

63. Frederick B. Wiener, *Briefing And Arguing Federal Appeals* 117 (1961).
64. Edward D. Re, *Brief Writing and Oral Argument* at 145.
65. Girvan Peck, *Writing Persuasive Briefs* at 150.
66. Helene S. Shapo et al, *Writing and Analysis in the Law* at 325.
67. Nancy L. Schultz and Louis J. Sirico, Jr., *Legal Writing and Other Lawyering Skills* at 298.
68. Richard K. Neumann, Jr., *Legal Reasoning and Legal Writing: Structure, Strategy, and Style* at 383.
69. U.S. Supreme Court Rule 24.1(h).
70. Brief Amicus Curiae of the Association of American Publishers, Inc. in_Support of Petitioners at 5, Harper & Row Publishers v. Nation Enters., 471 U.S. 539 (1984) (No. 831632) (emphasis added).
71. Brief Amici Curiae of the Gannett Co. in Support of Respondents at 4-5, Harper & Row, Publishers v. Nation Enters., 471 U.S. 539 (1984) (No. 83-1632) (emphasis added).
72. *Rhetorica ad Herennium* at 31.
73. U.S. Supreme Court Rule 24.1(i).
74. 3 Quintilian, *Institutio Oratoria* at 7.
75. Aristotle, *Rhetoric* at 235-36.
76. 3 Quintilian, *Institutio Oratoria* at 11.
77. *Rhetorica Ad Herennium*, at 189.
78. 3 Cicero, *De Oratore* at 421 (E. Sutton and H. Rackham trans. 1942).
79. Girvan Peck, *Writing Persuasive Briefs* at 133.
80. Robin S. Wellford, *Legal Reasoning, Writing and Persuasive Argument* 300 (2002).
81. Linda Edwards, *Legal Writing: Process, Analysis, and Organization* at 330.
82. Nancy L. Schultz and Louis J. Sirico, Jr., *Legal Writing and Other Lawyering Skills* at 307.
83. Girvan Peck, *Writing Persuasive Briefs* at 142.
84. Helene S. Shapo et al, *Writing and Analysis in the Law* at 359-360.
85. Robin S. Wellford, *Legal Reasoning, Writing and Persuasive Argument* at 333.
86. 2 Cicero, *De Inventione*, at 123.
87. Richard K. Neumann, Jr., *Legal Reasoning and Legal Writing: Structure, Strategy, and Style* at 306.
88. Linda Edwards, *Legal Writing: Process, Analysis, and Organization* at 325-6.
89. 3 Cicero, *De Oratore* at 421.
90. U.S. Supreme Court Rule 24.1(i).
91. 3 Quintilian *Institutio Oratoria* at 7.
92. Gannett amicus brief, *Harper & Row Publishers v. Nation Enterprises*, 471 U.S. 539 (1984) (No. 83-1632) at 4.

Chapter 4

Ethos, Pathos and Legal Audience

EMOTION AND ADVOCATE CREDIBILITY

When preparing their arguments, modern lawyers sometimes fail to consider how their own credibility or the emotional aspects of their case affect a judge or jury. Instead, they focus their attention on the substantive and logical integrity of their arguments. They are far more interested in logical and organizational coherence than in the emotional climate within which they argue or in their own credibility while arguing a case. By focusing on logic and organization, they ignore two especially effective non-rational means of persuading judges and juries to accept their arguments: emotional appeals based on the facts of the case and personal appeals based on the advocate's own credibility.

Although appellate advocacy handbooks occasionally discuss the persuasive effects of emotion and lawyer credibility, it is trial advocacy handbooks and manuals that provide the fullest treatment of the topic.[1] Trial lawyers repeatedly emphasize how important emotion and lawyer credibility are in persuading courts and juries to the lawyer's point of view.[2] And, in their periodical literature and journals, trial lawyers frequently remind one another, formally and informally, that legal arguments are not won solely on the basis of their substantive merits. They know that intangible, non-substantive factors often affect the outcome of a case.

The trial bar clearly understands that they must tailor their arguments to suit multiple audiences and that this skill must be learned and practiced. Their interest in audience is reflected in everything from detailed instructions about jury selection and managing exhibits to miscellaneous advice about particular judges, lines of argument, and jury dynamics. By focusing on the importance of audience, emotion and lawyer credibility, modern trial lawyers, perhaps instinctively, are adhering to time-honored rhetorical techniques that were first described by Aristotle, Cicero and Quintilian.

GRECO-ROMAN APPROACHES TO PERSUASION

Aristotle's *Rhetoric* is the earliest authoritative analysis of persuasive discourse and the source of Cicero's and Quintilian's multi-volume treatises on the topic. According to Quintilian, these treatises were written for inexperienced advocates and for anyone who might sometime argue a case in court.[3] Based on his close observations of human nature and his own considerable legal experience, he and other classical rhetoricians analyzed persuasive discourse in exhaustive detail.

In effect, these treatises were practice manuals intended for use by all members of the educated classes.[4] For the most part, they were descriptive, rather than prescriptive, in force. They were consistent with one another in many respects, including their heavy emphasis on audience. Most of them contained detailed discussions of how to manipulate judges and juries.

For purposes of analysis, Aristotle, Cicero, and Quintilian divided legal arguments into three categories: logical arguments (*logos*), emotional arguments (*pathos*), and arguments based on an advocate's ethical appeal or credibility (*ethos*).[5] Although each type of argument has unique qualities, classical rhetoricians never treated them as completely separable from one another. In their view, each type of argument is connected to and affects the others. To be successful '[t]here are ... three aims which the [advocate] must always have in view; he must instruct, move, and charm his hearers.'[6]

Because they thought that emotional arguments and lawyer credibility were critically important, they devoted fully as much attention to those topics as they did to logical, substantive, or organizational components. They were especially interested in how *logos* is affected by *pathos* and *ethos* because they knew that logical arguments frequently fail when advocates ignore or fail to recognize the important non-rational factors at play in their case.

Beginning with Aristotle, classical rhetoricians repeatedly emphasize that advocates must be sensitive to the needs of their audience. In his *Rhetoric*, Aristotle observes that:

> the individual man is as truly a judge or decider as an entire audience; so, in the wider sense, whoever it is you have to persuade is 'judge' ... [Y]ou compose your speech for an audience, and the audience is the 'judge.' As a rule ... the term 'judge' means simply and solely one of the persons who decide the issue in the disputes of civil life, where, as in law-suits, there is a question of fact to be settled, or, as in deliberations of State, a question of policy.[7]

However, although he emphasizes the importance of audiences, Aristotle does not always have a very high opinion of their analytical abilities or fairness. In fact, much of his advice regarding advocacy assumes that legal audiences are insufficiently educated and trained. Consequently, they are too easily influenced by charming advocates who appeal to their emotions. He was dismayed that 'external matters,' such as emotion, 'count for [so] much, because of the sorry nature of an audience.'[8]

GRECO-ROMAN AUDIENCES

The Roman rhetoricians shared Aristotle's general skepticism regarding the legal acumen of judges and juries. In large part, this skepticism arose from the fact that in both Greek and Roman systems the judges who heard routine civil cases were usually not professional jurists but regular citizens.

In Athens, for example, the judicial system was scrupulously non-professional. It:

> was manned by juries of male citizens over thirty years old, chosen by lot to serve for a year ... A randomly chosen cross-section of the male citizen body, six thousand men in all ... were distributed into individual juries as needed to handle the case load ... There were no judges to instruct the jurors and usually no prosecutors or defense lawyers to harangue them ... All trials were conducted in a single day, and jurors made up their own minds after hearing speeches by the persons involved.[9]

In Rome, judges were typically drawn from the upper classes and heard only a few cases in their entire lifetimes.[10] Under Roman law, for example:

> [t]he trial of an action under the *legis actio* procedure ... was characterized by a remarkable division of the proceedings into two states, the first of which took place before the magistrate, under whose supervision all the preliminaries were arranged, while the second in which the issue was actually decided, was held before a *iudex* (judge), who was neither a magistrate nor a professional lawyer, but a layman agreed on by the parties and appointed by the magistrate.[11]

Most judges were amateurs because 'it was a part of the philosophy of the Romans that the duty of a citizen included taking his share of the burdens of the law: acting as judge, arbitrator or juror and supporting his friends in their legal affairs by coming forward as witness, surety and so on.'[12] Most judges, acting out of a sense of duty, 'were members of the Roman upper class, for even public and political office were only incidents in lives of leisure, and it was therefore an amateur activity just as much as being a historian or an agricultural expert.'[13]

If the judges had technical questions about the law, they could consult a 'line of celebrated *iurus predentes* (legal experts) ... [Their] *responsa prudentium*, the "answers of the learned" counted as one of the sources of the law.'[14] These jurists were widely respected and were considered 'the best, authoritative, sources of evidence of the law.'[15]

Although most cases were heard by a single judge, 'many [notorious or important] civil actions went before a much bigger jury, the Court of One Hundred, *centumviri* ... The *centumviri* had no exclusive competence in any particular field; inheritances, for example, could equally well go before a single *iudex* (judge).'[16] Sometimes, in the case of international disputes, cases of particular urgency, or social importance, a panel of judges known as *recuperatores* heard the case.[17]

Given the amateur status of both the judges and juries who decided legal disputes, Greek and Roman rhetoricians understandably stressed persuasive techniques based on emotional arguments and the advocate's personal credibility instead of relying solely on legal arguments. Much of their assessment of what would persuade judges and juries was grounded in basic human psychology rather than statutory law or jurisprudential philosophy. Consequently, throughout their works, they emphasized rhetorical and psychological strategy as much as they did legal strategy. *Pathos* and *ethos* were at the heart of all their analyses of persuasive discourse.

EMOTION AND ARGUMENT: *PATHOS*

In his *Rhetoric*, Aristotle analyzed legal arguments in terms of both rational and non-rational or affective methods of persuading an audience. The *Rhetoric* examines legal arguments in terms of 'human nature, with its ways of reasoning, its habits, desires, and emotions.'[18] In effect, his treatise is a 'practical psychology' handbook, which provides a detailed examination of human nature as the Greeks and Romans understood it.[19]

Although Aristotle's psychological assumptions may occasionally strike modern readers and professional psychologists as over-simplified, they are nonetheless grounded on his keen insights into how hate, love, pity, anger, impatience, boredom, and inattentiveness affect a judge or jury's reasoning abilities and legal decisions. Any shortcomings attributable to Aristotle's somewhat 'mechanistic' psychology are more than compensated for by his close analysis of the interplay between emotion and argument and his detailed advice regarding how to measure an audience and manipulate its emotions.

To begin with, Aristotle and later rhetoricians frequently decry the effect emotions have on judges, but grudgingly concede that, since emotions often have a profound effect, advocates should exploit them whenever possible. For example, near the beginning of his *Rhetoric*, Aristotle says that 'the man who is to judge should not have his judgment warped by speakers arousing him to anger, jealousy, or compassion. One might just as well make a carpenter's rule crooked before using it as a measure.'[20] Nonetheless, he later notes that while 'strict justice ... would lead us ... to seek no more [of an emotional effect] than that we should avoid paining the hearer without alluring him' and that 'the case should, in justice, be fought on the strength of the facts alone ... [n]evertheless ... external matters do count for much, because of the sorry nature of an audience.'[21]

Quintilian makes a similar point when urging advocates to identify and exaggerate emotion-triggering facts:

> Meanwhile I will content myself with the observation that the aim of appeals to emotion is not merely to shew the bitter and grievous nature of ills that actually are so, *but also to make ills which are usually regarded as tolerable seem unendurable ...* For the force of eloquence is such that it not merely compels the judge to the conclusion toward which the nature of the facts lead him, but awakens emotions which either do not naturally *arise from the case or are stronger than the case would suggest.*[22]

When discussing how emotions affect arguments, Aristotle and his successors took it as a commonplace that:

> the same thing does not appear the same to men when they are friendly and when they hate, nor when they are angry and when they are in gentle mood; in these different moods the same thing will appear either wholly different in kind, or different as to magnitude.[23]

Elsewhere Aristotle observes that, '[a]ppeals to the hearer aim at securing his good will, or at arousing his anger; sometimes at engaging his attention, or, on occasion, at diverting it – since engaging it is not always an advantage, and for that reason a speaker will often try to set his audience laughing.'[24]

Aristotle's suggestion that advocates should deliberately try to manipulate a judge and jury's emotions is echoed by his successors. Cicero, for instance, emphasized the importance of emotions when he observed that one 'potent factor' in the successful argument of a case is 'the feelings of the tribunal ... [which must] be won over, as far as possible, to goodwill towards the advocate and the advocate's client as well.'[25] He too recommended playing on the court's emotions and, like Aristotle, suggested that advocates speak in a way that 'excites and urges the feelings of the tribunal towards hatred or love, ill-will or well-wishing, fear or hope.'[26]

Quintilian, Cicero's great admirer, made similar recommendations, primarily because he thought that emotional arguments have the greatest appeal of all. In fact, he claimed that 'this emotional power ... dominates the court[;] it is this form of eloquence that is queen of all.'[27] And, like Aristotle, he thought that 'the duty of the [advocate] is not merely to instruct: the power of eloquence is greatest in emotional appeals.'[28]

Aristotle and later rhetoricians not only identified a few emotions (hate, love, anger, fear, hope, pity) as being especially powerful in creating strong arguments; they also thought that judges and juries reacted to those emotions in predictable ways.[29] It is here that the Greco-Roman analysis seems overly simplistic. Cicero, for instance, thought that 'love' is won based primarily on the justness of the advocate's cause or the court's own self-interest:

> [S]ince the emotions which eloquence has to excite in the minds of the tribunal ... are most commonly love, hate, wrath, jealousy, compassion, hope, joy, fear or vexation, we observe that love is won if you are thought to be upholding the interests of your audience, or to be working for good men, or at any rate for such as that audience deems good and useful.[30]

Quintilian makes a similar observation when he describes how a defendant's social class and courtroom demeanor may provoke the court's jealousy, hatred, or anger. He asserts that '*jealousy* will be produced by the *influence* of the accused, *hatred* by the *disgraceful nature of his conduct,* and *anger by his disrespectful attitude toward the court.*'[31]

Quintilian may have overstated his point by suggesting that the defendant's cause or rank or conduct always produces the same emotions in the judge. Nevertheless, his analysis of how to manipulate a judge's emotions was based on his own considerable courtroom experience. Both he and Cicero provide numerous 'real life' examples of how they identified and manipulated the emotional crosscurrents in their cases. Notwithstanding their sometimes simplistic and somewhat dogmatic assertions about how emotion affects judges and juries, their observations and advice are generally sound.

EMOTION AND THE CHARACTER OF THE JUDGE

Both rhetoricians were equally interested in analyzing the temperament and psychology of judges. As part of their pre-trial preparations, they routinely investigated the work habits and vulnerabilities of the judges. Cicero, for example, said that:

> when setting about a hazardous and important case, in order to explore the feelings of the tribunal, I engage wholeheartedly in a consideration so careful, that I scent out with all possible keenness their thoughts, judgements, anticipations and wishes, and the direction in which they seem likely to be led away most easily by eloquence.[32]

Quintilian also recommended learning as much as possible about the 'character' of the judges. To increase his chances of success, Quintilian thought it was 'desirable to enlist [the judges'] temperaments in the service of our cause, where they are such as like to be useful, or to mollify them, if they are like to prove adverse, just according as they are harsh, gentle, cheerful, grave, stern, or easy-going.'[33]

He gave numerous suggestions about how to 'enlist' a judge's sympathies. He suggests '[f]or instance, in pleading for a man of good birth we shall appeal to his (the judge's) own high rank, in speaking for the lowly we shall lay stress on his sense of justice.'[34] Almost ruefully he reminded advocates that 'it would be folly for me to warn speakers not to say or even hint anything against [the judge], but for the fact that such things do occur.'[35]

Although both Cicero and Quintilian began by investigating individual judges, their trial preparations did not end there. Both of them also stressed the need for mid-trial flexibility and developed flexible trial strategies based on their study of recurring judicial attitudes and behavior.

Quintilian, for example, was especially sensitive to the fact that an advocate's argument may not coincide with the judge's view of the case: 'Above all it is important, whenever we suspect that the judge desires a proof other than that on which we are engaged, to promise that we will satisfy him on the point fully and without delay ...'[36] Quintilian further observed that impatient judges especially dislike digressions in the statement of the facts because:

> as soon as he has heard the facts set forth in order, the judge is in a hurry to get to the proof and desires to satisfy himself of the correctness of his impressions at the earliest possible moment. Further, care must be taken not to nullify the effect of the statement by diverting the minds of the court to some other theme and wearying them by useless delay.[37]

Elsewhere, he noted that most judges are usually in a hurry to reach the most important point in the case: 'If he has a patient disposition he will merely make a silent appeal to the advocate, whom he will treat as bound by his promise [to get to the point.] On the other hand, if he is busy, or holds exalted position, or is intolerant by nature, he will insist in no very courteous manner on [the advocate] coming to the point.'[38]

Quintilian also warned against boring the judge with all the available arguments,[39] against 'dry repetition of facts' which may suggest the advocate's lack of confidence in the judge's memory,[40] and against 'over-elaboration' of arguments, a practice which makes judges suspect that the advocate is not confident about the argument.[41] These observations and others attest to Quintilian's own courtroom experience and to the timeless verities of his 'judicial profiles.'

EMOTION AND ORGANIZATION

Greco-Roman analysis of how judges respond to emotional appeals was closely linked to the classical five-part structure for legal arguments.[42] Based on their observation that legal arguments usually follow predictable patterns, they described the function of each part and its logical connection to the overall argument. They did not, however, limit their analysis to the logical interrelationships among the parts. They also discussed the emotional effects appropriate to each part and a judge's tendency to become impatient, bored, inattentive, or distracted unless he is also emotionally engaged in the case.

A. Opening Statement

Aristotle was skeptical about whether advocates even needed to provide an *exordium* or introduction for their arguments. He considered them:

> extraneous to a speech. They are for the audience, an audience that is weak enough to accept utterances beside the point; and if audiences were not what they are, there would be no need of any *proem* (opening statement) beyond a summary statement of the matter in question ...'[43]

Nonetheless, he grudgingly conceded that advocates can use the introduction to engage the audience's attention or 'on occasion, divert it.' In his view, a good introduction may help make an 'audience receptive.'[44]

Later rhetoricians, however, attached much more importance to introductions, primarily because they help create an emotional interest in the case. Cicero thought that emotion was 'especially important in the exordium; it is essential that [the exordium] should have the power of stirring the minds of the audience ... [because it has] a very great effect in persuading and arousing emotion.'[45] He also noted that arousing the judge's emotions is 'easier in the introduction, because the audience [is] most attentive when [it has] the whole of the speech to look forward to, and also [it is] more receptive at the start' because the advocate's position is usually clearer at the beginning than in the middle of the argument.[46]

Like Cicero, Quintilian thought that the introduction exercised a 'valuable influence in winning the judge to regard us with favor.'[47] Quintilian also suggested that advocates should use a temperate or low-key delivery in their introduction: '[I]n our opening any preliminary appeal to the compassion of the judge must be made sparingly and with restraint.'[48] And, to pique and maintain an impatient judge's interest, he suggested that advocates should 'create the impression that [they] shall not keep [the judge] long and intend to stick closely to the point ... The mere fact of such attention makes the judge ready to receive instruction from [them], but [they] shall contribute still more to this effect if [they] give a brief and lucid summary of the case which [they have] to try.'[49]

B. Statement of the Case

In contrast to his skepticism about the usefulness of *exordia*, Aristotle was very enthusiastic about the persuasive value of the Statement of the Case or *narratio*. Aristotle thought that it offered advocates a unique opportunity to create a favorable impression of their clients and made numerous suggestions about how to do so. He emphasized that '[t]he narration should depict the *ethos* (character) [of the client]. One thing that will give this quality is the revelation of moral purpose; for the quality of the *ethos* is determined by the quality of the purpose revealed, and the quality of this purpose is determined by its end.'[50]

The most thorough analysis of ways to exploit the emotional or affective content of the Statement of the Case comes from Quintilian. He thought that 'the purpose of the statement of the facts is not merely to instruct, but rather to persuade the judge.'[51] Quintilian made the traditional observations about the importance of clarity, conciseness, and relevance:

> We shall achieve lucidity and clearness in our statement of the facts, first by setting forth our story in words which are appropriate, significant and free from any stain of meanness, but not on the other hand farfetched or unusual, and secondly by giving a distinct account of facts, persons, times, places and causes, while our delivery must be adapted to our matter, so that the judge will take in what we say with the utmost readiness.[52]

But he also included warnings against excessive concision, especially as it affects a listening audience:

> We must avoid ... terseness ... and shun all abruptness of speech, since a style which presents no difficulty to a leisurely reader, flies past a *hearer* and will not stay to be looked at again; and whereas the reader is almost always a man of learning, the judge often comes to his panel from the countryside and is expected to give a decision on what he can understand.[53]

He also offered suggestions about how to avoid tediousness: 'Division of our statement into its various heads is another method of avoiding tedium ... Such a division will give the impression of ... short statements rather than [a] long one.'[54]

Finally, in keeping with his conviction that emotion, more than logic or justice, is the primary ground on which cases are decided, Quintilian focused on emotion's place in the *narratio*. He stressed, for instance, that 'there is no portion of a[n] [argument] at which the judge is more attentive, and consequently nothing that is well said is lost. And the judge is, for some reason or other, all the more ready to accept what charms his ear and is lured by pleasure to belief.'[55]

And, in rebuttal of those who discounted the importance of the statement of the case, he said:

> I am ... surprised at those who hold that there should be no appeal to the emotions in the statement of the facts ... [W]hy, while I am instructing the judge, should I refuse to move him as well? Why should I not, if it is possible, obtain that effect at the very opening of the case which I am anxious to secure at its conclusion, more especially in view of the fact that I shall find the judge far more amenable to the cogency of my proof, if I have previously filled his mind with anger or pity?[56]

C. Argument Summary, Argument, Closing Argument

When discussing the argument summary (*partitio*) and the argument itself (*confirmatio*), classical rhetoricians understandably focused more on the logic and substantive coherence of the argument than on its emotional content. Even so, like Cicero, they thought that 'all arguments must be rounded off either by enlarging on your points or by *arousing the feelings of the judge or calming them down*.'[57] In Quintilian's view, '[t]here is scope for an appeal to the emotions ... in every portion of a speech.'[58]

Quintilian suggested that while an argument summary sometimes allays a judge's fears[59] or makes him more attentive and receptive,[60] it should be omitted if the advocate will be making unique or unpopular arguments:

> Sometimes we shall even have to hoodwink the judge and work upon him by various artifices so that he may think that our aim is other than what it really is. For there are cases when a proposition may be somewhat startling: if the judge foresees this, he will shrink from it in advance, like a patient who catches sight of the surgeon's knife before the operation. On the other hand, if we have given him no preliminary notice and our words take him unawares, without his interest in them having been previously roused by any warning, we shall gain a credence which we should not have secured had we stated that we were going to raise the point.[61]

Despite their disagreements about the necessity or usefulness of argument summaries, classical rhetoricians all agreed that the closing argument or *peroration* was an extremely important place for exploiting the emotional content of the case. Aristotle said that advocates should use their closing argument to 'put the audience in the right state of emotion' and that they should 'make the audience feel the right emotions – pity, indignation, anger, hatred, envy, emulation, antagonism.'[62]

Quintilian concurred and insisted that '[t]he peroration is the most important part of forensic pleading, and in the main consists of appeals to the emotions.'[63] Moreover, given its placement at the end of the case, it 'provides freer opportunities for exciting the passions of jealousy, hatred, or anger.'[64] Although the *peroration* also gives advocates a chance to refresh the judge's memory,[65] its principal purpose is to play on the feelings of the court:

> [I]n the *peroration* we have to consider what the feelings of the judge will be when he retires to consider his verdict, for we shall have no further opportunity to say anything ... It is therefore the duty of both parties to seek to win the judge's goodwill and to divert it from their opponent, as also to excite or assuage his emotions ...[66]

Quintilian especially recommended using the *peroration* to play on the fears of the court, 'The appeal to fear ... occupies a more prominent place in the peroration than in the exordium ...'[67]

Not only did these rhetoricians analyze ways to manipulate the emotions of the court, they also gave technical advice about how to orchestrate those emotions. Aristotle noted that advocates vary their emotional appeals depending on their purpose: 'Appeals to the hearer aim at securing his good will, or at arousing his anger; sometimes at engaging his attention, or, on occasion, at diverting it – since engaging it is not always an Advantage ...'[68] Cicero too noted that advocates must vary the emotional climate of their argument according to need:

> But closely associated with this [other style] is that dissimilar style of speaking which, in quite another way, excites and urges the feeling of the tribunal towards hatred or love, ill-will or well-wishing, fear or hope ... or by it they are prompted to whatever emotions are nearly allied and similar to these passions ...[69]

Quintilian was even more specific about just what approach should be used in each part of the argument. He thought the *exordium* and *peroration* were distinguishable in that in our opening any preliminary appeal to the compassion of the judge must be made sparingly and with restraint, while in the *peroration* we may give full rein to our emotions, place fictitious speeches in the mouths of our characters, call the dead to life, and produce the wife or children of the accused in court, practices which are less usual in *exordia*.[70] He also stressed that advocates must emphasize the emotional connections between the statement of the facts and the closing argument:

> If you wait for the *peroration* to stir your hearer's emotions over circumstances which you have recorded unmoved in your statement of facts, your appeal will come too late. The judge is already familiar with them and hears their mention without turning a hair, since he was unstirred when they were first recounted to him. Once the habit of mind is formed, it is hard to change it.[71]

As the foregoing analysis shows, classical rhetoricians regarded *pathos* as one of the most important rhetorical tools in legal argument. While they sometimes decried its effects, they nonetheless thought emotion was a critical tool for emphasizing sympathetic facts and for controlling how judges perceive those facts. Accordingly, they developed a comprehensive system for using emotion to cultivate goodwill toward both advocates and their clients. This system included suggestions about which emotions to use for particular causes of action, particular classes of clients, and particular kinds of conduct. It also stressed the importance of investigating the judge's background and predispositions before the trial and of showing sensitivity to the judge's emotional state during the trial.

They knew that emotion is an important part of every trial, but that it has slightly different effects depending on whether it appears in the opening statements (*proem* or *exordium*), the statement of the case (*narratio*), the argument itself (*confirmatio*), or in closing argument (*peroratio*). Opening statements and the statement of the case are important in creating good first impression of the advocate, disclosing the client's good character, and showing the justness of his cause. Closing arguments are critical in establishing a favorable emotional climate just before the conclusion of the trial and for refreshing the judge's memory regarding sympathetic facts and arguments.

Throughout their analysis, flexibility is a key theme. Each emotion has a particular purpose and must suit a particular context. Above all, it must suit the audience to whom it is addressed. Given the breadth and depth of their analysis of *pathos*, classical rhetoricians clearly thought it played an important part in persuasive discourse.

ETHOS AND LAWYER CREDIBILITY

Under classical theory, effective legal arguments depend almost as much on the advocate's character and credibility, or *ethos*, as they do on logical integrity (*logos*) or emotional content (*pathos*). Moreover, for Aristotle, and for Cicero and Quintilian after him, *projecting* the proper *ethos* is as important as actually possessing it:

> [T]he speaker must not merely see to it that his [argument] shall be convincing and persuasive, but he *must give the right impression of himself* ... This is [especially] true in forensic speaking ...; [F]or in conducing to persuasion it is highly important that the speaker should evince a certain character, and that the judges should *conceive him* to be disposed towards them in a certain way ...[72]

Given the importance he attached to projecting character or credibility, Aristotle offered some practical suggestions about how to create the right impression: '[T]here are three things that gain our belief, namely, intelligence, character, and good will ... This being so, the means by which one may give the *impression* of intelligence and good character are to be found in our analysis of the virtues.'[73]

Within his analysis of these 'virtues,' Aristotle noted that affective or emotional arguments (*pathos*) frequently depend on an advocate's *ethos*. Accordingly, he advised advocates to exploit the connections between *pathos* and *ethos* in order to make the judge more attentive: '[Y]ou may use each and all of these means [of emotional arguments] ... with a view to making your audience receptive, and withal give an impression of yourself as a good and just man, for good character always commands more attention.'[74]

And, at the risk of appearing to encourage duplicity and trickery, Aristotle warned advocates against inadvertently betraying their manipulative intentions: '[P]resent yourself from the outset in a distinctive light, so that the audience may regard you as a person of this sort, your opponent as of that; *only do not betray your design*. It is easy to give the right impression.'[75] All in all, Aristotle was convinced that an advocate could control the court's perception of his character as effectively as he controlled its emotions or the logic of his own arguments. In Aristotle's view, *ethos*-control is as much an acquired skill as it is an inherent characteristic of the advocate.

Both Cicero and Quintilian accepted and elaborated on Aristotle's basic premises regarding the part *ethos* plays in legal argument. Like Aristotle, they emphasized *projecting* good character as much as they did *possessing* it. And, like Aristotle, they seemed to approve a certain deliberate disingenuousness by advocates who want to disguise their intentions. For instance, when Cicero listed virtues which contribute to an attractive or convincing *ethos*, – 'a mild tone, a countenance expressive of modesty, [and] gentle language,' – he added that advocates should also develop the 'faculty of *seeming* to be dealing reluctantly and under compulsion with something you are really anxious to prove.'[76] Occasionally, Cicero offered specific advice on how to project the proper *ethos*. He believed, for instance, that:

> much is done by good taste and style in speaking, [so] that the speech *seems* to depict the speaker's character. For by means of particular types of thought and diction, and the employment besides of a delivery that is unruffled and eloquent of good nature, the speakers *are made to appear* upright, well-bred and virtuous men.[77]

However, mindful of the need to vary delivery depending on audience and purpose, Cicero also stressed that advocates must sometimes abandon the restrained or temperate *ethos* and adopt instead the passionate emotions they are trying to instill in their audience:

> [I]t is impossible for the listener to feel indignation, hatred or ill-will, to be terrified of anything, or reduced to tears of compassion, unless all those emotions, which the advocate would inspire in the arbitrator, are visibly stamped or rather branded on the advocate himself.[78]

Moreover, an advocate's emotions must be genuine, not feigned:

> [I]t is not easy to succeed in making an arbitrator angry with the right party, unless he first sees you on fire with hatred yourself; nor will he be prompted to compassion, unless you have shown him the tokens of your own grief by word, sentiment, tone of voice, look and even by loud lamentation.[79]

To illustrate this point, Cicero provides an example from one of his cases in which:

> [o]n seeing [my client] cast down, crippled, sorrowing and brought to the risk of all he held dear, I was myself overcome by compassion before I tried to excite it in others. Assuredly I felt that the Court was deeply affected when I called forward my unhappy old client, in his garb of woe, and when I did those things ... *not by way of technique* ... but under stress of deep emotion and indignation – I mean my tearing open his tunic and exposing his scars.[80]

Cicero also noted that in a complex case an advocate must frequently vary his approach and intermingle temperate and passionate emotions.[81] According to Cicero, success in controlling these emotions and the court's reaction depends on the technical skills and 'personal urbanity of the advocate.'[82]

Quintilian approached the topic of *ethos* in much the same way as Aristotle and Cicero. Like Aristotle, he believed that 'the strongest argument in support of a speaker is that he is a good man.'[83] And, like Cicero, he offered copious advice on how to cultivate a convincing *ethos*. Quintilian thought that an advocate's credibility depended mainly on his perceived motives for taking a particular case: 'It is ... preeminently desirable that he should be believed to have undertaken the case ... [from a] moral consideration.'[84] Credibility also depends on avoiding 'the impression that we are abusive, malignant, proud or slanderous toward any individual or body of men, especially as cannot be hurt without exciting the disapproval of the judges.'[85]

Like the others, Quintilian paid considerable attention to the artfulness or skill needed to create credibility. One technique he recommended was a kind of false humility, that is, 'representing that we are weak, unprepared, and no match for the powerful talents arrayed against us.'[86] For maximum effect, this false humility can be accompanied by a 'certain simplicity in the thoughts, style, voice and look of the speaker ...'[87]

He also warned advocates against burdening 'the judge with all the arguments we have discovered since by so doing we shall at once bore him and render him *less inclined to believe us*.'[88] And, finally, to be persuasive an advocate should present the entire case with an air of confidence: 'Our advocate must ... adopt a confident manner, and should always speak as if he thought his case admirable.'[89]

During his analysis of how an advocate's confidence creates credibility, Quintilian repeated his predecessors' warnings against noticeable disingenuousness or excessive self-assurance. He pointed out the dangers of appearing too confident: 'For as a rule [a] judge dislikes self-confidence in a pleader, and conscious of his rights tacitly demands the respectful deference of the orator.'[90]

Quintilian's advice about cultivating appearances is accompanied by several warnings about what happens when a judge discovers that an advocate has been deceptive or insincere. He notes, first, that disguising artfulness is extremely difficult: '[T]o avoid all display of art in itself requires consummate art.'[91] Elsewhere, while discussing the statement of the facts, Quintilian stresses how careful advocates must be:

> It is ... specially important in this part of our speech to avoid anything suggestive of artful design, for the judge is never more on his guard than at this stage. Nothing must seem fictitious, nought betray anxiety; everything must seem to spring from the case rather than the art of the orator.[92]

As the foregoing analysis shows, persuasive arguments depend as much on the advocate's character and credibility *(ethos)* as they do on their legal or emotional content. According to Quintilian, the perfect orator is a good man speaking well.[93] Under classical theory, an advocate's credibility depends primarily on the perception that he accepted his case from good or moral considerations and that he is completely confident in its outcome. It also depends on his ability to convince the court that he is intelligent, has goodwill toward others, and is of upright character.

Given the importance of *ethos*, classical rhetoricians felt that projecting the proper *ethos* was as important as actually possessing it. For them, *projecting* the proper *ethos* was an acquired skill, an art that disguised art. And, like the skillful manipulation of arguments or emotions, it requires flexibility and constant practice. They encouraged advocates to look for ways to connect their *ethos* to the emotional undercurrents of a case and to develop the ability to deliver arguments in a restrained or an impassioned manner, depending on the circumstances.

If the occasion demands it, they even sanction certain types of disingenuousness, so long as the deceptions go undetected. And, they illustrate how difficult it is to project and control the proper *ethos* by showing how advocates lose their credibility by over-elaboration of trivial arguments, excessive self-assurance, or unseemly arrogance. Throughout their discussion of *ethos*, classical rhetoricians repeatedly remind advocates that their success depends heavily on the judge's assessment of their character.

ETHOS AND *PATHOS*: THE MODERN VIEW

When compared with the analysis in classical treatises, modern analysis of how *pathos* and *ethos* affect legal audiences is sketchy and disorganized. It lacks the overarching theoretical framework that the classical rhetorical treatises provide. Although modern authorities discuss many of the topics covered in the classical texts, they do so in a less comprehensive and clearly organized fashion.

Notwithstanding these shortcomings, modern trial advocacy handbooks, practice manuals, and even some recent law review articles repeatedly testify to the enduring importance of *pathos* and *ethos* in legal discourse. These articles and treatises also demonstrate that audience awareness is as important to modern trial lawyers as it was to Aristotle, Cicero and Quintilian. It is especially important to trial lawyers because they argue their cases before dual audiences: an amateur jury and a professional judge.

Because modern trial lawyers argue their cases before lay juries, their general approach to advocacy is similar to the classical approach. In fact, a few modern writers even cite Cicero and Quintilian when discussing persuasion techniques.[94] While their explicit reliance on classical sources is usually, and understandably, limited, the major classical themes still survive, albeit in altered, and sometimes diminished, form. Like their classical sources, they too stress the importance of emotion (*pathos*) and lawyer credibility (*ethos*) especially when they analyze and describe overall trial strategy, jury selection, opening statements, and closing arguments.

A. Modern Audience Assessment

Unlike Greek and Roman advocates who argued their cases before judges who were inexperienced amateurs, modern lawyers argue their cases before a mixed audience: an experienced, professional judge and an inexperienced, amateur jury. Consequently, their task of audience assessment is more difficult. Nonetheless, their basic approach resembles that of their classical predecessors since both emphasize the importance of thoroughly investigating the prospective audience.

In the classical period, most litigants had the benefit of selecting a judge who was agreeable to both parties.[95] By contrast, modern advocates have little say in the matter and usually must argue before whichever judge is assigned to the case.[96] Moreover, whereas the classical advocate, faced with an amateur, inexperienced judge, investigated the judge's personal qualities and background, the modern advocate, faced with a professional judge, analyzes and investigates the judge's professional background or track record. This investigation takes many avenues, but frequently revolves around questions like:

> Is he plaintiff- or defense-oriented in personal injury cases? What kind of judgments has he entered in similar civil cases? Do his trial rulings have any particular bent? In criminal cases, is he prosecution- or defense-minded? Does he have known attitudes in certain types of cases? What sentencing disparity does he have between bench and jury trials?[97]

Others suggest that '[t]he advocate should know the background of the judge, what organizations he or she belonged to as a private lawyer before going on the bench, what his or her *professional* experience was, and what attitudes the judge has manifested since going on the bench. Argument should then be shaped as much as possible to convince that particular judge [or judges].'[98] Or they recommend that '[i]f you are unfamiliar with the judge who will try the case, find out how much latitude will be allowed in asking questions [during *voir dire*], or if it will be the judge who asks all questions.'[99]

While the process of investigating a judge's decision-making habits is undoubtedly supplemented by advocates' informal inquiries about personal habits and traits, their overall focus is on the judge's professional, rather than personal behavior. In this respect, it differs from the classical practice.

It differs also in the fact that modern lawyers focus their pre-trial investigations on jurors, rather than on judges. In some ways, the modern jury selection process resembles the Roman judge selection process. However, instead of selecting a mutually agreeable judge, modern advocates select mutually agreeable jurors. The judge-centered approach of the classical period has been transformed to a juror-centered approach in the modern era.[100] Despite these differences, audience assessment is critical to both approaches.

Armed with elaborate questionnaires and sometimes with the research findings of social scientists, modern lawyers try to determine 'the ideal type of juror in a given case.'[101] To that end, advocates investigate what they regard as 'predictors of likely attitudes: age, education, employment history, residence history, marital and family history, hobbies and interests, reading and television habits, [and membership in] organizations.'[102] Occasionally, their investigation even extends to assessments of jurors' 'body language,' likability,' and predisposition to be a 'leader or follower.'[103]

In the classical period, the principal purpose of audience investigation was to help advocates tailor their arguments to suit the judge. This 'tailoring' function is retained in the modern jury selection practice because it helps lawyers select sympathetic or neutral jurors and disqualify unsympathetic or biased jurors.

In sum, modern lawyers have a more difficult audience assessment task than their classical counterparts. Instead of investigating only one type of audience, modern lawyers must investigate two – one amateur (the jury) and one professional (the judge). When investigating the judge, modern lawyers usually focus on professional, not personal, background information. However, when investigating the jury, they modify the classical practice and focus on the jurors' personal and professional background. In doing so, they transform the judge-oriented approach of the classical period to the jury-oriented approach of today.

B. Advocate Credibility

Since lawyer credibility is so important, most modern trial advocacy handbooks devote considerable attention to listing and analyzing 'credibility factors.' According to one authority, '[t]he only thing a trial lawyer has to sell to the jury is his credibility.'[104] Most modern lists of 'credibility factors' resemble the Greco-Roman lists of those 'virtues' that contribute to an advocate's *ethos.*

Cicero, for example, found '[i]t is very helpful to display the tokens of good-nature, kindness, calmness, loyalty and a disposition that is pleasing and not grasping or covetous, and all the qualities belonging to men who are upright, unassuming ...'[105] Modern lawyers get the same advice. They become more credible once they can establish their 'expertise, trustworthiness, impartiality, dynamism, similarity to jurors and personal attractiveness.'[106] In various ways, they are repeatedly reminded that 'the image of you in the jurors' minds ... should be one of fairness, honesty, sincerity, courteousness and the desire for justice.'[107]

Modern handbooks also stress that successful lawyers usually possess a non-arrogant confidence in and enthusiasm for their cases. Given the importance of self-confidence, modern authorities suggest that lawyers consciously demonstrate their 'enthusiasm about trying the case' whenever possible.[108] To be most effective, this enthusiasm must also be coupled with a 'total conviction in [the] case and [an] unwavering commitment to [the client's] side.'[109] Aristotle, Cicero, and Quintilian made essentially the same points regarding confidence and enthusiasm. According to Cicero, a successful advocate's enthusiasm for his case must be 'visibly stamped or rather branded on the advocate himself.'[110]

Classical rhetoricians also emphasized the importance of *projecting* the proper *ethos.* That is, effective advocacy depends on the audience perceiving the lawyers as intelligent, knowledgeable, honest and fair. Classical authorities reluctantly conceded that advocates must sometimes feign these qualities, either by assuming a false humility or by appearing reluctant to make an argument they are in fact eager to make. But they regarded false humility and feigned reluctance as exceptions to the general emphasis on enthusiasm, confidence, and intelligence.

Modern authorities also recognize that lawyer credibility depends on appearing to be intelligent and knowledgeable about the law and the case. They too think that appearing to be 'fair' increases a lawyer's credibility:

First, appear interested in helping the jurors decide the case in a fair manner, rather than just appearing as a partisan advocate. Second, show fairness to all parties and witnesses.[111]

Echoing the classical rhetoricians' advice regarding appearances, modern experts suggest that lawyers should 'strive to create an atmosphere of sincerity – that you and your client are honest and moral people. Throughout the trial, it is important to avoid exaggeration and deception.'[112] In addition, many experts think that a lawyer's credibility is increased by candid admissions of weaknesses in the case:

> Confronting weaknesses has two advantages. First, your weaknesses are your opponent's strengths. By addressing them first, you can in part deflate his later argument ... Take the wind out of his sails by raising his points first, and they will sound hollow and tired when he argues them. Second, the jury will respect your honesty and candor when openly and candidly discussing those weaknesses. Since your credibility as an advocate is critically important, this consideration should not be downplayed.[113]

As the foregoing discussion shows, classical and modern authorities agree that merely possessing the proper *ethos* or character is not sufficient. The advocate must also take steps to insure that the audience perceives or appreciates the fact that the advocate possesses it. Although there are some small differences between the classical and modern experts regarding which attributes or approaches affect credibility, they nevertheless agree that lawyer credibility is critically important.

Even though classical and modern experts usually agree regarding which factors affect an advocate's credibility, they differ somewhat on the importance of non-verbal communication. Classical rhetoricians linked credibility to how advocates delivered their argument. They stressed that voice, eye contact, gestures, mannerisms, and stance affect the reception of legal argument. Aristotle focused on voice: 'The art of delivery has to do with the voice: with the right management of it to express each several emotion – as when to use a loud voice, when a soft, and when the intermediate ...'[114] Cicero was convinced that '[d]elivery ... is the dominant factor in oratory.'[115] For him 'delivery is wholly the concern of the feelings, and these are mirrored by the face and expressed by the eyes ...'[116] He even gave detailed instructions regarding gesture: 'All these emotions must be accompanied by gesture not this stagy gesture reproducing the words but one conveying the general situation and idea not by mimicry but by hint ...'[117]

Quintilian noted that '[a]ll emotional appeals will inevitably fall flat, unless they are given the fire that voice, look, and the whole carriage of the body can give them.'[118] He thought that '[a]ll delivery ... is concerned with two different things, namely, voice and gesture ...'[119] Quintilian's discussion of voice and gesture is comprehensive.[120] When discussing voice he analyzes the effects of enunciation, volume, rhythm, and tone as well as a host of other topics. His discussion of gesture includes, among other things, an advocate's posture, hands, gait and clothing.

Building on many of these same techniques of non-verbal communication, modern analysts also add discussions based on psychology and sociology. Their analysis sometimes even includes the concepts and terminology of elocution coaches: 'Since so little communication is grounded on bare word content, lawyers must understand how kinesics (posture, gestures, movement, eye contact, and use of space), para-linguistics (voice inflection) and personal appearance affect whether verbal communication will be persuasive.'[121] According to them, a lawyer's credibility can depend on intangibles as small as a smile:

> Whether out of nervousness or aloofness, some lawyers forget such friendly but important gestures as a smile. Let the jurors know that you are a human being, that you have a sense of humor, and that no matter how important your client's case is to you, you still can remember the basic courtesies which people should extend to one another.[122]

Given their assumption that a lawyer's rapport with the audience depends on non-verbal communication, they stress even small details, such as when to maintain good eye contact,[123] where to stand while addressing the jury,[124] and why it is inadvisable to read an argument.[125] They are convinced that attention to such details will ingratiate advocates with their audience and make their arguments more persuasive.

Their emphasis on a just a few non-verbal factors affecting a lawyer's credibility differs from the classical rhetoricians' heavy emphasis on an advocate's character and personal integrity. At its most simplistic, the modern approach resembles a course in advanced elocution. It reduces *ethos* to common courtesy and careful staging. At best, it equates *ethos* with general competence or professionalism.

Even so, modern and classical authorities agree on the importance of lawyer credibility. They agree on which personal qualities are most important, on which attitudes must be conveyed, and even, in some cases, on which techniques are most effective. And, finally, they agree that projecting personal integrity is as important as actually possessing it.

However, they part ways on the subject of non-verbal communication. Modern authorities rely heavily on theories and testing that did not exist in the classical period. Even so, their treatment of such subjects as eye contact, posture, voice inflection are not nearly as thorough as their classical predecessors.

C. Arguments from Emotion

In their analysis of how emotion affects persuasive discourse, modern authorities also differ somewhat from their classical counterparts. Even though classical rhetoricians preferred appeals to reason, they recognized the power of appeals to emotion. They disapproved of such appeals, however, because emotion impairs an audience's ability to reach a well-reasoned decision. While modern experts also recognize that emotion may impair the ability to reason logically, they are more tolerant of non-rational 'reasoning' than their predecessors.

In part, this modern tolerance springs from recent research regarding the non-logical ways people 'reason' or think. Many modern authorities, for instance, believe that 'people are affective, not cognitive, thinkers. That is, most people are emotional, symbol-oriented, selective perceivers of information who base their decisions largely on previously held attitudes about people and events.'[126]

This explanation is simply another way of explaining how emotion and reasoning are inevitably intermingled. Moreover, if people are 'affective, not cognitive thinkers,' appeals to an audience's emotions are, in one sense, appeals to reason. Thus, even if an advocate's arguments are logical and 'well-reasoned,' the audience's emotional response may be stronger than its cognitive response. Consequently, appeals to emotion become unavoidable and just as important as appeals to reason.

Despite different analytical approaches, classical and modern authorities agree that persuasive discourse depends on controlling the audience's emotions and the emotional climate of the trial. And, like their predecessors, modern authorities recognize that this emotional climate fluctuates during the trial. At the beginning, for example, jurors are anxious, curious, receptive, and looking for someone to trust.[127] They are also more likely to be interested and attentive.[128] By the end of the trial, however, both the judge and the jury will be tired, perhaps bored, and occasionally confused.[129] Good lawyers realize this and vary their arguments depending on which part of the trial is taking place.

D. Voir Dire and Opening Statements

Beginning with jury selection and their opening statement, experienced lawyers try to set the emotional tone of the trial and begin to orchestrate the audience's emotions. As the preceding analysis has shown, the emotional tone of the case is closely connected to the advocate's credibility. Because of this connection, modern authorities recommend that lawyers relieve jury anxiety during *voir dire* and 'become the jurors' friend and guide by helping them understand the trial system, by reassuring them that they do belong here, and by letting them know that their participation is important to [them] and [their] party.[130] Moreover, modern experts point out that '*voir dire* examination is arguably your best contact with the jurors ... [T]his is the only phase at which you can speak with them. During the questioning, you can engage in a dialogue with the jury and develop personal rapport with them.'[131]

This emotional rapport is especially important during the advocate's opening statement. Both classical and modern authorities agree that a strong and emotionally engaging opening statement may determine the outcome of the case. In fact, some modern authorities believe that '80% of jurors make up their minds during opening and never change their opinions.'[132]

Modern analyses of opening statements resemble classical analyses of *exordia* in that both stress the importance of first impressions: 'As in life generally, the psychological phenomenon of primacy applies, and initial impressions become lasting impressions.'[133] Moreover, a good opening should 'heighten' the jury's attention.[134] For the most part, these first impressions come from the lawyer's overview of the case and from the statement of the facts.

E. Statement of the Facts

Like their classical predecessors, modern experts think that lawyers should use the emotional facts of the case to predispose the judge and jury in the client's favor. To accomplish this, they recommend that the story be about the 'people, not the legal problems. Jurors want to know who to silently root for, who wears the white hat. Jurors want to feel good about their decisions ... and reach a verdict consistent with their feelings about those people.'[135]

A lawyer's storytelling style is also an important tool for exploiting the audience's emotions. A lawyer's 'storytelling should be emotional and dramatic, since you want to draw the jurors into your story and create empathy for your party. Vivid, dramatic, emotional storytelling is engaging and holds the jury's attention.'[136]

Although they tend to concentrate on the jurors, modern analysts also note that while 'the judge may know a good deal about the law governing the case; and the judge may even have presided at similar trials in the past ... the judge may be a complete stranger to the facts in the instant case.'[137] Consequently, like lay jurors, judges may be responsive to the emotional aspects of the case and lawyers should narrate the facts with this in mind.

F. Closing Argument

Like the classical rhetoricians, modern authorities attach a great deal of importance to the closing argument and regard it as one of the best opportunities for playing on the court's emotions. Ideally, a good closing argument is 'logic and emotion brought together.'[138] They stress that closing argument gives advocates an opportunity for demonstrating their own emotional involvement with the case, but warn that '[s]howing honest emotion does not mean crying or other histrionics. Rather, it means ... demonstrat[ing] the appropriate emotional response to the content of the closing argument whether it be sadness, happiness, anger or indignation.'[139] They also note that 'the delivery style that accomplishes this is as varied as trial lawyers are numerous. Some lawyers are emotional and passionate; others quietly compelling ...'[140]

Ever mindful of the audience, they frequently remind lawyers that a closing argument should not be so long that it bores or confuses the audience.[141] And, given the audience's limited attention span, 'key ideas should be repeated, since repetition is so important for retention.'[142]

Although most authorities regard the closing as a good place for emotional argument, some of them warn lawyers about the attendant dangers:

> Psychological studies show that appeals to reason are better than appeals to emotion. They [are] ... more lasting. [V]ery strong emotions block out almost completely the ability to reason. [I]f a person is caught up in a storm of emotion, he will have ... little memory of what was said. He remembers his feelings about the subject matter, but he will not be in a position to defend those feelings in the jury room.[143]

In sum, like their classical predecessors, modern authorities stress sensitivity to and use of the fluctuating emotional climate of the case. They too urge lawyers to exploit the audience's emotions strategically, depending on what stage of the trial (*voir dire*, opening statement, closing argument, etc.) is taking place.

The modern tolerance of emotion's place in persuasive discourse represents the biggest difference between classical and modern approaches. In part, this tolerance springs from modern experts' conviction that most people reason in an affective (emotional, symbol-oriented), rather than a cognitive, fashion. In addition, modern experts stress the overlapping effects of emotion and lawyer credibility in ways that differ from the classical sources.

SIMILARITIES AND DIFFERENCES

In their systematic and comprehensive analysis of legal discourse, Greco-Roman rhetoricians divided legal argument into three equal and mutually dependent components: *logos, pathos*, and *ethos*. Even though they emphasized the importance of logic, they realized that judges and juries also make their decisions based on non-rational factors such as their sense of the advocate's personal integrity or the emotional content of the case. Taking these factors into account, classical rhetoricians devoted as much attention to these non-rational means of persuasion as they did to logic.

For them, advocacy was an art and could only be learned by practice. Using examples drawn from their own considerable experience, they emphasized audience assessment techniques, strategic approaches, recurring problems, and the importance of flexibility. Above all, they stressed the importance of *projecting* the advocate's personal integrity and exploiting the emotional climate of the case. Their overall approach was focused on humanizing the case in ways that would favorably affect the judge's decision.

Modern analysts, especially trial advocacy specialists, also realize the importance of *ethos* and *pathos* in persuasive discourse. In their discussions of trial strategy, they implicitly (and sometimes explicitly) endorse classical rhetorical principles and discuss many of the same topics as classical rhetoricians. Very often, they reach the same conclusions about what is effective and what is not.

However, to suit new circumstances, modern lawyers must sometimes depart from classical principles. For example, both classical and modern rhetoricians think an audience-oriented focus is important. But modern trial lawyers have a more difficult task than their predecessors because they have two audiences – the judge (a professional) and the jury (non-professionals). Despite this difference, modern lawyers and their classical predecessors both agree that advocates must tailor their arguments to suit the audience. Occasionally, modern authorities adopt a somewhat different approach to non-verbal persuasion techniques. They differ too when they discuss the importance of *affective* reasoning instead of cognitive reasoning. Even then, they are building on principles that were first introduced in the classical treatises.

Although there are substantial similarities between Greco-Roman and modern ideas of the persuasive effects of *pathos* and *ethos*, modern authorities do not discuss these effects very systematically. Unlike their predecessors, they do not provide an overarching theoretical framework within which to analyze the non-rational factors in legal argument. This lack of a systematic approach presents several dangers. First, it results in an over-emphasis on logic in most formal analyses of legal argument. It also misleadingly relegates *ethos* and *pathos* to positions of secondary importance.

These dangers are likely to continue because law students and most new lawyers do not have ready access to discussions of *ethos* and *pathos*. Instead, they must glean this information from journal articles, parts of trial advocacy treatises, and from more experienced lawyers. To correct this deficiency and to speed up the educational process, modern lawyers should familiarize themselves with the rhetorical works of Aristotle, Cicero, and Quintilian. If they do so, they will soon see how the timeless concepts of *ethos* and *pathos* fit into a practical, experience-based theoretical framework.

Notes

1. Appellate advocacy treatises focus on these topics with a judicial audience in mind, whereas trial advocacy texts focus on both judicial and jury audiences. Appellate advocacy texts deal with the subject of lawyer credibility by focusing on the advocate's command of substantive matters or by emphasizing the advocate's 'professionalism' and personal 'style.' Although they sometimes discuss emotion in connection with the statement of the case, the subject is not treated in great detail.

    For a representative sampling of appellate advocacy books treating these matters, see Carole C. Berry, *Effective Appellate Advocacy: Brief Writing and Oral Advocacy* (3rd ed. 2003); Board of Student Advisers, Harvard Law School, *Introduction to Advocacy* 84 (7th ed. 2002); Charles R. Calleros, *Legal Method and Writing* 341 (3rd ed. 1998); David C. Frederick, *The Art of Oral Advocacy* (2003) and *Supreme Court and Appellate Advocacy* (2003); Wesley Gilmer, Jr., *Legal Research, Writing and Advocacy* 258 (1987); Richard K. Neumann, Jr., *Legal Reasoning and Legal Writing* 399 (4th ed. 2001); Karen K. Porter et al., *Introduction to Legal Writing and Oral Advocacy* 175 (1989); Edward D. Re, *Brief Writing and Oral Argument* 167 (6th ed. 1987); Helene S. Shapo et al., *Writing and Analysis in the Law* 370 (4th ed. 1999) and Steven D. Stark, *Writing to Win: The Legal Writer* (1999).

2. '[C]redibility is the only thing a lawyer has to sell.' Thomas Mauet, *Fundamentals of Trial Techniques* 46, 48 (3rd ed. 1992).

3. In addition to serving these functions, classical rhetorical treatises also described a comprehensive educational curriculum and provided detailed instruction on public speaking for ceremonial and political occasions.

4. For a fuller description of the typical treatise-user see 1 Quintilian, *Institutio Oratoria* 5-19 (H.E. Butler trans. 1954); Susan Miller, 'Classical Practice and Contemporary Basics,' in *The Rhetorical Tradition and Modern Writing* 46 (James J. Murphy ed. 1982); Donovan J. Ochs, 'Cicero's Rhetorical Theory,' in *A Synoptic History of Classical Rhetoric* 96 (James J. Murphy ed. 1983).

5. Aristotle, *Rhetoric* at 8.

6. 1 Quintilian, *Institutio Oratoria* at 397.

7. Aristotle, *Rhetoric* at 141.

8. Aristotle, *Rhetoric* at 183-84.

9. Thomas R. Martin, *Ancient Greece: From Prehistoric to Hellenistic Times* 110 (2000). H.C. Lawson-Tancred also describes the size and composition of the Athenian court: '[It was] popular in the sense that it was open to all citizens, unlike the aristocratic Areopagus,

and it also had a jury that was huge by modern standards ... [T]he juries ... were regularly five hundred strong.' Aristotle, *The Art of Rhetoric* 10 (H.C. Lawson-Tancred trans. 1991).

10. 'At Rome, most private suits were heard by a single judge, the *iudex privatus* or arbiter.' George Kennedy, *The Art of Rhetoric in the Roman World* 198 (1972). 'Each iudex was appointed to serve only in a particular case, some might have been called on frequently; when called on it was their duty to serve, for the office of iudex was a public office which could be declined only for valid reasons.' Kennedy, *Art of Rhetoric in the Roman World* at 231.

11. H.F. Jolowicz and Barry Nicholas, *Historical Introduction to the Study of Roman Law* 176 (1972).

12. J.A. Crook, *Law and Life of Rome* 33 (1967). See also Bruce W. Frier, *The Rise of the Roman Jurists: Studies in Cicero's Pro Caecina* 96 (1985), where the author notes that, 'The normal judge in a Roman civil case was emphatically not a legal professional, nor even a magistrate, but instead a layman with no special training in the law.'

13. Crook, *Law and Life of Rome* at 89.

14. Crook, *Law and Life of Rome* at 40.

15. Alan Watson, *The Spirit of Roman Law* 60 (1995).

16. Alan Watson, *The Spirit of Roman Law* at 79-80.

17. George Kennedy, *The Art of Rhetoric in the Roman World* at 198-99.

18. Aristotle, *Rhetoric* at xxi.

19. Aristotle, *Rhetoric* at xvii.

20. Aristotle, *Rhetoric* at 2.

21. Aristotle, *Rhetoric* at 183-84. See also 2 Quintilian, *Institutio Oratoria* at 155: 'There have been certain writers of no small authority who have held that the sole duty of the orator was to instruct: in their view appeals to the emotions were to be excluded for two reasons, first on the ground that all disturbance of the mind was faulty, and secondly that it was wrong to distract the judge from the truth by exciting his pity, bringing influence to bear, and the like. Further, to seek to charm the audience, when the aim of the orator was merely to win success, was in their opinion not only superfluous for a pleader, but hardly worthy of a self-respecting man.'

22. 2 Quintilian, *Institutio Oratoria* at 431 (emphasis added).

23. Aristotle, *Rhetoric* at 91.

24. Aristotle, *Rhetoric* at 223.

25. 3 Cicero, *De Oratore* 327.

26. 3 Cicero, *De Oratore* at 331.

27. 2 Quintilian, *Institutio Oratoria* at 419.

28. 2 Quintilian, *Institutio Oratoria* at 139.

29. 2 Quintilian, *Institutio Oratoria* at 13. In several places, Quintilian hinted at some of the techniques he used to stir the court's emotions: 'Sometimes it is desirable to set forth [the client's] merits ... Sex, age and situation are also important considerations, as for instance, when women, old men or wards are pleading in the character of wives, parents or children. For *pity* alone may move even a strict judge.'

30. 3 Cicero, *De Oratore* at 349.

31. 2 Quintilian, *Institutio Oratoria* at 391 (emphasis added).

32. 3 Cicero, *De Oratore* at 331.

33. 2 Quintilian, *Institutio Oratoria* at 15.

34. 2 Quintilian, *Institutio Oratoria* at 15.

35. 2 Quintilian, *Institutio Oratoria* at 11.

36. 2 Quintilian, *Institutio Oratoria* at 147.
37. 2 Quintilian, *Institutio Oratoria* at 125-127.
38. 2 Quintilian, *Institutio Oratoria* at 141-143.
39. 2 Quintilian, *Institutio Oratoria* at 303: 'We must not always burden the judge with all the arguments we have discovered, since by so doing we shall at once bore him and render him less inclined to believe us.'
40. 2 Quintilian, *Institutio Oratoria* at 383: '[T]he points selected for enumeration (in the closing argument) must be treated with weight and dignity, enlivened by apt reflexions and diversified by suitable figures; for there is nothing more tiresome than a dry repetition of facts, which merely suggests a lack of confidence in the judge's memory.'
41. 2 Quintilian, *Institutio Oratoria* at 343.
42. For a fuller discussion of classical theory on the proper organization of legal argument, see Chapter Three.
43. Aristotle, *Rhetoric* at 224.
44. Aristotle, *Rhetoric* at 223-24 (emphasis added).
45. 3 Cicero, *De Oratore* at 435.
46. 3 Cicero, *De Oratore* at 443.
47. 2 Quintilian, *Institutio Oratoria* at 19.
48. 2 Quintilian, *Institutio Oratoria* at 21.
49. 2 Quintilian, *Institutio Oratoria* at 25.
50. Aristotle, *Rhetoric* at 230. Aristotle's advice, and his sense of drama, even extended to small details of wording as when he observed, 'things that impart character are the traits that belong to each type; thus: "Still talking, on he went" – which reveals the type of blusterer and boor.' Aristotle, *Rhetoric* at 231. And, elsewhere, he advised advocates to 'employ the traits of emotion. Use symptoms familiar to all, and any special signs of emotion in the defendant or his adversary. For example: "With a scowl, he left me" ... These touches carry conviction; the hearer knows them, and, to him, they evince the truth of what he does not know.' Aristotle, *Rhetoric* at 231.
51. 2 Quintilian, *Institutio Oratoria* at 61.
52. 2 Quintilian, *Institutio Oratoria* at 69-71. In another passage, Quintilian suggests that '[t]he statement of facts will be brief, if in the first place we start at that point of the case at which it begins to concern the judge, secondly avoid irrelevance, and finally cut out everything the removal of which neither hampers the activities of the judge nor harms our own case.' 2 Quintilian, *Institutio Oratoria* at 73.
53. 2 Quintilian, *Institutio Oratoria* at 75 (emphasis added).
54. 2 Quintilian, *Institutio Oratoria* at 77.
55. 2 Quintilian, *Institutio Oratoria* at 115.
56. 2 Quintilian, *Institutio Oratoria* at 111.
57. 3 Cicero, *De Oratore* at 449 (emphasis added).
58. 2 Quintilian, *Institutio Oratoria* at 417.
59. 'For it not only makes our arguments clearer by isolating the points from the crowd in which they would otherwise be lost and placing them before the eyes of the judge, but *relieves his attention* by assigning a definite limit to certain parts of our speech ... For it is a pleasure to be able to measure how much of our task has been accomplished, and the knowledge of what remains to do stimulates us to fresh effort over the labour that still awaits us.' 2 Quintilian, *Institutio Oratoria* at 149.
60. 'Partition may be defined as the enumeration in order of our own propositions, those of our adversary or both. It is held by some that this is indispensable on the ground that it makes the case clearer and the judge more attentive and more ready to be instructed, if he

knows what we are speaking about and what we are going subsequently to speak about.' 2 Quintilian, *Institutio Oratoria* at 137.

61. 2 Quintilian, *Institutio Oratoria* at 139.
62. Aristotle, *Rhetoric* at 240.
63. 2 Quintilian, *Institutio Oratoria* at 417.
64. 2 Quintilian, *Institutio Oratoria* at 391.
65. Aristotle, *Rhetoric* at 240. Aristotle said that advocates should use the epilogue to 'refresh their memories.' See also 2 Quintilian, *Institutio Oratoria* at 383, where Quintilian observes: 'There are two kinds of peroration, for it may deal either with facts or with the emotional aspect of the case. The repetition and grouping of the facts ... serves to both refresh the memory of the judge and to place the whole of the case before his eyes ...'
66. 2 Quintilian, *Institutio Oratoria* at 389.
67. 2 Quintilian, *Institutio Oratoria* at 391.
68. Aristotle, *Rhetoric* at 223.
69. 3 Cicero, *De Oratore* at 331.
70. 2 Quintilian, *Institutio Oratoria* at 21.
71. 2 Quintilian, *Institutio Oratoria* at 113.
72. Aristotle, *Rhetoric* at 91 (emphasis added).
73. Aristotle, *Rhetoric* at 92. The 'virtues' Aristotle had in mind are best summarized in a list Cicero provides: 'It is very helpful to display the tokens of good-nature, kindness, calmness, loyalty and a disposition that is pleasing and not grasping or covetous, and all the qualities belong to men who are upright, unassuming ...' 3 Cicero, *De Oratore,* at 329.
74. Aristotle, *Rhetoric* at 224.
75. Aristotle, *Rhetoric* at 231 (emphasis added).
76. 3 Cicero, *De Oratore* at 327-29 (emphasis added).
77. 3 Cicero, *De Oratore* at 329 (emphasis added).
78. 3 Cicero, *De Oratore* at 333.
79. 3 Cicero, *De Oratore* at 335.
80. 3 Cicero, *De Oratore* at 339 (emphasis added).
81. 'But these two styles, which we require to be respectively mild and emotional, have something in common, making them hard to keep apart. For from that mildness, which wins us the goodwill of our hearers, some inflow must reach this fiercest of passions, wherewith we inflame the same people, and again, out of this passion some little energy must often be kindled within that mildness: nor is any style better blended than that wherein the harshness of strife is tempered by the personal urbanity of the advocate, while his easy-going mildness is fortified by some admixture of serious strife.' 3 Cicero, *De Oratore* at 355.
82. 3 Cicero, *De Oratore* at 355.
83. 2 Quintilian, *Institutio Oratoria* at 303. Quintilian also observed that although an advocate 'may be modest and say little about himself, yet if he is believed to be a good man, this consideration will exercise the strongest influence at every point of the case.' 2 Quintilian, *Institutio Oratoria* at 9.
84. 2 Quintilian, *Institutio Oratoria* at 9.
85. 2 Quintilian, *Institutio Oratoria* at 11.
86. 2 Quintilian, *Institutio Oratoria* at 11.
87. 2 Quintilian, *Institutio Oratoria* at 37.
88. 2 Quintilian, *Institutio Oratoria* at 303. Elsewhere Quintilian said: 'There is another serious fault into which pleaders fall: the anxious over-elaboration of points. Such a procedure makes his case suspect to the judges, while frequently arguments which, if

stated without more ado, would have removed all doubt, lose their force owing to the delay caused by the elaborate preparations made for their introduction, due to the fact that the advocate thinks that they require additional support.' 2 Quintilian, *Institutio Oratoria* at 343.

89. 2 Quintilian, *Institutio Oratoria* at 343.

90. 2 Quintilian, *Institutio Oratoria* at 37.

91. 2 Quintilian, *Institutio Oratoria* at 37.

92. 2 Quintilian, *Institutio Oratoria*. at 119.

93. 2 Quintilian, *Institutio Oratoria* at 9.

94. For a representative sampling, see Robert F. Hanley, 'Brush Up Your Aristotle,' 12 Litigation 39, No. 2 (Winter, 1986) (a regrettably short essay stressing both the accessibility and applicability of the Greco-Roman rhetorical principles discussed in this Article); Anthony G. Amsterdam and Randy Hertz, 'An Analysis of Closing Arguments to a Jury,' 37 New York Law School Law Review 55 (1992) (quoting Aristotle, Cicero and Quintilian while analyzing rhetorical structure of closing arguments); James J. Brosnahan, 'Overview: Basic Principles of Advocacy,' in *Master Advocates' Handbook* 29 (D. Lake Rumsey, ed. 1986) (periodically quoting Cicero during essay); Jeffrey J. Hartje and Mark E. Wilson, *Lawyer's Work* 305 (1984) (quoting Aristotle, Cicero, and Quintilian in a chapter devoted to persuasive discourse).

95. H.F. Jolowicz and Barry Nicholas, *Historical Introduction to the Study of Roman Law* 179 (1972), '[T]he appointment [of a judge] was ... made by the magistrate, but ... he would in practice take account of the wishes of the parties, and ... would not force any particular [judge] on an unwilling party.' (Emphasis added). See also J. A. Crook, *Legal Advocacy in the Roman World* 78 (1995) '[W]e hear sometimes of humble [judges], chosen no doubt by humble litigants. If the parties did not have anyone in particular in mind, or could not agree, the praetor would propose names from the annual list of select jurors ...'

96. In the Federal system, advocates must prove that a judge is biased before he or she can be removed. In some states, advocates have a right to one peremptory challenge; thereafter, the advocate must file an affidavit alleging cause. Advocates have greater latitude regarding judges under some Alternative Dispute Resolution procedures. That is, the parties may decide to hire a retired judge who is mutually satisfactory.

97. Thomas Mauet, *Fundamentals of Trial Techniques* 14 (3rd ed. 1992) Some professional news services even offer to sell lawyers 'profiles' of judges. But see J.P. Vero, 'Nine Secrets for Living with Judges,' 17 Litigation 18 (1991). Vero, not content with examining the professional record of the judge, classifies judges according to 'type' and offers advice as to how to accommodate each type.

98. James J. Brosnahan, 'Overview: Basic Principles of Advocacy,' in *Master Advocates' Handbook* 30 (D. Lake Rumsey, ed. 1986).

99. Peter Perlman, 'Jury Selection,' *Master Advocates' Handbook* 51 (D. Lake Rumsey, ed. 1986).

100. Thomas Mauet, *Fundamentals of Trial Techniques*, at 376.

101. Lawrence A. Dubin and Thomas F. Guernsey, *Trial Practice* 15 (1991). The authors also note that '[t]he scientific selection of juries became popular in the early 1970s. Market researchers developed methods for conducting mock trials and testing the salability of a case in much the same way a product is tested before being distributed in the marketplace.'

102. Mauet, *Fundamentals* at 25.

103. Mauet, *Fundamentals* at 27. See also Perlman, 'Jury Selection' for the proposition that '[t]here are various proper and ethical means which provide lawyers information about

prospective jurors. Many jurisdictions provide jury lists which contain the jurors' names, addresses, marital status, children, and occupations. Various public records may also be helpful. These include voter registration lists and various cross-reference directories.

More sophisticated techniques include the use of expert handwriting analysts, market research studies, and community attitude surveys. Such studies provide a juror matrix summary through which the attitudes of various jurors are classified and assigned a probability rating.' Perlman, 'Jury Selection,' *Master Advocates' Handbook* at 50.

104. Thomas A. Mauet, *Trial Techniques* (6th ed. 2002) at 69.

105. 3 Cicero, *De Oratore* at 329.

106. Mauet, *Fundamentals* at 379.

107. Lawrence A. Dubin and Thomas F. Guernsey, *Trial Practice* at 20.

108. Mauet, *Fundamentals* at 42.

109. Mauet, *Trial Techniques* at 414. See also Stuart M. Speiser, 'Closing Argument,' in *Master Advocates' Handbook* at 236. ('The most compelling summations I have heard are those that convey a deep personal conviction of [sic] the client's cause, coupled with exposition of the evidence in light of the judge's final instructions.')

110. 3 Cicero, *De Oratore* at 333.

111. Lawrence A. Dubin and Thomas F. Guernsey, *Trial Practice* at 171.

112. Speiser, 'Closing Argument' at 243; and Hon. James C. Hill, 'The Importance of Sincerity,' in *Master Advocates' Handbook* 13 (D. Lake Rumsey ed. 1986).

113. Mauet, *Trial Techniques* at 413. *See also* Lawrence A. Dubin and Thomas F. Guernsey, *Trial Practice* at 40: '[Y]ou are usually better off revealing significant weaknesses before the opponent does. To allow opposing counsel to raise damaging information runs the risk that the jury will feel you have unfairly attempted to hide relevant information.' And Perlman 'Jury Selection' at 53: 'Exposing weaknesses and mitigating their damaging effect frequently disarms the opponent. At the same time, it confirms your sincerity and credibility.'

114. Aristotle, *Rhetoric* at 183.

115. 4 Cicero, *De Oratore* at 169.

116. 4 Cicero, *De Oratore* at 177.

117. 4 Cicero, *De Oratore* at 177.

118. 4 Quintilian, *Institutio Oratoria* at 245.

119. 4 Quintilian, *Institutio Oratoria* at 249.

120. 4 Quintilian, *Institutio Oratoria* at 243-349.

121. Mauet, *Fundamentals* at 379. See also Lawrence A. Dubin and Thomas F. Guernsey, *Trial Practice* at 42 ('The pitch, pace, tone, and volume of your voice should convey *credibility* and *sincerity*') (emphasis added) and Ronald L. Carlson and Edward J. Imwinkelried, *Dynamics of Trial Practice: Problems and Materials* 75 (1989).

122. Robert J. Jossen, 'Opening Statements,' in *Master Advocates' Handbook* at 69.

123. Jossen advises practitioners to 'Look at the jurors ... and show them that you care about them as well as about your case. It is important to *look* at as many different jurors as possible ...; do not devote all of your attention to one or two individuals.' See also Perlman, 'Jury Selection' at 54 ('[C]ounsel must maintain eye contact with the jury ...') and Lawrence A. Dubin and Thomas F. Guernsey, *Trial Practice* at 173 ('Reading notes will preclude the opportunity for good eye contact with the jurors.')

124. Mauet, *Fundamentals* at 49. See Lawrence A. Dubin and Thomas F. Guernsey, *Trial Practice*, at 42 ('Where possible ... it may create a warmer, more trusting atmosphere to stand in front of the first row of jurors or to the side of the podium').

125. 'The ideal closing argument is organized, planned and delivered without notes. A reliance on notes relegates a closing argument into a formal speech ... Reading notes will preclude the opportunity for good eye contact with the jurors.' Lawrence A. Dubin and Thomas F. Guernsey, *Trial Practice* at 173.
126. Thomas A. Mauet, *Trial Techniques* 43 (6th ed. 2002).
127. Mauet, *Trial Techniques* at 62.
128. Carlson and Imwinkelried, *Dynamics of Trial Practice* at 40.
129. Mauet, *Fundamentals* at 277. See also Lawrence A. Dubin and Thomas F. Guernsey, *Trial Practice* at 177.
130. Mauet, *Fundamentals* at 23. See also Lawrence A. Dubin and Thomas F. Guernsey, *Trial Practice* at 20 ('A legitimate and significant goal of voir dire is to begin the process of establishing your credibility to the prospective jurors') and Perlman, at 49 ('[Jurors] are suddenly thrust into a totally unfamiliar and intimidating atmosphere in which they are unsure what is expected of them. They have a deep-seated need for guidance, self assurance, and recognition of their involvement in the process.')
131. Carlson and Imwinkelried, *Dynamics of Trial Practice* at 40.
132. Carlson and Imwinkelried, *Dynamics of Trial Practice* at 64 (citing Jossen, 'Opening Statements: Win it in the Opening,' 10 The Docket, 6 (1986). The authors dispute Jossen's assertion which is based on findings of the Chicago Jury Project in the 1960s, but add that 'common sense and psychological theory point to the importance of the opening ...' *Id.* See also Mauet, *Trial Techniques* at 61 ('Trial lawyers agree that opening statements often make the difference in the outcome of a case. Studies have shown that jury verdicts are ... consistent with the initial impressions made by the jury during opening statements.')
133. Mauet, *Trial Techniques* at 61. See also Lawrence A. Dubin and Thomas F. Guernsey, *Trial Practice* at 33: 'Psychologists tell us that what we hear first and last have the persuasive impact on us. If you, as plaintiff's counsel make an effective opening statement, immediately after it the jury should want to find for your client.'
134. Mauet, *Fundamentals* at 44. This function is similar to that served by the classical *partitio* or argument summary.
135. Mauet, *Trial Techniques* at 26. See also Mauet, *Fundamentals* at 4: 'Most opening statements are based on storytelling, usually giving a chronological overview of "what happened" from either the plaintiff's or the defendant's viewpoint ...'
136. Mauet, *Trial Techniques* at 65.
137. Carlson and Imwinkelried, *Dynamics of Trial Practice* at 65.
138. Mauet, *Trial Techniques* at 407.
139. Lawrence A. Dubin and Thomas F. Guernsey, *Trial Practice* at 174.
140. Mauet, *Trial Techniques* at 414.
141. Lawrence A. Dubin and Thomas F. Guernsey, *Trial Practice* at 177 ('What you do not want is an argument longer than necessary. Do not either *bore or confuse* the jurors') (emphasis added). See also Mauet, *Trial Techniques* at 407 ('Most closing arguments last 20-40 minutes. Using more time is counterproductive: Jurors will be overwhelmed by details and will respond by *shutting you out.*') (emphasis added).
142. Mauet, *Fundamentals* at 279. Cicero and Quintilian thought that repetition betrayed a lack of confidence in the judge.
143. Carlson and Imwinkelried, *Dynamics of Trial Practice* at 229. See also Speiser, 'Closing Argument' at 243: 'One thing must always be kept in mind: overuse of emotional appeal may be disastrous. Loud, bombastic oratory should never be used. When emotion is used, it must be natural and sincere. If you switch into a highly theatrical delivery, the jury may interpret the emotional appeal as a substitute for reason or a screen for lack of confidence.'

Chapter 5

Greco-Roman Analysis
of Metaphoric Reasoning

Frequently and almost instinctively lawyers use figurative and metaphoric language when they want to emphasize or crystallize their analysis or arguments.[1] When they rely on familiar metaphoric clichés – the law as a 'seamless web,' cases with 'progeny,' corporations with 'veils,' and constitutional 'penumbras' – they reveal not only their appreciation for the power of figurative language, but also their substantial reliance on metaphoric reasoning. Generally speaking, 'metaphoric reasoning' is the use of metaphors and similes to explain, describe, persuade, or emphasize.

Lawyers' predilection for figurative language in what are otherwise rather dry and logical arguments has recently prompted some legal analysts to examine the impact and place of metaphors in forensic discourse.[2] Most modern commentary centers on the issues raised by Justice Cardozo's oft-cited admonition that '[m]etaphors in law are to be narrowly watched, for starting as devices to liberate thought, they end often by enslaving it.'[3] Those who 'narrowly watch' how metaphors affect legal reasoning generally spend most of their time explaining how metaphors either 'liberate' thought or 'enslave' it.

However, resourceful as they are in discovering the connections between metaphors and the law, modern analysts seldom rely on the works of classical rhetoricians who studied the matter in considerable detail and whose analysis goes far beyond the 'liberate/enslave' dichotomy. Aristotle's *Rhetoric* and his *Poetics*, Cicero's *De Oratore*, the *Rhetorica ad Herennium*, and Quintilian's *Institutio Oratoria*, for example, all include extensive discussions of the analytical and persuasive value of metaphors in forensic discourse.[4] Their analysis of how metaphors work and when they are appropriate reveals more about legal reasoning than do most modern commentaries on the topic.

Moreover, in addition to discussing the logical value of metaphoric reasoning, these classical treatises also examine its persuasive and aesthetic impact. While their focus on the aesthetics of legal discourse may strike modern analysts as somewhat odd, classical rhetoricians regarded aesthetics as a natural, proper, and necessary component of legal analysis and argument. From a classical perspective, metaphors had a clear logical and emotional function in legal discourse. They were also directly linked to an advocate's credibility and helped legal audiences evaluate his character.

Classical rhetoricians thought metaphors contributed to the logical proof of legal arguments partly because they are subtle, concise and intellectually engaging and partly because they provide a unique intellectual dimension without sacrificing logical integrity. They also thought that well-chosen metaphors contribute important emotional and aesthetic qualities, help capture the audience's attention, ease the demands on the audience's intelligence and make the experience pleasurable. Classical rhetoricians were so convinced of the emotional impact of certain metaphors that they categorized them according to effect, suitability, proper placement and persuasive value. And, finally, under classical theory, an advocate's choice and use of metaphors provides valuable insights into his character, resourcefulness, probity, genius and even his aesthetic sensibility.

Although numerous parallels exist between classical and modern opinions about the place of metaphors in legal discourse, most modern analysts still regard them with suspicion. Their suspicions focus almost exclusively on the very emotional and intellectually intuitive qualities that attracted classical rhetoricians. These differences notwithstanding, several modern approaches to legal metaphors, especially those based on language theory and cognitive psychology, have their roots in classical sources.

CLASSICAL APPROACHES TO METAPHOR

Greek and Roman rhetoric handbooks and treatises address every aspect of legal discourse.[5] They were by no means monolithic in their approaches and advice. In fact, they frequently differ from one another as to particular strategies and techniques. Even so, they agreed with one another about basic principles. For example, they were all convinced of the importance of style, including metaphors, in forensic discourse. They all assumed that legal arguments and analysis do not succeed or depend solely on their logical integrity.

Quintilian stresses this point when he observes that 'oratory in which there is no guile fights by sheer weight alone.'[6] In large part, the 'guile' Quintilian had in mind was an advocate's exploitation of all available stylistic resources. He was convinced that rhetoric teachers should concentrate on style:

> since it cannot possibly be acquired without the assistance of the rules of art: it is this which is the chief object of our study, our exercises and all our efforts at imitation, and it is to this that we devote the energies of a lifetime; it is this that makes one orator surpass his rivals, this that makes one style of speaking preferable to another.[7]

Because of its importance and difficulty, Quintilian and others focused a great deal of attention on the place of style or 'diction' in legal discourse. By far the longest and most detailed parts of their treatises are devoted to style since, according to Aristotle, 'it is not enough to know what to say – one must also know how to say it.'[8] And, according to Quintilian, style 'cannot possibly be acquired without the assistance of the rules of art.'[9] Classical rhetoricians described these stylistic 'rules of art' in exhaustive detail, even to the point of recommending specific syntactic and semantic forms to suit specific rhetorical purposes.[10]

In tacit recognition of the intrinsically figurative nature of all language, Greek and Roman analysts treated metaphors, similes and other figurative devices as both figures of speech and figures of thought.[11] That is, metaphors help audiences understand arguments even as they respond to their 'charm.'

Consequently, within the larger context of their analysis of inductive and deductive reasoning, classical rhetoricians devoted considerable attention to metaphors as figures of thought. As figures of thought, metaphors were regarded as valid and perfectly 'natural' devices for analysis and argumentation, rather than as mere belletristic embellishments. Quintilian called attention to how intrinsic and pervasive metaphors are in everyday discourse when he said:

> Let us begin [our analysis of tropes] ... with the commonest and by far the *most beautiful of tropes*, namely, metaphor, the Greek term for our *translatio*. It is not merely so natural a turn of speech that it is often employed unconsciously or by uneducated persons, but it is in itself so attractive and elegant that however distinguished the language in which it is embedded it shines forth with a light that is all its own.[12]

Even while acknowledging that language is intrinsically figurative, Quintilian understood that metaphors are not uniquely figurative. Nevertheless he thought they were the 'most beautiful' of all rhetorical figures.

By characterizing them as the 'most beautiful of tropes,' Quintilian is not simply repeating Aristotle's observations about language in general and metaphors in particular. He adds to and comments on the Aristotelian position. Aristotle's high regard for metaphors sprang from his conviction that metaphors help compensate for the stylistic deficiencies of prose. In Aristotle's view 'all the more attention must be devoted to metaphors because ... [in forensic prose] the resources of the writer are less abundant than in verse.'[13] Cicero agreed and said that use of metaphors 'sprang from necessity due to the pressure of poverty and deficiency [of prose].'[14]

However, by Quintilian's time, metaphors were considered the 'supreme ornament' of forensic discourse and figured prominently in his approach to legal argument.[15] He, along with the other rhetoricians, assumed that metaphorical language was as integral to legal thinking as the language of logic.

A. Logos

Although classical rhetoricians devoted comparatively little attention to the contributions that metaphors make to the logical integrity (*logos*) of legal arguments, they nonetheless assumed that metaphors do have persuasive and logical value. For example, within the context of classical logical conventions, metaphors operate almost like examples do in inductive proofs.[16] Quintilian understood them in this way when he noted that similes (a form of metaphor) 'are designed for insertion among our arguments to help our proof.'[17] Under classical theory, metaphors clarify legal arguments primarily by means of comparisons in which meanings in one context are transferred to another context. According to Quintilian, this transference occurs when '[a] noun or verb is transferred from the place to which it properly belongs to another where there is either no literal term or the transferred [term] is better than the literal. We do this ... because it is necessary ... to make our meaning clearer ...'[18]

All metaphors are analogies, and most classical rhetoricians include them with other analogical tropes, like similes, whose principal effects arise from the creation of comparisons. Analogical tropes function by means of 'reciprocal representation' in which 'both subjects of comparison [are placed] before our very eyes, displaying them side by side.'[19] This comparison gives the audience cognitive insights not usually achievable by linear or syllogistic reasoning. Aristotle saw metaphors as vehicles with 'which we give names to nameless things.'[20] In a similar vein, Cicero observed that 'when something that can scarcely be conveyed by the proper (literal) term is expressed metaphorically, the meaning we desire to convey is made clear by the resemblance of the thing that we have expressed by the word that does not belong.'[21] That is, in some cases, a metaphor may be the only way to make or emphasize a particular point.

Aristotle was attracted to metaphors because they challenge the audience to seek resemblances where none usually exist. Metaphors are intellectually engaging in ways that differ from the usual deductive and inductive methods. He thought that, because metaphors provide insights not achievable by other means, they must spark cognitive intuitions available only through a discovery process. For him, the act of understanding or 'solving' a metaphor is similar to solving a riddle. In both cases the solving is itself an act of learning.[22] In Aristotle's view 'the charm of metaphor, and with it that of ornament in general, is primarily cognitive.'[23]

Cicero focused on a related but slightly different source of intellectual attraction when he recommended using metaphors because they increased the rhetorical impact of intellectual insights without compromising logical integrity. According to him, the audience's 'thoughts are led to something else and yet without going astray, which is a very great pleasure.'[24] The *Rhetorica ad Herennium* makes a slightly different point by claiming that metaphors can be used 'for purpose of proof':

> Neither can an untrained horse, however well-built by nature, be fit for the services desired of a horse, nor can an uncultivated man, however well-endowed by nature, attain to virtue. This *idea has been rendered more plausible*, for it becomes easier to believe that virtue cannot be secured without culture, when we see that not even a horse can be serviceable if untrained.[25]

That is, the plausibility of the logical point is increased by use of figurative language. Here, as elsewhere, the comparison functions as both a figure of speech and a figure of thought.

Classical rhetoricians were also attracted to metaphors because they were concise, subtle, and provided a unique 'wholeness' of insight. According to Aristotle, metaphors achieve their effect in part because they can convey 'fresh knowledge' almost as fast as they are stated.[26] Cicero too commended metaphors for their ability to convey complex ideas concisely. According to him, 'metaphors serve to achieve brevity, for instance, "If the weapon slipped from his hand": it was not possible to express the unintentional nature of the discharge of the missile more briefly by employing the proper words than it is conveyed by a single word used metaphorically.'[27]

Quintilian too observed that metaphors work subtly: 'For although it may seem that proof is infinitesimally affected by the figures (of speech) employed, none the less those same figures lend credibility to our arguments and steal their way secretly into the minds of the judges.'[28] In addition to their conciseness and subtlety, metaphors give the audience a greater sense of the '*whole meaning* of the matter, whether it consists in an action or a thought.'[29]

B. Pathos

The 'wholeness' of meaning that classical rhetoricians had in mind included the emotional aspects of the case. Although modern theories of legal discourse generally disfavor patently emotional arguments, classical theory recognized the inevitability of emotional appeals and approved of their use. Aristotle, for instance, emphasizes *pathos* as one of the three means of persuasion at an advocate's disposal: 'Persuasion is effected through the audience, when they are brought by the [argument] into a state of emotion; for we give very different decisions under the sway of pain or joy, and liking or hatred.'[30]

Although Aristotle recognized the emotional component in legal arguments, he did not endorse arguments based solely on the emotions. Instead, he insisted that decisions should be based on 'right reason' and that 'the man who is to judge should not have his judgment warped by [advocates] arousing him to anger, jealousy, or compassion. One might just as well make a carpenter's rule crooked before using it as a measure.'[31] Even though Aristotle clearly recognized the dangers of emotion-based arguments, he nevertheless provided detailed descriptions of how and when to use them.[32]

Within classical analysts' discussion of emotional arguments, metaphors play a small but significant part. According to Quintilian and other Greco-Roman rhetoricians, metaphors are inherently emotional. He noted that a '[m]etaphor is designed to move the feelings'[33] and that 'there is no more effective method of exciting the emotions than an apt use of figures [like metaphors].'[34]

Classical analysts were fascinated with the ability of metaphors to produce emotional and intellectual pleasure. Aristotle, for instance, says 'we may start from the principle that we all take a natural *pleasure* in learning easily; so, since words stand for things, those words are *most pleasing* that give us fresh knowledge ... Accordingly, it is metaphor that is in the highest degree instructive and *pleasing*.'[35] Cicero makes a similar observation when he notes that 'everybody derives more *pleasure* from words used metaphorically and not in their proper sense than from the proper names belonging to the objects.'[36] He thinks the pleasure may arise from the fact that the audience's 'thoughts are led to something else and yet without going astray, which is a *very great pleasure*.'[37] Quintilian too thought that:

> rhetorical ornament[s] contribute not a little to the furtherance of our case. ... For when our audience finds it a *pleasure* to listen, their attention and their readiness to believe what they hear are both alike increased, while they are generally *filled with delight*, and sometimes even transported by admiration.[38]

Classical rhetoricians' analysis of metaphors' emotional impact also includes a detailed examination of the sources of this pleasure. Aristotle, for instance, thinks that they are pleasurable in part because they make intellectual tasks easier and in part because they challenge the mind to seek resemblances.[39] He was intrigued by their paradoxical qualities.

Aristotle and other rhetoricians also think that metaphors achieve many of their strongest effects by means of novel insights and pleasurable surprise. Aristotle notes that 'liveliness through the use of metaphor is ... gained when there is an added element of surprise.'[40] Quintilian observes that 'the more remote the [metaphor] is from the subject to which it is applied, the greater will be the impression of novelty and the unexpected which it produces.'[41]

They also devoted considerable attention to metaphors' aesthetic qualities. Even though they admired the intellectual impact of metaphors, they were equally fascinated by their ability to make prose more interesting. They repeatedly allude to metaphors' 'charm' and 'distinction,'[42] and their 'agreeable and entertaining qualities.'[43] In addition to metaphors' other virtues, Quintilian thought that they acted as an 'ornament to oratory, and serve[d] to make it sublime, rich, attractive or striking.'[44]

Unlike most analyses of aesthetic value, which eventually degenerate into expressions of personal taste, classical rhetoricians agreed not only on how metaphors please but also on a number of other points. They agreed, for instance, that most effective metaphors are based on sight, rather than hearing, taste or touch. Cicero said that metaphors have a 'direct appeal to the senses, especially the sense of sight'[45] and Quintilian thought that metaphors were designed to 'give special distinction to things and place them vividly before the eye.'[46]

Understandably, given the analogical nature of metaphors, they also agreed with Aristotle's assertion that successful metaphors depend on the degree of correspondence or proportion between the metaphor and the subject to which it is applied.[47] Quintilian takes Aristotle's point regarding correspondence and his observation that 'metaphors are of four kinds'[48] as the basis for a four-part classification system: 'In the first we substitute one living thing for another ... Secondly, inanimate things may be substituted for inanimate ... or inanimate may be substituted for animate ... or animate for inanimate.'[49] Quintilian's categories demonstrate the classical rhetorician's acute sensitivity to subtle distinctions and appreciation for the logical and aesthetic values of symmetry and asymmetry.

Aristotle's provides one important variation on this principle of correspondence. For him, concision and contrast are critical:

> The more concise and antithetical the saying, the better it pleases, for the reason that, by the contrast, one learns the more, and, by the conciseness, learns with the greater speed ... [W]hen the words are metaphorical, and the metaphor is the right kind, and there is antithesis with balanced structure, and a sense of activity as well [the livelier is the effect] ...[50]

Classical rhetoricians also devote considerable attention to a special class of metaphor: the simile. Generally speaking, they regard similes as just another kind of analogical trope. Sometimes they see them as mere decorative embellishments.[51] At other times, they see them as integral parts of the argument.[52] Aristotle had a low regard for similes, in part because they are less subtle and sophisticated than metaphors. He noted that:

> [t]he simile ... is a metaphor, differing from it only in that the simile adds the phrase of comparison, which makes it longer, and hence less pleasing. Nor does it, like the metaphor, say 'this *is* that'; and hence the mind of the hearer does not have to seek the resemblance.[53]

Cicero, however, thought highly of similes because 'a simile can be drawn from everything – a single word supplied by it that comprises the similarity, if used metaphorically, will give brilliance to the style.'[54] Quintilian too thought that '[t]he invention of similes has ... provided an admirable means of illuminating our descriptions' and required only that 'the subject chosen for our simile [be] neither obscure nor unfamiliar: for anything that is selected for the purpose of illuminating something else must itself be clearer than that which it is designed to illustrate.'[55] Aristotle's reservations notwithstanding, most rhetoricians analyzed and used similes in the same way they did other metaphors.

As the preceding summary reveals, classical rhetoricians generally agreed that all figurative language, and especially metaphors and similes, should be symmetrical and precise. They also agreed on matters such as the sensory appeal of metaphors and the proper degrees of correspondence and antithesis. And, finally, they agreed that certain kinds of metaphors had specific emotional effects[56] and had fixed opinions about where they should appear.[57]

Fond as they were of metaphors, they nevertheless recognized their potential for offending, confusing, or emotionally abusing an audience. Consequently, they devoted almost as much attention to improper use of metaphors as they did to their proper use. Aristotle said that 'faulty metaphors arise when they are either too grand or too obscure.'[58] Cicero warned against using metaphors 'where there is no real resemblance' or which are 'too farfetched.'[59] Quintilian concluded that 'while a temperate and timely use of metaphor is a real adornment to style, on the other hand, its frequent use serves merely to obscure our language and weary our audience, while if we introduce them in one continuous series, our language will become allegorical and enigmatic.'[60] He was particularly critical of cliches and cautioned against 'those hackneyed phrases of forensic pleading, "to fight hand to hand," "to attack the throat," or "to let blood" ... [because] they do not strike the attention: for it is novelty and change that please in oratory.'[61]

The range and type of emotional effects these rhetoricians envisaged is reflected in their own use of metaphors. They themselves frequently created metaphors to illustrate various rhetorical effects and stylistic alternatives. Like Aristotle explaining that metaphors should closely resemble their objects, classical rhetoricians sometimes make their point metaphorically and then explain the resemblance.[62] Or, relying on Cicero's observation that good metaphors make an advocate's meaning clearer, they leave their metaphors unexplained.[63] Classical handbooks are filled with illustrative metaphors.

Quintilian, for example, illustrates his point regarding a 'bold, manly and chaste' style of embellishment with a long, rigorously symmetrical metaphor. He begins by asking a rhetorical question:

> [I]s beauty an object of no consideration in the planting of fruit trees? Certainly not! For my trees must be planted in due order and at fixed intervals. What fairer sight is there than rows of trees planted in echelon which present straight lines to the eye from whatever angle they be

> viewed? But it has an additional advantage, since this form of plantation enables every tree to derive an equal share of moisture from the soil. When the tops of my olive trees rise too high, I lop them away, with the result that their growth expands laterally in a manner that is at once more pleasing to the eye and enables them to bear more fruit owing to the increase in the number of branches.[64]

Even when not explicitly discussing matters of style, they reflexively use metaphors to illustrate their points.[65] Cicero, for instance, uses water imagery to assert that all rhetorical eloquence has a single source: '[E]loquence is one, into whatever shores or realms of discourse it ranges ... the flow of language though running in different channels does not spring from different sources, and wherever it goes, the same supply of matter and equipment of style go with it.'[66]

At the very beginning of his description of how legal arguments should be organized, Quintilian illustrates his point by noting that:

> just as it is not sufficient for those who are erecting a building merely to collect stone and timber and other building materials, but skilled masons are required to arrange and place them, so in speaking, however abundant the matter may be, it will merely form a confused heap unless arrangement be employed to reduce it to order and to give it connexion and firmness of structure.[67]

As these and countless other metaphors attest, classical rhetoricians regarded metaphors not just as stylistic embellishments but also as a modes of thought. While their metaphors may not evoke the same emotions in modern audiences that they did in ancient ones, their choice and placement of metaphors nonetheless demonstrate their conviction that the aesthetic components of language provide an important emotional complement to its purely logical components. For them, metaphors possess an inherently aesthetic appeal and a quantifiable emotional impact that good advocates use in the same way they use other rhetorical resources.

C. Ethos

Under classical theory, the emotional effect of an argument was closely linked to the credibility of the person who makes it. For Greco-Roman rhetoricians, an advocate's *ethos* was just as important as the logical (*logos*) or emotional (*pathos*) content of his argument. Aristotle stressed this point when he said that 'we might almost affirm that [an advocate's] character (*ethos*) is the most potent of all the means to persuasion.'[68] However, he also stressed that an advocate's credibility should not depend on 'an antecedent impression that the speaker is this or that kind of man.'[69] Rather, credibility 'should be created by the speech itself.'[70] That is, the advocate must deliberately strive to create and project a particular *ethos* by means of the speech he makes.

Within the speech itself, an advocate's character is revealed as much by his stylistic choices as by his choice of substantive points: 'Character is manifested in choice [in what men choose to do or avoid]; and choice is related to end or aim.'[71] All classical rhetoricians emphasized the importance of selecting specific styles to achieve specific rhetorical effects. Quintilian, for instance, thought style selection was a two-step process:

> [W]e must consider first our ideal of style, and secondly how we shall express this ideal in actual words. The *first* essential is to realize clearly what we wish to enhance or attenuate, to express with vigour or calm, in luxuriant or austere language, at length or with conciseness, with gentleness or asperity, magnificence or subtlety, gravity or wit. The *next* essential is to decide by what kind of metaphor, figures, reflexions, methods and arrangement we may best produce the effect which we desire.[72]

By focusing on the advocate's deliberate decisions about what to emphasize and which style to use, Quintilian stresses that metaphor selections are as much a matter of premeditation as they are of inspiration. Good advocates do not just hope that an apt metaphor will occur to them. Instead, they consciously create the proper metaphor to achieve a specific rhetorical effect.

Although both Aristotle and Cicero thought stylistic decisions, including decisions about which metaphors to use, contributed significantly to an advocate's *ethos*, they made only modest claims for those contributions. Aristotle does suggest that good metaphor selection demonstrates an advocate's resourcefulness and insight: '[T]he adept will perceive resemblances even in things that are far apart.'[73] In his *Poetics*, however, Aristotle posits a stronger and clearer connection between good metaphors and *ethos*. During his discussion of poetic diction he asserts that:

> [i]t is a matter of great importance to use each of the [stylistic] forms ... in a fitting way, ... but by far the most important matter is to have skill in the use of metaphor. This skill alone it is not possible to obtain from another; and it is, in itself, a *sign of genius*. For the ability to construct good metaphors implies the ability to see essential similarities.[74]

Cicero does not go quite so far as Aristotle, but he too thought an advocate's choice of metaphors reflected on his *ethos*. For him, good metaphors are a 'mark of cleverness' in a writer.[75]

Quintilian, on the other hand, thought that good metaphors make an appreciable contribution to an advocate's *ethos*. In his view, an advocate commends both himself and his argument by skillful selection and use of figurative language:

> [B]y the employment of skillful ornament (including metaphors) the orator commends himself at the same time [as he commends his argument], and whereas his other accomplishments appeal to the considered judgment, this gift appeals to the

enthusiastic approval of the world at large, and the speaker who possesses it fights not merely with effective, but with flashing weapons.[76]

With his use of the 'flashing weapons' metaphor, Quintilian illustrates how the emotional appeal of 'commending' oneself complements the logical appeal to 'considered judgment.' By skillfully cultivating a close relationship between logical and emotional appeals an advocate can make the substantive merits of his case even more compelling than they would otherwise be.

Not only does an advocate's *ethos* depend on the careful selection of good metaphors, it also depends on avoiding enigmatic, obscure, allegorical or cliched metaphors or overusing metaphors to the point they 'weary the audience.'[77] Although classical rhetoricians seldom make the point directly, they implicitly recommend that advocates avoid misusing metaphors.

For them, good legal arguments depend as much on stylistic choices as they do on substantive ones. They assume that selecting good metaphors, and avoiding bad ones, is integral to an advocate's *ethos* and that *ethos* is just as important as *logos* or *pathos*.

Classical rhetoricians clearly understood that metaphors are a natural, important, and even essential, stylistic resource in legal argument. They also understood that good metaphors make unique contributions to the intellectual integrity, emotional wholeness, and general credibility of all arguments. Their insights into the intrinsically figurative nature of language allowed them to find and exploit all the available links between particular legal arguments and particular rhetorical effects.

MODERN ANALYSIS OF LEGAL METAPHORS

When classical analysts discussed the effect of metaphors on legal discourse they focused their attention almost exclusively on legal arguments, oral or written. Most of their examples are drawn from real cases, their own or famous arguments from the past. Frequently, they made their selections from cases that had significant social or legal implications.

In modern times, however, the focus has switched from famous legal arguments to famous judicial opinions. In part this is because modern judicial opinions have a greater social and legal impact than almost any other form of legal discourse. Inevitably these opinions contain figurative language of many sorts, including metaphors. Recently, modern scholars have begun examining the power these metaphors have on the thinking processes of judges.[78] A few of them even link their analysis to the concepts and terminology of classical rhetoric.[79]

However, the classical principles must be applied cautiously, with due allowances for the differences in point of view and legal context. Classical theory was based on metaphors drawn from oral arguments by passionate advocates, not from written opinions by impartial judges.

Even so, analyzing the metaphors that appear in modern judicial opinions can sometimes reveal a great deal about a judge's reasoning processes and judicial temperament. For example, the metaphors chosen by Judge Goldberg of the 5th Circuit in a routine First Amendment case (*Shanley v. Northeast Indiana School District*) reveal his highly emotional reaction to the case. They also reveal insights into his thought processes and contribute to his distinctive judicial *persona*.[80]

The *Shanley* case involved high school students who distributed an underground newspaper near a school. The court ruled that the students had a First Amendment right to do so and decided the case against school officials who tried to prevent the distribution. In reaching its decision, the court relied in part on another First Amendment case also defending high school students' First Amendment rights, *Tinker v. Des Moines School District*.[81] Beginning with a pun, Judge Goldberg employs an extended metaphor to make his point:

> *Tinker's* dam to school board absolutism does not leave dry the fields of school discipline. This court has gone a considerable distance with the school boards to uphold its disciplinary fiats where reasonable. ... *Tinker* simply irrigates, rather than floods, the fields of school discipline. It sets canals and channels through which school discipline might flow with the least possible damage to the nation's priceless topsoil of the First Amendment ...[82]

Like Quintilian's metaphor featuring neatly distributed fruit trees, Judge Goldberg's irrigation metaphor features neatly distributed 'canals and channels.' Both writers use the subtle emotional connotations of a quasi-pastoral metaphor to strengthen their arguments.[83] Classical analysts would maintain that by selecting this, rather than a different metaphor, Judge Goldberg is consciously attempting to increase his own credibility or *ethos* by drawing on the emotional associations or *pathos* of a particular metaphor. That is, by associating Americans' long-held reverence for agriculture and farming with his own position on an abstract First Amendment principle, he is making a metaphoric argument for his position.

He subtly equates the First Amendment protections provided by the *Tinker* opinion with a dam that prevents a flood of uncontrolled and oppressive school discipline that could overwhelm students' rights. Moreover, the 'canal and channel' metaphor helps Goldberg appear even-handed. It demonstrates that he knows that schools need some sort of internal controls.

His metaphor also depends on other, less explicit, associations: farmers' natural fear of floods and their understandably protective attitudes about topsoil; the aesthetic appeal of symmetrical canals, etc. all of which contribute in less direct ways to his legal argument. The purpose of these and other associations is not susceptible to definitive analysis and raises the problems common to all interpretation – interpreter's bias, over-interpretation, auctorial intent. As with all extensive analysis, it risks ignoring or devaluing the reasons why writers use legal metaphors in the first place, for their non-rational or intuitive impact.

The persuasive impact of this particular metaphor depends on a number of variables, including the overall context in which the metaphor appears and its associations with other metaphors in the opinion. Of course, some of these same context problems arise when interpreting other forms of legal discourse, whether the discourse in question is a statute, a regulation, a contract, or a municipal ordinance. It also depends on the audience's general susceptibility to metaphors and its feelings about the outcome of the case. If the audience does not like the outcome, it probably will not like the metaphor either.[84]

These variables notwithstanding, metaphor analysis of this sort discloses emotional overtones and credibility strategies that a strictly logical analysis might not reveal. This does not mean that analysis of the logical content of a metaphor is less important. In fact, it is crucial. But, by concentrating primarily on the logic of legal metaphors, modern analysts may overlook insights into how these metaphors affect the emotional impact of legal arguments and an author's credibility. Whatever the audience's response to it, Judge Goldberg's metaphor reflects a basic seriousness about the subject matter and the case.

Legal metaphors in other judicial opinions are amenable to the same sort of analysis and provide equally interesting insights into the judge's reasoning processes, stylistic strategies, and judicial *ethos*. Judge Goldberg's underlying seriousness contrasts strongly with the irreverent, frequently patronizing spirit behind Justice Michael Musmanno's metaphors in the case of *Pavlicic v. Vogtsberger*.[85] In *Pavlicic*, George Pavlicic, 80, sued Sara Jane Mills, 28, for recovery of gifts he gave her in anticipation of their marriage. During the course of their lengthy engagement, Pavlicic gave Mills several gifts, including a house, a car and the down payment on a saloon, each time with the understanding that he gave the gift because Mills agreed to marry him. Before giving Mills the house, for example, Pavlicic said, 'If you marry me, I will take the mortgage off.' She said: 'Yes.'[86] However, Mills did not marry Pavlicic. Instead, she left town with the down payment for the saloon, bought a saloon, and then married another man.

In deciding that the Pavlicic matter was a conditional gift case, not a breach of contract-to-marry case, Justice Musmanno explains his decision using a variation of the traditional 'sea of matrimony' metaphor:

> A gift delivered by a man to a woman on condition that she sail the sea of matrimony with him is no different from a gift based on the condition that the donee sail on any other sea. If, after receiving the provisional gift, the donee refuses to leave the harbor – if the anchor of contractual performance sticks in the sands of irresolution and procrastination – the gift must be restored to the donor. How much more applicable is this principle of justice when the donee not only refuses to voyage with the donor, but, on the contrary, transfers to another ship and sails away with the donor's rival![87]

The droll tone of Musmanno's 'sea of matrimony' metaphor reveals something very distinctive about his temperament and judicial *ethos*. As he interweaves technical contract principles into his maritime metaphor, he seems to be primarily interested in amusing himself. Moreover, this metaphor is similar in tone to others in the same opinion. Elsewhere, he notes that Sara Jane Mills had previously been married to a 'young man and their matrimonial bark had split on the rocks of divorce,'[88] and that '[t]o allow Sara Jane to retain the money and property which she got from George by dangling before him the grapes of matrimony which she never intended to let him pluck would be to place a premium on trickery, cunning, and duplicitous dealing.'[89] Musmanno's 'sea of matrimony' metaphor, especially when combined with his other mock-serious metaphors, creates the picture of a particularly self-indulgent judge, one who takes excessive pride in his own cleverness.

Justice Musmanno's irreverence persists even while he attempts to bias the *pathos* or emotional content of the case against Mills. Mills refuses to 'leave the harbor,' her 'anchor' of contractual performance sticks in the 'sands of irresolution,' she 'refuses to voyage' and, finally, she 'sails away with the donor's rival.' Musmanno characterizes Mills and Pavlicic's pre-marital agreement as a simple business relationship and portrays Mills as ungrateful, stubborn and deceitful, a fickle procrastinator whose real motives are mercenary not romantic. With these and other metaphors, Musmanno paints a too-clever-by-half picture of himself.

By projecting this kind of judicial *ethos*, Musmanno creates his own 'judicial profile' and thereby provides careful and resourceful advocates with information they need when preparing their written or oral arguments. The *ethos* created by Musmanno's frequent and self-satisfied willingness to treat a serious subject unseriously contrasts sharply with the *ethos* created by Judge Goldberg. Their judicial temperaments are markedly different. A strictly logical analysis of either the Goldberg or the Musmanno opinion, however, would disregard the *ethos* implications of the metaphors and focus instead on the governing legal principle, thereby overlooking potentially useful aspects of the case.

While Musmanno could have made his criticisms of Mills' conduct by simply using a list of pejorative adjectives, he creates a qualitatively different emotional climate by using metaphors instead. As was the case with Judge Goldberg's metaphors, it is a matter of opinion whether Justice Musmanno's metaphors persuade or illuminate where his logic would not. Or whether his metaphors engage or alienate his readers. In either case, additional insights into his judicial temperament and reasoning are revealed by examining the metaphors from a classical perspective.

MODERN THEORIES OF METAPHORIC REASONING

Despite a recent upsurge of interest in the topic, only a few modern legal analysts attempt a systematic study of metaphors in legal discourse. Those who do address the topic fall roughly into two groups: those who think metaphors are imprecise and inessential rhetorical embellishments whose principal, if not only, purpose is to emphasize a logical point and make it more memorable, and those who think metaphors and 'metaphoric reasoning' are an important, even central, cognitive factor in almost all legal reasoning. Although both groups offer useful insights into how metaphors work and when they are appropriate, neither group seems to rely on classical theories about metaphoric reasoning. Moreover, neither group addresses the subject as systematically or thoroughly as the classical rhetoricians.

A. Metaphoric Embellishment and Imprecision

Those in the first group usually disfavor the use of metaphors in legal discourse. Generally speaking, they minimize the positive qualities of metaphors and focus instead on their potential for abuse. Their skepticism about metaphor use is epitomized in Justice Cardozo's oft-cited admonition that '[m]etaphors in law are to be narrowly watched, for starting as devices to liberate thought, they end often by enslaving it.'[90] He and several other U.S. Supreme Court justices have strong reservations about introducing the 'mists of metaphor' into judicial opinions.[91] Judicial skepticism about metaphors usually centers on metaphors' capacity for oversimplifying complex legal doctrines as well as stifling further thought and encouraging 'uncritical' acceptance of received dogmas.[92] Given judges' concerns about illogical reasoning, imprecise or uncritical analysis, and their own susceptibility to the emotional effects of metaphors, this judicial skepticism is understandable.

Moreover, this general skepticism about metaphors extends even to those who write treatises on the subject of effective advocacy. Like their classical counterparts, these writers are interested in the rhetorical impact of all language. However, although they share with classical writers a common interest in rhetorical language, they devote little or no attention to the careful selection, creation, or placement of metaphors in legal discourse and almost none to metaphors' contribution to legal reasoning.

They are generally adverse to placing metaphors in legal briefs or memoranda. For the most part, they think metaphors should be used solely to emphasize points and make them memorable noting that '[metaphors] are useful in adding color and impact to an assertion,' or that '[m]etaphor, simile, and other figures of speech can enliven your argument,' and '[m]etaphors create ... a more concrete picture in the reader's mind, and concreteness increases memory.'[93]

Moreover, they ignore the positive qualities of metaphors and focus instead on their stylistic shortcomings and potential for abuse. Echoing the classical rhetoricians, they warn against over-using metaphors or using them in a self-consciously 'literary' or belletristic manner.[94] They think that metaphors sometimes call unnecessary attention to themselves or that they are inexact or imprecise. Even while conceding that sometimes 'judgments require use of metaphors and images, they add that metaphors are] – a way of thinking that hardly commends itself as precise and scientific ... [m]etaphors and causal imagery may represent a mode of thought that appears insufficiently rational in an era dominated by technological processes.'[95] At best, metaphors are subject to multiple interpretations. At worst, they are uncontrollable and evoke reasoning or associations the advocate did not intend.[96] These and other criticisms generally treat metaphors as inessential and distracting embellishments that detract from logical argument and analysis. Taking the most extreme view, some even assert that '[s]imiles and metaphors will never win an argument; they are, in fact, no argument at all.'[97]

Even when they do think metaphors make a meaningful contribution to legal analysis or argument, these writers usually ignore the *pathos* and *ethos* components that are so important in the classical approach. A few exceptions exist. They note with approval Aristotle's observation that 'the ability to create metaphor ... is the surest sign of originality.'[98] Some writers concede that '[c]areful selection of imagery can also introduce the emotional aspect of your message ...' and that '[a]lthough the way imagery enhances persuasion is not clear, it does enhance an argument.'[99] They do not, however, explain how this 'enhancement' takes place. A few others discuss the place metaphors have in ostensibly 'rational' legal reasoning and insist that a purely 'rational' world view:

> fails to see the poetic, the imaginative, the analogical, the emotive, the whimsical, the affective. Men and women are bigger than mere rationality, we express ourselves as more than logical creatures. Law is not insulated from life and so too the judicial opinion with all its logic is imaginative, metaphorical, and poetic.[100]

Most often, however, they focus on the quasi-logical effects of metaphors. If they mention the emotional effect of metaphors at all, it is usually in a negative context. Trite or 'poorly chosen figures of speech [are] likely to irritate the reader.'[101] 'Too many figures of speech make for ornate and confusing prose' or 'obscure' illustration.[102] Using metaphors for their 'own sake can be distracting rather than emphatic, or embarrassing rather than impressive.'[103] 'Too many mental pictures flashed before the reader in rapid succession become wearying.'[104] By focusing on metaphors' negative effects, these critics frequently ignore the positive ones.

Quintilian offered many of the same criticisms when he observed that, 'while a temperate and timely use of metaphor is a real adornment to style, on the other hand, its frequent use serves merely to obscure our language and weary our audience, while if we introduce them in one continuous series, our language will become allegorical and enigmatic.'[105] Notwithstanding these problems, he still favored using metaphors in legal arguments. Far too often, metaphor-averse modern critics focus on the negative and either minimize or fail to examine the intellectual pleasure that a well-chosen metaphor creates in a reader.

B. Inherent Metaphors and Cognitive Psychology

Despite widespread skepticism about using metaphors in legal discourse, some analysts take a more sympathetic view. Employing a combination of literary theory and cognitive psychology, they analyze the effect of metaphors in ways that resemble the classical techniques. Some recent commentators on metaphors reject the view that metaphors are merely superficial stylistic devices. They assert that 'it is now well established that the tropes, especially the metaphor, are not simply rhetorical flourishes used to embellish discourse.'[106] Instead, they claim that metaphors are essential devices for achieving certain sorts of intellectual insights.

By taking this view of metaphors, they disregard Justice Cardozo's warning that metaphors can 'enslave' thought and focus instead on his observation that metaphors start 'as devices to liberate thought.'[107] Cardozo's allusion to the 'liberating' effect of metaphors echoes classical rhetoricians' claims that metaphors provide insights or 'fresh knowledge'[108] that can 'scarcely be conveyed'[109] by other means. Under this view, metaphors become important intellectual components of legal analysis, rather than mere mnemonic or focusing devices.

Like their classical counterparts, these modern analysts base their assertions about the intellectual importance of metaphors on the fact that language is intrinsically figurative. They reach the same conclusions that Cicero and Quintilian reached when they noted the frequent and natural occurrence of metaphors in everyday speech.[110]

And, like the classical analysts, they conclude that metaphors are, in effect, repositories of universal wisdom and emotional power that should be exploited whenever possible.

Citing the authority of British attorney and linguist Owen Barfield, they stress the importance of metaphors and the intrinsically figurative nature of language:

> One of the first things that a student of etymology – even quite an amateur student – discovers for himself is that every modern language, with its thousands of abstract terms and its nuances of meaning and association, is apparently nothing, from beginning to end, but an *unconscionable tissue of dead, petrified metaphors.*[111]

From a slightly different perspective, James B. White illustrates the 'unconscionable tissue of dead, petrified metaphor' point using the traditional vocabulary of case analysis:

> [A] problem has parts which fit together to make a whole; arguments have strengths and weaknesses; interests have bulk or weight, which permit them to be measured, weighed, and balanced; general rules, like boxes, have lots of specific rules inside them; every rule has a reason (or a policy) which determines its proper course ... conflicts between rules can be harmonized ... every case presents a problem with a solution; and so on.[112]

This example, and others like it, have led White to conclude that spatial metaphors 'may be inherent in language. In language in general, abstract concepts are formed in spatial terms. They arise out of experiences in the world.'[113] Burr Henly makes a similar point:

> [M]etaphors portray one part of experience by borrowing terms associated with another part. Thus, they require a jump from one category of experiences and related descriptive terms to another. Metaphors that are overtly spatial involve the most obvious kind of category jump. With such spatial metaphors, legal ideas are described and discussed as if they existed in two-or even three-dimensional form ...[114]

Modern claims about the concrete, experiential source of metaphoric language are reminiscent of Cicero's assertion that metaphors have a 'direct appeal to the senses.'[115] Metaphors have a visceral, emotional impact in part because they originated in the world of the senses. Because of this, their effects are as physiological as they are logical.

The inherently metaphoric nature of language has led some legal analysts to examine metaphors in light of cognitive psychology theories. Cognitive theories attempt to explain how metaphors contribute to our 'reasoning' processes. Starting with the assumption that all metaphors involve some measure of transferred meaning from one subject to another, these theories suggest that metaphors 'foster insights' that demand a 'simultaneous awareness of both subjects (of comparison) that is not reducible to any mere comparison between the two. It is this insight that gives metaphor its cognitive value – the very insight that is lost when one foregoes the metaphorical and remains stuck in the literal and the literal only.'[116]

Others agree that metaphors provide insights that are impossible to achieve with literal language, but think that metaphors are capable of converting or transferring 'chunks' of information from the vehicle to the topic, enabling us to talk about experience which cannot be literally described.[117] For them, metaphors function as translators of experience.

Relying on both literary theory and cognitive psychology, some analysts think that our very thought processes are metaphorical and that we should think of metaphor use:

> as a cognitive function – that is, as the imaginative means by which we conceive the multiple relations of a complex world. In that event, we will no longer ask what metaphor 'obscures' as if there were some determinate reality 'behind' the metaphor. Rather, the renunciation of the traditional opposition between metaphor and reality allows us to recognize that metaphors are our way of having a reality and, therefore, that the important question about any metaphor is, which (partial) reality does it enable?[118]

In sum, the conclusions that metaphors 'foster insights,' or that they transfer 'chunks' of information, or that they are 'imaginative means' of 'conceiving ... multiple relations,' and 'liberate' the imagination are not substantially different from those of Aristotle, Cicero and Quintilian. Aristotle also saw metaphors as a means of giving 'names to nameless things.'[119] Cicero noted that metaphors have the capacity for expressing what can 'scarcely be conveyed' by a literal term.[120] Quintilian thought that one of metaphors' central functions was to transfer information and insights from one place to another.[121]

All three noted that metaphors provide a unique 'wholeness' of insight that is absent from merely literal reasoning. Cicero, for instance, thought that metaphors 'better convey the *whole* meaning of the matter, whether it consists in an action or a thought ...' and with 'a single word ... suggest the thing and a picture of the *whole* ...'[122] It is this 'wholeness' of insight that is missing in most modern analysis. The missing parts are usually some kind of analysis of how metaphors affect *ethos* and *pathos* in a particular case.

Regrettably, even those who think metaphors are essential to legal reasoning neglect their *pathos* and *ethos* effects. The closest modern analysts come is when they analyze the metaphoric patterns in a few, narrowly limited groups of constitutional law cases. For example, in his analysis of rhetorical figures in recent U.S. Supreme Court cases on First Amendment protections for students and teachers, Haig Bosmajian asserts that '[t]he metaphors and other tropes relied upon by the opposing Justices provide us with some insight into their respective views on education, especially when we look at their approaches to education as "inculcation".'[123] Bosmajian's point regarding how metaphor choices reveal character resembles Aristotle's claim that '[c]haracter is manifested in choice [in what men choose to do or avoid]; and choice is related to end or aim.'[124] That is, an advocate's *ethos* is revealed through the metaphoric language he uses.

To support his contention that metaphors provide 'insights ... into [a judge's] views on education,' Bosmajian points out that 'again and again the language quoted from ... landmark decisions are the figurative expressions, the tropes, especially the metaphors and metonymies.'[125] As an example, he quotes several passages from Justice Jackson's opinion in the case of *West Virginia State Board of Education v. Barnette*, which have been repeatedly used 'in arguments defending the First Amendment rights of students and teacher.'[126] Jackson wrote:

> If there is any *fixed star in our constitutional constellation*, it is that no official, high or petty, can prescribe what shall be orthodox in politics, nationalism, religion, or other matters of opinion or force citizens to confess by word or act their faith therein.[127]

Bosmajian traces numerous references to this 'fixed star' metaphor in subsequent cases confronting the same issues. He also interprets numerous other metaphors in related cases and ultimately concludes that the 'course of the law ... [may be] decided not so much on the intricacies of the application of the arcane abstractions of the first amendment as it is upon the greater or lesser appeal of the tropes involved in the various opinions.'[128] His point is that metaphors reflect both the character (*ethos*) of their author and the character of writers who subsequently rely on them.

Another analyst, Burr Henly, makes a similar point in connection with what he regards as the 'most important and puzzling ... metaphor in American constitutional law ... Justice William O. Douglas "penumbra" from *Griswold v. Connecticut*.'[129] He traces the various uses of 'penumbra' in legal discourse from its first appearance in Oliver Wendell Holmes' *The Theory of Torts* to its appearance in *Griswold*.[130] After a detailed survey of how 'penumbra' has been used or interpreted by various Supreme Court justices, Henly concludes that 'the penumbra metaphor has often been used as a shorthand for the *limits* of judicial reasoning. Just as often ... judges have used the penumbra metaphor to convey their *discretion*.'[131] Given these multiple and contradictory interpretations of 'penumbra,' Burr's analysis seems to confirm Cardozo's and other judges' suspicions that metaphors can promote 'uncritical' acceptance of received dogma.

The studies of both Henly and Bosmajian illustrate the subtle power that metaphors undeniably exercise on the legal imagination and the force they have in determining how legal concepts are evaluated. In a more limited way, they also show how metaphors reveal the character of the judge who selects them and the emotional attraction of certain metaphors. And, finally, their studies show that metaphors play a substantial part in many important constitutional law cases. Their work, as well as the work of analysts who rely on literary analysis and cognitive psychology theories, helps explain how figurative language, especially metaphors, affects legal reasoning.

SIMILARITIES AND DIFFERENCES

Both modern and classical analysts agree that legal reasoning relies more heavily on figurative language than is commonly recognized. They also agree that substantive legal points are sometimes necessarily or best expressed in figurative or metaphoric language because merely logical or literal language is unequal to the task. However, unlike classical analysts, modern analysts have generally restricted their analysis to explaining the quasi-logical impact of metaphors and have ignored how metaphors evoke emotional responses and contribute to an author's credibility. In so doing, they ignore two important aspects of metaphoric reasoning. Moreover, they do not satisfactorily explain why certain metaphors capture the legal imagination and others do not.

According to classical rhetoricians, the 'why' is closely linked to the emotional effects created by metaphors and the reader's trust in the person who created them. They understood that the force of a metaphor depends as much on the credibility of its author as it does on the audience's intellectual pleasure or surprise at the metaphor's aptness, concision, or subtlety. This intellectual pleasure, combined with trust in the writer, makes metaphors emotionally as well as intellectually engaging. It also helps create a sense of wholeness or completeness.

Until modern analysts examine more fully both the emotional effects of metaphors and the issue of authorial credibility, their analyses will be incomplete. This incompleteness could be rectified by a close re-examination and use of classical analytical techniques and approaches. Rather than invent or construct an entirely new critical apparatus, modern analysts can modify the pre-existing apparatus and insights provided by Greco-Roman rhetoricians.

Notes

1. Numerous modern definitions of metaphor exist, ranging from Robert Frost's that a metaphor is 'saying one thing and meaning another,' James B. White, *The Legal Imagination: Studies in the Nature of Legal Thought and Expression* 57 (1973), to that of the *Princeton Encyclopedia of Poetry and Poetics* 490 (Alex Preminger ed. 1965), which defines metaphor as '[a] condensed verbal relation in which an idea, image, or symbol may, by the presence of one or more other ideas, images, or symbols, be enhanced in vividness, complexity, or breadth of implication ... The metaphorical relation has been variously described as comparison, contrast, analogy, similarity, juxtaposition, identity, tension, collision, [and] fusion ...'

2. Michael R. Smith, *Advanced Legal Writing: Theories and Strategies in Persuasive Writing* (2002) (discussing how *logos*, *pathos*, and *ethos* intersect with metaphor); Haig Bosmajian, *Metaphor And Reason in Judicial Opinions* (1992); Steven L. Winter, 'Transcendental Nonsense, Metaphoric Reasoning and the Cognitive Stakes for Law,' 137 University of Pennsylvania Law Review 1105 (1989).

3. Berkey v. Third Avenue Railway Company, 244 New York 84, 155 N.E. 58 (1926).

4. Aristotle, *Aristotle's Poetics: A Translation and Commentary for Students of Literature* (Leon Golden, trans. 1968).

5. Although Greco-Roman commentaries on legal discourse assumed a listening rather than a reading audience, their observations regarding metaphors apply as fully to the written as to the spoken word. See Richard Enos, *The Literate Mode of Cicero's Legal Rhetoric* 60 (1988): 'Oral and written expression were so inextricably bound in ancient discourse that its unity was an unquestioned presumption upon which theories of rhetoric were developed.' This presumption was based on the fact that silent reading was rare (especially for Greeks) and that most writing was intended to be presented orally. Enos, *The Literate Mode* at 60.

6. 3 Quintilian, *Institutio Oratoria* at 359.

7. 3 Quintilian, *Institutio Oratoria* at 185-6.

8. Aristotle, *Rhetoric* at 182.
9. 3 Quintilian, *Institutio Oratoria* at 185.
10. Aristotle, *Rhetoric* at 194-196 and 202-206; 3 Quintilian, *Institutio Oratoria* at 349ff.
11. Aristotle, *Rhetoric* at 204-5 (discussing how style is 'pleasing also because of its ... logic ...')
12. 3 Quintilian, *Institutio Oratoria* at 303 (emphasis added). Cicero also notes that 'the use of metaphor is of wide application.' 4 Cicero, *De Oratore* at 121. A trope is 'a deviation from the ordinary and principal signification of a word.' Edward P.J. Corbett, *Classical Rhetoric for the Modern Student* 461 (1971).
13. See Aristotle, *Rhetoric* at 187.
14. 4 Cicero, *De Oratore* at 121.He then illustrates his point metaphorically: 'For just as clothes were first invented to protect us against cold and afterwards began to be used for the sake of adornment and dignity as well, so the metaphorical employment of words was begun because of poverty, but was brought into common use for the sake of entertainment.'
15. 3 Quintilian, *Institutio Oratoria* at 199: 'Metaphor ... which is the supreme ornament of oratory, supplies words to things with which they have strictly no connexion.'
16. For a description of how Greco-Roman advocates used 'examples' see Aristotle, *Rhetoric* at 147-149; 2 Cicero, *De Inventione* at 89-91 (H.M. Hubbell trans. 1949); and 2 Quintilian, *Institutio Oratoria* at 275.
17. 3 Quintilian, *Institutio Oratoria* at 251.
18. 3 Quintilian, *Institutio Oratoria* at 303. See also Quintilian's observation that all tropes (including metaphors) transfer 'expressions from their natural and principal signification to another' or transfer 'words and phrases from the place which is strictly theirs to another to which they do not properly belong.' Quintilian, *Institutio Oratoria* at 351.
19. Quintilian, *Institutio Oratoria* at 255.
20. Aristotle, *Rhetoric* at 188.
21. 4 Cicero, *De Oratore* at 123.
22. Aristotle, *Rhetoric* at 213.
23. Aristotle, *The Art of Rhetoric* at 42.
24. 4 Cicero, *De Oratore* at 125.
25. *Rhetorica ad Herennium* at 359.
26. Aristotle, *Rhetoric* at 206-207.
27. 4 Cicero, *De Oratore* at 125.
28. 3 Quintilian, *Institutio Oratoria* at 359.
29. 4 Cicero, *De Oratore* at 125 (emphasis added). Cicero later says that metaphors are pleasurable 'because a single word in each case suggests the thing and a picture of the whole.' 4 Cicero, *De Oratore* at 127.
30. Aristotle *Rhetoric* at 9.
31. Aristotle, *Rhetoric* at 2.
32. Aristotle, *Rhetoric* at 92ff.
33. 3 Quintilian, *Institutio Oratoria* at 311.
34. 3 Quintilian, *Institutio Oratoria* at 359.
35. Aristotle, *Rhetoric* at 206 (emphasis added).
36. 4 Cicero, *De Oratore* at 125 (emphasis added).
37. 4 Cicero, *De Oratore* at 125 (emphasis added).
38. 3 Quintilian, *Institutio Oratore* at 213 (emphasis added).
39. Aristotle, *Rhetoric* at 206-207.
40. Aristotle, *Rhetoric* at 212.

41. 3 Quintilian, *Institutio Oratoria* at 253.
42. Aristotle, *Rhetoric* at 187.
43. 4 Cicero, *De Oratore* at 121.
44. 3 Quintilian, *Institutio Oratoria* at 253.
45. 4 Cicero, *De Oratore* at 127. Cicero prefers visual metaphors because the sense of sight is 'keenest' and because they 'virtually plac[e] within the range of our mental vision objects not actually visible to our sight.'
46. 3 Quintilian, *Institutio Oratoria* at 311.
47. Aristotle, *Rhetoric* at 187.
48. Aristotle, *Rhetoric* at 208.
49. 3 Quintilian, *Institutio Oratoria* at 305-07.
50. Aristotle, *Rhetoric* at 214-215.
51. *Rhetorica ad Herennium* at 141. 'Embellishment consists of similes, examples, amplifications, previous judgements, and the other means which serve to expand and enrich the argument ...'
52. 3 Quintilian, *Institutio Oratoria* at 359.
53. Aristotle, *Rhetoric* at 207 (emphasis in original).
54. 4 Cicero, *De Oratore* at 127.
55. 3 Quintilian, *Institutio Oratoria* at 251.
56. See Aristotle, *Rhetoric* at 187 for Aristotle's list of 'effects.' Also see *Rhetorica ad Herenium* at 343: 'Metaphor is used for the sake of creating a vivid mental picture ... for the sake of brevity ... for the sake of avoiding obscenity ... for the sake of magnifying ... for the sake of minifying ... [and] for the sake of embellishment.'
57. A 'metaphor should always either occupy a place already vacant, or if it fills the room of something else, should be more impressive than that which it displaces.' 3 Quintilian, *Institutio Oratoria* at 311. See also 4 Cicero, *De Oratore* at 129: '[T]he metaphor ought to have an apologetic air, so as to look as if it had entered a place that does not belong to it with a proper introduction, not taken it by storm, and as if it had come with permission, not forced its way in.'
58. Aristotle, *Rhetoric* at 192. See also Cicero's observation: 'I deprecate a metaphor that is on a bigger scale than the thing requires – "a hurricane of revelry" or on a smaller scale the revelling of the hurricane.' 4 Cicero, *De Oratore* at 129.
59. 4 Cicero, *De Oratore* at 127. See also *Rhetorica ad Herennium* at 143: 'A simile is defective if it is inexact in any aspect, and lacks a proper ground for the comparison, or is prejudicial to him who presents it.'
60. 3 Quintilian, *Institutio Oratoria* at 307-309.
61. 3 Quintilian, *Institutio Oratoria* at 331.
62. Aristotle, *Rhetoric* at 212: 'Metaphors ... should be drawn from objects that are related to the object in question, but not obviously related; [in rhetoric] as in philosophy the adept will perceive resemblances even in things that are far apart. Thus [the philosopher] Archytas said that an arbitrator and an altar were the same, since both are a refuge for the injured.'
63. To stress his point regarding resemblances, Cicero quotes a passage personifying the elemental forces of a storm: 'A shivering takes the sea,/Darkness is doubled, and the murk of night/And stormclouds blinds the sight, flame 'mid the cluds/Quivers ...' 4 Cicero, *De Oratore* at 123.
64. 3 Quintilian, *Institutio Oratoria* at 215-217.
65. Aristotle, for instance, compared judgement warped by emotion to a carpenter's rule made crooked before use. Aristotle, *Rhetoric* at 2.

66. 4 Cicero, *De Oratore* at 19-21.
67. 3 Quintilian, *Institutio Oratoria* at 3.
68. Aristotle, *Rhetoric* at 9.
69. Aristotle, *Rhetoric* at 9.
70. Aristotle, *Rhetoric* at 8.
71. Aristotle, *Rhetoric* at 46.
72. 3 Quintilian, *Institutio Oratoria* at 233 (emphasis added).
73. Aristotle, *Rhetoric* at 212.
74. Aristotle, *Aristotle's Poetics: A Translation and Commentary for Students of Literature* 41 (Leon Golden, trans. 1968) (emphasis added).
75. 4 Cicero, *De Oratore* at 125.
76. 3 Quintilian, *Institutio Oratoria* at 213.
77. 3 Quintilian, *Institutio Oratoria* at 307-309.
78. Haig Bosmajian, *Metaphor and Reason in Judicial Opinions*; William Domnarski, *In the Opinion of the Court* 97ff (1996).
79. Michael R. Smith, *Advanced Legal Writing: Theories and Strategies in Persuasive Writing* 79-221 (2002); Henry Weihofen, *Legal Writing Style* 118 (2nd ed. 1980) noting that Aristotle regarded the ability to create metaphors as the 'surest sign of originality.'
80. Shanley v. Northeast Indiana School District. 462 F.2d 960 (5th Cir. 1972).
81. Tinker v. Des Moines School District, 393 U.S. 503 (1969).
82. Shanley at 978.
83. 3 Quintilian, *Institutio Oratoria* at 215-217.
84. See Haig Bosmajian, *Metaphor and Reason in Judicial Opinions* 181 (1992) whose treatise focuses on the connections between legal metaphors and judicial reasoning. He criticizes Judge Goldberg's metaphor, apparently because he mixes metaphors and because metaphors should be unobtrusive:

    > One problem with this water-control extended metaphor is that while earlier in the court's opinion the Plessy decision was personified as having progeny, the Tinker decision is depersonalized into a structure, a dam. Further, the extended metaphor brings too much attention to itself, what with 'irrigates,' 'floods,' 'fields of school discipline,' 'canals and channels,' and 'topsoil of the First Amendment.'
    >
    > Bosmajian's criticisms depend on the assumption that legal writing style, including use of figurative language, should not call attention to itself and that mixing metaphors betrays aesthetic insensitivity or an indefensible inconsistency.

85. Pavlicic v. Vogtsberger, 136 A.2d 127 (Pa. 1957).
86. Pavlicic, 136 A.2d 127 at 128.
87. Pavlicic, 136 A.2d 127 at 130.
88. Pavlicic, 136 A.2d 127 at 128.
89. Pavlicic, 136 A.2d 127 at 130.
90. Berkey v. Third Avenue Railway Company, 244 N.Y. 84, 155 N.E. 58 (1926).
91. Haig Bosmajian, 'The Judiciary's Use of Metaphors, Metonymies and Other Tropes to Give First Amendment Protection to Students and Teachers,' 15 Journal of Law and Education 443 (1986). Bosmajian quotes several U.S. Supreme Court justices, including Justices Potter Stewart, Felix Frankfurter, and Oliver Wendell Holmes, on the inadvisability and dangers of metaphors in judicial opinions. Holmes 'observed in 1912: 'It is one of the misfortunes of the law that ideas become encysted in phrases and therefore for a long time cease to provoke further analysis.' Hyde v. United States, 225 U.S. 347, 391 (1912).

92. Bosmajian, 'The Judiciary's Use of Metaphors,' at 443. He quotes Justice Potter Stewart's observation that 'the Court's task is not responsibly aided by the uncritical invocation of metaphors like the "wall of separation," a phrase nowhere to be found in the Constitution.' Engel v. Vitale, 370 U.S. 421, 445 (1962) (emphasis added).

93. The following is a representative sampling of writers who think metaphors serve principally to emphasize and memorialize: '[Metaphors] are useful in adding color and impact to an assertion, making your point much more vivid and memorable to the reader.' William P. Statsky and R. John Wernet, Jr., *Case Analysis and Fundamentals of Legal Writing* 294 (3rd ed. 1989); 'Metaphor, simile, and other figures of speech can enliven your argument, especially in introductions or conclusions.' And '[Metaphors] create ... a more concrete picture in the reader's mind, and concreteness increases memory.' Mary Barnard Ray and Barbara J. Cox, *Beyond the Basics: A Text for Advanced Legal Writing* 236 (1991).

94. '[Metaphors] should be used sparingly and cautiously.' Statsky and Wernet at 294. 'There is nothing wrong with using metaphors and similes in legal writing, but they should be used judiciously and sparingly.' Robert B. Smith, *The Literate Lawyer: Legal Writing and Oral Advocacy* 19 (1986); '[Metaphors] must be used with discrimination and restraint.' Henry Weihofen, *Legal Writing Style* 119 (1980); 'As with any technique, you also need to guard against overuse.' Ray and Cox, *Beyond the Basics* at 237.

95. George P. Fletcher, 'Fairness and Utility in Tort Theory,' 85 Harvard Law Review 571-73 (1972).

96. George P. Fletcher, at 571-573.

97. Statsky and Wernet, *Case Analysis* at 294.

98. Weihofen, *Legal Writing Style* at 118.

99. Ray and Cox, *Beyond the Basics* at 236.

100. James E. Murray, 'Understanding Law as Metaphor,' 34 Journal of Legal Education 714, 718 (1984).

101. Statsky and Wernet, *Case Analysis* at 294.

102. Girvan G. Peck, *Writing Persuasive Briefs* at 23 (1984).

103. Ray and Cox, *Beyond the Basics* at 237.

104. Weihofen, *Legal Writing Style* at 119.

105. 3 Quintilian, *Institutio Oratoria* at 307-309.

106. Bosmajian, 'Judiciary's Use of Metaphor' at 441.

107. Berkey v. Third Avenue Railway Company, 244 N.Y. 84, 94; 155 N.E. 58, 61 (1926).

108. Aristotle, *Rhetoric* at 206.

109. 4 Cicero, *De Oratore* at 123.

110. 3 Quintilian, *Institutio Oratoria* at 303 (noting that metaphors are 'so natural a turn of speech that it is often employed unconsciously or by uneducated persons'); 4 Cicero, *De Oratore* at 121 notes that 'the use of metaphor is of wide application.'

111. Owen Barfield, *Poetic Diction: A Study in Meaning* 63-64 (1964) (emphasis added).

112. James B. White, *The Legal Imagination: Studies in the Nature of Legal Thought and Expression* 695 (Boston, 1973); Peck, *Writing Persuasive Briefs* at 21 illustrates the frequency of metaphors with a short extract from Justice Cardozo's opinion in Meinhard v. Salmon, 249 N.Y.458, 164 N.E. 545, 546 (1928). He also provides metaphoric word lists which reinforce the point made in James B. White's quotation. Peck, *Writing Persuasive Briefs* at 22-23.

113. White, *Legal Imagination* at 707.

114. Burr Henly, '"Penumbra": The Roots of a Legal Metaphor,' 15 Hastings Constitutional Law Quarterly 82 (1987).

115. 4 Cicero, *De Oratore* at 127.

116. James E. Murray quoting with approval Edward L. Murray, 'The Phenomenon of the Metaphor: Some Theoretical Considerations,' 2 Duquesne Studies in Phenomenological Psychology 288 (A. Giorgi, C. Fischer and E. Murray, eds. 1975).

117. Bosmajian, Metaphor and Reason at 44 quoting A. Paivo, *Psychological Processes in the Comprehension of Metaphor* (emphasis added).

118. Steven L. Winter, 'Death is the Mother of Metaphor,' 105 Harvard Law Review 745, 759 (1992) (emphasis added) reviewing Thomas C. Grey, *The Wallace Stevens Case: Law and the Practice of Poetry* (1991).

119. Aristotle, *Rhetoric* at 188.

120. 4 Cicero, *De Oratore* at 123.

121. 3 Quintilian, *Institutio Oratoria* at 304.

122. 4 Cicero, *De Oratore*, at 125 and 127 (emphasis added).

123. Bosmajian, 'Metaphor, Metonymies' at 457 (emphasis added).

124. Aristotle, *Rhetoric* at 46.

125. Bosmajian, 'Metaphor, Metonymies' at 444.

126. Bosmajian, 'Metaphor, Metonymies' at 444.

127. West Virginia State Board of Education v. Barnette, 319 U.S. 642 (emphasis added).

128. Bosmajian, 'Metaphor, Metonymies' at 463.

129. Burr Henly, '"Penumbra": The Roots of a Legal Metaphor', 15 Hastings Constitutional Law Quarterly 81, 83 (1987); Griswold v. Connecticut, 381 U.S. 479, 484 (1965).

130. Holmes, 'The Theory of Torts,' 7 American Law Review 652, 654 (1873), reprinted in 44 Harvard Law Review 773, 775 (1931).

131. Henly, 'Penumbra' at 100.

Chapter 6

Greco-Roman Elements of Forensic Style

CLASSICAL APPROACH TO ANTITHESIS AND PARALLELISM

Notwithstanding the importance of metaphor in their discussions of forensic style, classical rhetoricians also singled out other sentence-level rhetorical devices for special consideration. To make their arguments clearer and more persuasive, classical rhetoricians recommended using *similitudo*. *Similitudo* is a general term used to describe comparisons of all sorts, including parallelism and antithesis.[1] Because both devices make arguments more coherent, memorable, and emotionally appealing, they were especially favored for juxtaposing and contrasting rulings, facts, and policies.[2] Neither device was regarded as merely ornamental. Under classical theory, style serves a dual function. It is both a sentence-level technique for proving or refuting arguments and an emotion-generating technique for reinforcing and embellishing important points.

Moreover, according to Aristotle, style offers insights into an advocate's character and sense of propriety. This, in turn, directly affects how audiences respond to arguments: 'Your language will be appropriate, if it expresses (1) emotion and (2) character, and if it is (3) in proportion with the subject.'[3] Aristotle thinks that, like all other aspects of a well-constructed argument, even inconspicuous sentence-level stylistic choices contribute to an advocate's credibility.

Compared to Cicero's *De Oratore* and Quintilian's *Institutio Oratoria*, Aristotle's *Rhetoric* does not have a strong focus on style. Even so, Aristotle does single out antithesis as a device for making contrasting ideas easily felt. The author of the *Rhetorica ad Herennium* makes a similar claim for the importance of parallelism. He includes parallelism in his list of comparison techniques 'used to embellish or prove or clarify or vivify.'[4] Both Cicero and Quintilian also recommend using parallelism and antithesis in legal argument.[5]

Aristotle treats antithesis and parallelism as both figures of thought and figures of speech.[6] In his view, they both make arguments *felt* as well as understood:

> When the style is ... antithetical, in each of the two members ... an opposite is balanced by an opposite, or ... two opposites are linked by the same word. For example ... 'By nature citizens, by law bereft of their city ...' This kind of style is pleasing, because things are best known by opposition, and are all the better known when the opposites are put side by side; and is pleasing also because of its ... logic – for the method of refutation is the juxtaposition of contrary conclusions.[7]

According to Aristotle, the virtue of antithesis is that it enhances both the emotional impact ('is pleasing') and the comprehensibility (is 'known') of arguments. As for parallelism, Aristotle simply describes it and makes no explicit claims for its effects: '*Parisosis* [parallel structure] is having the two members of a period (sentence) equal in length. ...'[8] He does, however, observe of style generally that '[i]n respect to the style in which the argument is put, what they (the audience) like is antithesis and balance. ...'[9] This assertion is part of his recurring claim that style has measurable effects on an audience.

Focusing on logical rather than emotional effects, Quintilian claims that parallelism and antithesis are especially useful when proving a case based on likeness or dissimilarity:

> Since ... the majority of such [legal] arguments are based on similarity, we must make diligent search to discover if any discrepancy is to be found in what is put forward. It is easy to do this where points of law are concerned. For the law was drafted to cover cases quite other than the present, and consequently it is all the easier to show the difference between case and case.[10]

In Quintilian's opinion, both devices work well because they help advocates compare the facts, rules and policies of one case with another. Like Aristotle, he too regards antithesis as a figure of thought as well as a figure of style:

> Comparison is ... regarded as a [rhetorical] figure, although at times it is a form of proof, and at others the whole case may turn upon it, while its form may be illustrated by the following passage from the *pro Murena:* 'You pass wakeful nights that you may be able to reply to your clients; he that he and his army may arrive betimes at their destination. You are roused by cockcrow, he by the bugle's reveille' and so on. I am not sure, however, whether it is so much a figure of thought as of speech. For the only difference lies in the fact that universals are not contrasted with universals, but particulars with particulars.'[11]

According to Quintilian, the purpose of these rhetorical figures is 'to attract the attention of the audience and ... not allow it to flag, rousing it from time to time ...'[12] To reinforce his point, he offers detailed suggestions regarding sentence structure. He suggests that 'a number of clauses may begin with the same word for the sake of force and emphasis' or that they 'may end with the same words.'[13] He concludes by observing that 'in antithesis and comparisons the first words of alternate phrases are frequently repeated to produce correspondence ...'[14]

While Quintilian usually concentrated on short phrasal and clausal parallelisms, some of his examples are long and include multiple comparisons:

> If connexion with a male slave is disgraceful to the mistress of the house, so is the connexion of the master with the female slave. If pleasure is an end sought by dumb animals so also must it be with men ... But these arguments may readily be met by arguments from dissimilars: It is not the same thing for the master of the house to have intercourse with a female slave as for the mistress to have intercourse with a

male slave; nor does it follow that because dumb animals pursue pleasure, reasoning beings should do likewise.[15]

In Cicero's *Topica*, written at the request of a 'jurisconsult (legal expert) of some repute,' he stresses the logical function of both antithesis and parallelism.[16] Like many handbooks of the period, the *Topica* is both a practice manual for composing legal arguments and a philosophical treatise. In introducing the topic of *similitudo*, Cicero maintains that it is of more interest to philosophers than to jurists, but then illustrates how advocates commonly use it:

> For example, there are certain arguments from similarity which attain the desired proof by several comparisons, as follows: If honesty is required of a guardian, a partner, a bailee, and a trustee, it is required of an agent. This form of argument which attains the desired proof by citing several parallels is called induction ... Another kind of argument from similarity rests on comparison, when one thing is compared to one, equal to equal ...[17]

Elsewhere, he explains that in arguments based on *similitudo* 'comparison is made between things which are greater, or less or equal. And in this connexion the following points are considered: quantity, quality, value, and also a particular relation to certain things.'[18] For Cicero *similitudo* is simultaneously a way to prove and present an argument. The categories of quantity, quality, value, etc. not only help advocates discover all the available arguments but also help them organize arguments in a logical and pleasing fashion.

Like Cicero, the author of the *Rhetorica ad Herennium* offers detailed suggestions for increasing both the logical and the emotional impact of arguments by using parallelism and antithesis.[19] He emphasizes that rhetorical purpose dictates the form of presentation so that, depending on the purpose of the comparison, 'Contrast, Negation, Detailed Parallel or Abridged Comparison' may be used to 'embellish or prove or clarify or vivify.'[20]

According to the *Rhetorica ad Herennium*, these devices improve arguments by providing extensive and detailed embellishment of the subject and comparative part:

> A Comparison [can] be used for vividness, and be set forth in the form of a detailed parallel ... This comparison, by embellishing both terms, *bringing into relation* by a method of parallel description ... set[s] the subject vividly before the eyes of all. Moreover, the Comparison is presented in the form of a detailed parallel because, once the similitude has been set up, all like elements are related.[21]

By 'bringing into relation' the subject and comparative parts, parallelism acts as both a coherence and a mnemonic device. It refers to what has already been said and, by showing how like elements are related, allows authors to make complex comparisons without overburdening the audience's memory.

MODERN APPROACHES TO ANTITHESIS AND PARALLELISM

Modern scholars have also examined the connections between parallelism and antithesis and legal discourse, but seldom refer to classical sources when doing so. Some have suggested that symmetrical forms like parallelism and antithesis are 'innate forms of the mind' and that thought patterns like comparison, contrast, balance, and repetition are at the root of human experience.[22] Others note that 'the idea of justice carries with it the idea of balance and symmetry. We believe that the punishment should always be related to the crime. This idea is reflected in the [Biblical] maxim "An eye for an eye, a tooth for a tooth."'[23]

Still others approach the topic from an historical perspective. David Melinkoff's magisterial *The Language of the Law* examines the historical roots of legal writing in lexical as well as structural terms.[24] According to him, two traditions – one oral and one bilingual – account for many of the doublings, repetitions and parallelism that characterize modern legal prose.[25]

First, during the Anglo-Saxon period, an oral tradition in the law allowed an illiterate populace to participate in legal proceedings with memorized, formulaic pleadings and oaths. Repetitious legal rituals, especially alliterative ones, were easier to memorize and were consequently adopted. Moreover, these rituals carried with them a sort of word magic – alliterative, incantatory, and formulaic – which the following oath illustrates: 'In the name of Almighty God, as I here for N. in true witness stand, unbidden and unbought, so I with my eyes oversaw, and with my ears overheard, that which I with him say.'[26] Parallelism of this sort (alliteration, parallel prepositional phrases) functions as a mnemonic device, useful in oral proceedings.

A second, bilingual tradition accounts for those commonplace parallelisms that are linked, in the popular imagination, with the law: 'null and void,' 'aid and abet,' 'law and order,' 'last will and testament,' 'rest, remainder, and residue.' Pairings of this sort (verb/verb, noun/noun) reflect the bilingual origins of our legal language which has, at various times, been written in Latin and French, as well as in English. Because of this bilingualism, lawyers often used synonyms from two or three languages to ensure that their writings could be understood. This habit of doubling words and phrases has survived even though the necessity for it has not, in part because the rhythmical pairings of words and phrases carry with them their own emotional appeal.[27] Neither the oral nor bilingual tradition is closely linked to classical rhetoric, but both traditions exploit close connections between legal prose and antithesis and parallelism. Both traditions rely, as did the *Rhetorica ad Herennium*, on the fact that these devices 'embellish or prove or clarify or vivify' legal arguments and other forms of legal discourse and that they improve coherence and aid memory.[28]

Building on those traditions as well as the previously discussed 'current-traditional rhetorical' approach to stylistic 'correctness,' modern handbooks also recommend parallelism and antithesis. According to these handbooks, parallelism and antithesis help make arguments coherent, memorable, and persuasive:

[P]erhaps the most useful of all the devices in the lawyer's tool box is parallel structure. *Parallel phrases*, sentences, and clauses permit the brief writer to hold up one idea (phrased in a given sequence) against another idea (phrased in the same sequence) and then *to compare or contrast* them point for point. The *similarity* or *dissimilarity* will stand out because the parallel sequence invites a clear-cut comparison.[29]

Respecting parallelism, some handbooks emphasize that '[s]uch coordination promotes clarity and coherence.'[30] Others emphasize that it 'reflects the logical parallels of the content and also allows the writer to use [repetition] to emphasize a point'[31] or that it 'harmonizes your language with your thought,'[32] or that it improves 'readability.'[33]

As for antithesis, a few handbooks recommend it because it brings 'opposing ideas together in [a] way [that] makes them stand out with bold distinctness, and so has more impact on the reader.'[34] Even then, however, these handbooks do not explain just how this 'impact' is created. According to Aristotle, this 'impact' results from the intellectual challenge antithesis presents. Because antithesis requires readers to sort out the comparison to reach their own insights, they are 'pleased' when they have done so.

By contrast with the classical emphasis on the emotional effects of style, most modern handbooks ignore the topic, except by implication. Instead, they analyze both parallelism and antithesis using the 'correctness' principle of 'current-traditional rhetoric,' which emphasizes how proper usage, grammar, and style contribute to unity and coherence.[35] When, for example, they discuss 'faulty' parallelism, they identify the 'faults,' but do not discuss their emotional impact or how they affect an audience's opinion of the author, except to note that grammatical 'faults' reflect a lack of professionalism.[36] For them, proper parallelism reflects an orderly mind and imperceptibly creates confidence in the author. 'Faulty' parallelism has just the opposite effect.

Despite this general neglect of the topic of style and emotion, a few exceptions exist. Years ago, in his essay on 'Law and Literature,' Justice Cardozo identified both parallelism and antithesis as emotionally potent components in written advocacy: 'The [judicial] opinion will need persuasive force, or the impressive virtue of sincerity and fire, or the mnemonic power of *alliteration* and *antithesis* ...'[37] Other writers also connect parallelism with emotion: 'A writer can achieve *an emotional impact* by arranging words, phrases, or sentences in structurally similar groupings.'[38] Still others emphasize its rhythmic appeal, noting that parallelism increases readability because it introduces a rhythmic pattern that allows 'the reader's mind to anticipate how much attention will be required for each syllable to come.'[39] Some note that faulty parallelism discomforts readers: '[T]hey (faulty sentences) "jolt" us; something's "not quite right." This sensation is perhaps best illustrated by the "comfort" we feel in reading "To be, or not to be," compared to the "jolt" we receive in reading "To be, or not being."'[40] None of these writers, however, treat the subject with the thoroughness of the classical rhetoricians.

Moreover, only a few handbooks discuss how antithesis and other figures of speech provide insights into an advocate's character, or *ethos*. Those that do seem to embrace Quintilian's observation that eloquence can 'delight' an audience and note that '[w]hile the concept of arousing delight in an audience refers to the medium mood control function of eloquent language, the concept of inspiring admiration actually refers to a separate function: the ethos function.'[41] Antithesis is included in the list of *ethos*-enhancing figures of speech because it is a 'powerful tool for achieving emphasis ... [and its sometimes] aphoristic quality.'[42] Addressing the topic even more broadly, others invoke Aristotle for the precept that 'writing exhibits character ... it expresses what Aristotle calls *ethos*, an image of your character that affects the audience's response.'[43]

These exceptions notwithstanding, most modern legal writing and advocacy handbooks do not approach in scope or detail the classical attention to style as a tool for pleasing readers, keeping their interest, engaging their senses or increasing the writer's credibility. Instead, they restrict their attention to various analytical and 'usage' conventions. These 'conventions' should be modified to include more attention to how style affects emotion and advocate credibility. Experienced lawyers instinctively know this and rely heavily on both parallelism and antithesis when writing their briefs.

The evidence for this can be found in opposing briefs for the previously discussed case of *Harper & Row Publishers v. Nation Enterprises*. In that case, which pitted First Amendment rights against copyright in a 'fair use' case, lawyers from both sides used both parallelism and antithesis to increase the emotional impact of their arguments. At times, they rely on their formulaic, almost incantatory, appeal and, at other times, they use them to impose order on the temporal flow of experience. They use them to elevate the tone of their briefs and to analogize and distinguish cases on their facts. Most importantly, they use them to compare various rules, ideas, and lines of reasoning.

For example, in the Defendant *Nation* magazine's brief, the author uses these devices to contrast critical legal and analytical points, distinguishing 'momentous' affairs of state (pardoning a President) from 'well-established' principles of copyright law. In doing so, the author also uses them to emphasize the Plaintiff's misreadings of judicial opinions and misstatements of law:

> But if the roots of this action lie in momentous and unprecedented affairs of state, the decision of the Second Circuit ... rests firmly on a series of well-established and hardly controversial propositions of copyright law. Harper & Row's challenge to the judgment of the Court of Appeals is based upon a *misreading of the opinion* of the Second Circuit and a *misstatement of the law* of other circuits ...[44]

The author's use of both parallelism and antithesis places the legal arguments in clear relief, thereby enabling the reader to see their differences quickly. In Aristotle's words, 'the opposites are put side by side; ... [which] is pleasing also because of its ... logic – for the method of refutation is the juxtaposition of contrary conclusions.'[45]

Relying on the same techniques, an amicus brief supporting *Nation* magazine also uses parallelism to identify and contrast competing legal issues. 'In this case, this Court is asked to resolve the tension between the First Amendment's protection of news reporting and the protection afforded under the Copyright Act to nonfiction works written by former high public officials.'[46]

On the opposite side of the case, Plaintiff Harper & Row's brief uses parallel structure to focus on *Nation's* excessive and impermissible use of copyrighted material. In its statement of the case, facts damaging to *Nation's* argument are listed in parallel clauses:

> Defendants' trial testimony further demonstrated that defendants sought to, and did, copy Ford's expression. Mr. Navasky testified that *he quoted* Ford's portrait of Nixon because 'this was his (Ford's) own way of saying it ...' *He quoted* Ford's evaluation of the reasons for granting the pardon 'because of the absolute certainty with which he expressed himself ...' *He quoted* Ford's account of the negotiations with Ron Ziegler because '... when Ford writes about this as a narrator, it was the definitive quality of the statement that made me put it in ...' And *he quoted* Ford's account of Nixon's assurances of innocence because it was 'a much more powerful statement for the reader.'[47]

Anaphora (successive clauses beginning with the same word) of this kind has the cumulative and emotional effect of emphasizing that Navasky, *Nation's* editor, deliberately appropriated substantial portions of Ford's own words instead of paraphrasing the important points.

Following a similar pattern, the opening argument in the Harper & Row brief also uses anaphora to identify the mistakes that the circuit court made:

> Thus the [circuit court] held (a) *that* in works concerning news and history, the 'troublesome' concept of expression must be limited to 'its barest elements – the ordering and choice of the words themselves ...' (b) *that* facts coupled with expression cannot constitute a copyrightable totality, and (c) *that* almost unlimited paraphrasing from a work of non-fiction is permissible, unless the copier has 'borrowed virtually an entire work.'[48]

In this example, alphabetic tabulation, coupled with the rhythmic repetition of 'that' clauses, hammers home the writer's points.

In response, an amicus brief supporting Defendant *Nation* combines parallelism and antithesis to identify the mistakes that the circuit court avoided: 'The court below properly refrained from basing its decision upon its own subjective views of journalism: whether the journalism in the *Nation* article was "good" or, in the district court's revealing word, "poor" ... whether the article was necessary or superfluous.'[49]

Although these opposing briefs do not mirror one another's lines of argument, they do adhere to the same point/counterpoint pattern. On the issue of 'fair use,' for instance, Harper & Row uses antithetical gerund clauses to suggest that the circuit court mistakenly 'transformed a fair use question into an issue of copyrightability. There is a vast difference between sanctioning a use of material because the use is fair, and sanctioning such a use because the material is entitled to no protection at all.'[50]

In response, *Nation* uses antithesis ('factual'/'fictional') to add still another factor into the 'fair use' dispute: '[I]n analyzing the nature of a copyrighted work under the ... fair use [doctrine], *copying works of a factual nature* should be given broader leeway under the fair use doctrine than *copying works of a fictional nature.*'[51]

Varied as they are, all these examples closely adhere to classical stylistic principles as they draw parallels between cases, contrast groups of facts, and emphasize relationships among legal rules. Occasionally, they create passages as impressive as the following excerpt from an amicus brief for *Nation*:

> In answering that question, courts should apply ... doctrines that mediate between First Amendment rights and the interests protected by the Copyright act: *ideas*, as opposed to the form of expressing those ideas, *are not copyrightable*; facts, as opposed to the form of expressing those facts, *are not copyrightable*; works of the United States *are not copyrightable*; and material not original to the author *is not copyrightable*. These ... doctrines – especially the distinctions between ideas and expression and between facts and expression – should be applied so as to avoid questions of First Amendment violations.[52]

The rhetorical force of this passage depends heavily on parallelism and antithesis to maintain its almost architectonic symmetry and create its emotional effects.

As even this limited sampling shows, antithesis and parallelism are as prevalent and effective in modern legal argument as they were in classical times. Classical techniques and purposes inform the logic and organization of the arguments and allow lawyers to bring their arguments into emotional as well as logical focus. What is missing from the modern approach is a comprehensive theoretical framework within which to place this technique and teach it to others.

SIMILARITIES AND DIFFERENCES

The preceding discussion demonstrates a substantial correspondence between classical and modern rhetorical theory and practice. Further, it discloses a habit of mind and concern for rhetorical technique that seems inherent in all forensic discourse. Consciously or not, when classical and modern scholars analyze rhetoric, they are analyzing laws of thinking as much as they are analyzing rules for writing. When advocates make rhetorical choices, they are making argumentative choices as well.

As was seen in Chapter Three, the U.S. Supreme Court rules embody and tacitly endorse classical principles of organization and thereby testify to rhetoric's enduring value and importance. Chapters Five and Six show that classical principles of style are equally important and applicable to modern legal advocacy.

Unfortunately, through neglect and inattention, much of what both ancient and modern rhetoricians have discovered about sentence-level style has been lost or overlooked. As a consequence, advocates, through hard work and long experience, must discover for themselves what is readily available. As the analysis provided in this chapter demonstrates, a rekindled interest in and an application of classical rhetorical receipts is well worth the effort.

Notes

1. Marsh H. McCall, Jr., *Ancient Rhetorical Theories of Simile and Comparison* 59 (1969).
2. McCall, *Ancient Rhetorical Theories of Simile and Comparison* at 70.
3. Aristotle, *Rhetoric* at 197.
4. *Rhetorica ad Herennium* at 377.
5. Winifred Bryan Horner, *Rhetoric in the Classical Tradition* 312 (1988). Parallelism expresses similar or related ideas in similar grammatical construction. *Webster's Third New International Dictionary* 1637 (1981). Antithesis expresses a contrast or opposition of thoughts, usually in two phrases, clauses, or sentences. *Webster's Third International Dictionary* at 96. The following example uses parallel structure to distinguish the education and business experience of litigants in two different cases. 'In that case, the plaintiff was a construction worker with a limited education, who had no experience in business transactions. In this case, the plaintiff is an executive with an advanced degree, whose job it is to conduct business transactions.' Girvan Peck, *Writing Persuasive Briefs* at 49.
6. The *Rhetorica ad Herennium* follows Aristotle: 'As I have explained above, [antithesis] belongs either among the figures of diction ... or among the figures of thought ...' *Rhetorica ad Herennium* at 377.
7. Aristotle, *Rhetoric* at 204-05.
8. Aristotle, *Rhetoric* at 205.
9. Aristotle, *Rhetoric* at 207.
10. 2 Quintilian, *Institutio Oratoria* at 325.
11. 3 Quintilian, *Institutio Oratoria* at 437-439.
12. 3 Quintilian, *Institutio Oratoria* at 461.
13. 3 Quintilian, *Institutio Oratoria* at 463.
14. 3 Quintilian, *Institutio Oratoria* at 463.
15. 2 Quintilian, *Institutio Oratoria* at 293.
16. 2 Cicero, *Topica* at 378.
17. 2 Cicero, *Topica* at 413.
18. 2 Cicero, *Topica* at 433.
19. *Rhetorica ad Herennium* at 37.
20. *Rhetorica ad Herennium* at 377.
21. *Rhetorica ad Herennium* at 381-83 (emphasis added).
22. Kenneth Burke, *Counterstatement* 46 (1953).
23. Richard L. Graves, 'Symmetrical Form and the Rhetoric of the Sentence,' in *Essays on Classical Rhetoric and Modern Discourse* 171 (1984).
24. David Mellinkoff, *The Language of the Law* 43 (1963).
25. Mellinkoff, *Language of the Law* at 43.
26. Mellinkoff, *Language of the Law* at 43 (quoting I *Ancient Laws and Institutes of England* 181 B. Thorpe ed. 1840).
27. Mellinkoff, *Language of the Law* at 121.
28. *Rhetorica ad Herennium*, at 377.
29. Girvan Peck, *Writing Persuasive Briefs* at 49 (emphasis added).
30. Helene S. Shapo et al, *Writing and Analysis in the Law* at 174 (4th ed. 1999).
31. Mary Ray and Jill Ramsfield, *Legal Writing: Getting it Right and Getting it Written* 46, 135-36 (1987).
32. Bryan A. Garner, *Legal Writing in Plain English* 28 (2001).
33. Garner, *Legal Writing in Plain English* 100 (2001).

34. Henry Weihofen, *Legal Writing Style* 291 (1961).
35. See discussion of 'current-traditional rhetoric,' in Chapter One.
36. Richard K. Neumann, *Legal Reasoning and Legal Writing* at 223; Shapo et al, *Writing and Analysis* at 174-175.
37. Benjamin N. Cardozo, 'Law and Literature,' *Selected Writings* 342 (emphasis added).
38. Veda Charrow et al, *Clear and Effective Legal Writing* 174 (3rd ed. 2001) (emphasis added).
39. Lynn L. Squires et al, *Legal Writing in a Nutshell* 64 (2nd ed. 1996).
40. Teresa J. Reid Rambo and Leanne J. Pflaum, *Legal Writing by Design: A Guide to Great Briefs and Memos* 241 (2001).
41. Michael R. Smith, *Advanced Legal Writing*, at 227.
42. Michael R. Smith, *Advanced Legal Writing* at 234.
43. Stephen V. Armstrong and Timothy P. Terrell, *Thinking Like a Writer: A Lawyer's Guide to Effective Writing and Editing* 8-5 (1992).
44. Brief for Respondents at 4, *Harper & Row Publishers v. Nation Enterprises*, 471 U.S. 539 (1984) (No. 83-1632) (emphasis added).
45. Aristotle, *Rhetoric* at 204-05.
46. Gannett *amicus* brief, *Harper & Row Publishers v. Nation Enterprises*, 471 U.S. 539 (1984) (No. 83-1632) at 2.
47. Petitioner's brief, *Harper & Row Publishers v. Nation Enterprises*, 471 U.S. 539 (1984) (No. 83-1632) at 8 (emphasis added).
48. Petitioner's brief, *Harper & Row Publishers v. Nation Enterprises*, 471 U.S. 539 (1984) (No. 83-1632) at 10 (emphasis added).
49. Respondent's brief, *Harper & Row Publishers v. Nation Enterprises*, 471 U.S. 539 (1984) (No. 83-1632) at 11.
50. Petitioner's brief, *Harper & Row Publishers v. Nation Enterprises*, 471 U.S. 539 (1984) (No. 83-1632) at 17.
51. Gannett *amicus* brief, *Harper & Row Publishers v. Nation Enterprises*, 471 U.S. 539 (1984) (No. 83-1632) at 23 (emphasis added) (footnote omitted).
52. Gannett *amicus* brief, *Harper & Row Publishers v. Nation Enterprises*, 471 U.S. 539 (1984) (No. 83-1632) at 5 (emphasis added).

Chapter 7

The Rhetoric of Dissent:
A Greco-Roman Analysis

Despite an apparently inexhaustible interest in systematic analysis of judicial opinions, lawyers and legal scholars usually overlook the most comprehensive, adaptable, and practical analysis of legal discourse ever devised: the art of rhetoric. This is regrettable because classical rhetoric is the source of most modern theories on the topic of legal discourse. As the preceding chapters illustrate, classical rhetoric offers detailed and practical advice on how to analyze all forms of discourse and is particularly thorough on the subject of legal argument.

Although classical rhetoric has been largely neglected by legal scholars, scholars in other academic disciplines have increasingly turned their attention to the subject. In departments of English, Composition, Speech, and, of course, Rhetoric, they are returning to Greco-Roman sources for both inspiration and instruction in discourse analysis. In the past few years, dozens of books and articles have been written on the connections between modern and classical rhetorical principles.[1] None of them, however, focuses exclusively on legal rhetoric and most barely mention the topic.

As was noted in Chapter One, a few legal scholars, judges, and lawyers have recently begun to correct this omission. They recognize the value of classical rhetoric and occasionally rely on it to clarify or illustrate their points. They also recognize that, with some adaptations for modern taste and modern legal practice, the classical principles are as applicable today as they were for the Greeks and Romans.

Most of these commentators use classical rhetorical principles primarily to analyze the logic and persuasive value of legal arguments. Understandably, given their limited purposes, they rarely call attention to the larger context from which those principles were drawn. That is, they apply the principles without referring to the overall classical system, in part because they do not need to. As longtime lawyers and judges, they can rely on their own experience for much of the information and advice contained in the classical sources.

But law students and beginning lawyers do not have that experience to draw on. They need more information about the over-arching, experience-based, theoretical framework of the classical canon. Some of this information is included in the preceding chapters, which examine the classical topics of invention, factual analysis, argumentative strategies, legal reasoning, organizational patterns, audience analysis, stylistic conventions, and lawyer credibility.[2] And, on a limited basis, those chapters show how classical principles apply to modern legal discourse.

Although they provide a good starting point for understanding how classical rhetoric can benefit modern lawyers, those chapters are only a beginning. A fuller picture emerges when all forms of legal discourse, especially appellate briefs and judicial opinions, are analyzed from a classical perspective. Given the profound influence that they exercise on the law, it is especially important to apply that sort of analysis to judicial opinions. Above all other forms of legal discourse, they demonstrate the importance of a writer's rhetorical decisions.

LIMITS OF DISSENT

For many modern analysts of judicial opinions, 'rhetoric' is a pejorative term, frequently associated with '[l]anguage that is elaborate, pretentious, insincere, or intellectually vacuous.'[3] Critics use this definition of 'rhetoric' to criticize those whose opinions are unpopular or controversial. It is frequently invoked by those who disagree with the written opinions of Justice Antonin Scalia.[4]

Those who approve of Justice Scalia's opinions use a different definition. For them, rhetoric is '[s]kill in using language effectively and persuasively.'[5] Classical rhetoricians focused most of their attention on this second definition of rhetoric, but they were also aware that 'elaborate, pretentious, insincere' language impairs the quality of any legal argument.

Most discussions of Justice Scalia's rhetoric focus on the 'quotable' language in his dissenting opinions because that is where it is most noticeable. A good example of Scalia's distinctive writing style appears in his dissent in *PGA Tour, Inc. v. Martin*.[6] In that case, he disagreed with the Court's decision to allow disabled golfer Casey Martin to use a golf cart during professional tournaments. In his dissent, he contemptuously refers to the Court's creation of 'federal-Platonic golf'[7] and to its '*Kafkaesque* determination,'[8] its '*Alice in Wonderland* determination,'[9] and its '*Animal Farm* determination.'[10] It is this type of language that attracts public attention and helps create Justice Scalia's public reputation.

However, Justice Scalia's rhetorical skills consist of much more than his ability to find and employ a quotable phrase. The following analysis of Justice Scalia's dissent in the case of *United States v. Virginia* reveals both his rhetorical sophistication and his lapses of oratorical judgment.[11] It also demonstrates why it might be useful to analyze other judicial opinions from a classical perspective.

In the course of his dissent in that case, Scalia criticizes the Court's decision in language that makes his authorial voice the most distinctive on the U.S. Supreme Court. As he attacks the majority's decision to require, on equal protection grounds, the previously all-male Virginia Military Institute ('VMI') to admit qualified women, he accuses the majority of being 'illiberal,'[12] 'counter-majoritarian,'[13] and 'self-righteous.'[14] He asserts that the majority's equal protection jurisprudence is random,[15] that the Court 'load[s] the dice'[16] or plays 'Supreme Court peek-a-boo'[17] with the standards of review it applies, that it engages in 'politics-smuggled-into-law'[18] and 'do-it-yourself ... factfinding,'[19] that it re-writes the U.S. Constitution with 'custom-built tests,'[20] and 'ad-hocery,'[21] and that it employs 'fanciful description[s]' of its own decisions.[22] Language like this has gained Justice Scalia his well-deserved reputation for being a caustic and frequently sarcastic stylist.[23] It also helps create his very recognizable judicial *persona*.

Much of his rhetorical reputation arises from the language he uses when he is the sole dissenter. When he writes for the majority, his language is more formal and less controversial. In large part the language differences between his dissents and his majority opinions arise from the fact that majority opinions are 'corporate' or collaborative writing, that is, writing-by-committee (or, sometimes, writing-by-law clerks). Although the assigned Justice has considerable stylistic latitude in organizing and writing the opinion, the other Justices make both substantive and stylistic contributions.[24] The effect of these contributions is usually to dilute the personal writing style of the putative author and to produce an opinion with no distinctive authorial voice. Moreover, to ensure that the opinion appears as impartial as possible, most judges adopt an objective writing style that subordinates their personal voice.[25]

Dissents are a different matter. As a rule, dissenters are unhappy. After all, they have not persuaded their colleagues to their point of view.[26] They are unhappy about the majority's ruling, unhappy about its rationale, unhappy about its reading of the facts, treatment of the record, or understanding of the law. Consequently, they dissent. In their unhappiness, they use their dissents for sometimes dubious purposes and do so in the face of widespread skepticism about the usefulness or advisability of dissents generally.

As Bernard E. Witkin observes in his *Manual on Appellate Court Opinions*, '[t]he proponents and opponents of dissenting opinions are about evenly divided in number and in vehemence of their opinions on the subject.'[27] Witkin quotes numerous judges who offer two primary justifications for writing a dissent: they preserve legal principles for use at a later time, and they may prompt a court, on reflection, to correct its errors.[28]

In her *Judicial Opinion Writing Handbook*, Judge Joyce George maintains that '[a] dissent should be aimed at serving the law by raising unanswered issues and theories that more appropriately control the particular case. They may be used to guide a future court by suggesting the evolution of legal principles necessary to meet changed social conditions and concepts.'[29] She warns, however, that a dissent, '*depending upon its tone* ... may give the appearance of the existence of dissension among the members of the bench.'[30] As will be seen, the question of tone is central to any assessment of Justice Scalia's dissents.

Judges who think writing dissents is a bad idea give a number of reasons. They assert that dissents foster resentment in the losing party, encourage unnecessary appeals, and introduce uncertainty into the judicial process.[31] Frequent dissenters like Justice Scalia find these reasons unpersuasive.

As a rule, dissenters want to demonstrate that the majority was wrong to rule as it did. Frequently, they use the dissent to continue a debate on controversial topics or to test new (or old) ideas in the court of public opinion. Sometimes the dissent is intended to spur legislative action.[32]

Some judges, Justice Scalia among them, use their dissents to rebuke their colleagues publicly or to claim that bad consequences will inevitably flow from the ruling. Occasionally, a dissent functions as a sort of therapeutic venting for an unhappy judge.[33] In that sort of dissent:

> he (the dissenting judge) sometimes may indulge in sarcasm and far-fetched logic, unreasonable constructions and interpretations ... In some few cases personalities enter into it ... He wants to make his view stand out in bold relief, and by undue emphasis, unreasonable criticism, unfair interpretation, and a failure to follow the record he affords by his dissent much that makes good reading in the press, all to the harm of the court as a whole.[34]

Judge George makes a similar point when she insists that '[t]he dissenter should not personally attack the majority. The reasons compelling the dissent should be expressed clearly without intemperance, insinuations, or allegations of incompetence.'[35]

No matter what their purpose, dissenting judges – especially rhetorically sophisticated judges like Scalia – have a stylistic latitude that collaborative writers do not. Unalloyed by the substantive or stylistic contributions of other judges, the personal authorial voice of the dissenting judge emerges.[36] Frequently this authorial independence allows the judge's personality, or at least his or her judicial *persona*, to become much more visible. This in turn affects how the dissent is read.[37]

Not only does this judicial *persona* become visible, it is also transformed in character. In effect, the dissenting judge becomes an advocate as well as a judge, despite repeated admonitions against doing so. This type of dissenter ignores reminders that '[a] judge is not an advocate in robes. The judge may not extend his judicial activities so as to become, in effect, either an assisting prosecutor, an assisting defense attorney or a thirteenth juror. Nor should the judge's individual biases, values or morals be imposed upon others.'[38]

Unlike typical advocates, however, the dissenter is not addressing a court (or at least not his or her own court). The dissenter has already lost that battle. Instead, dissenting judges aim their arguments at other audiences.[39] In the hope of prompting them to action, dissenting judges write for other courts, and for legislative bodies, legal commentators, the media, and the general public. As judicial advocates, dissenting judges furnish these audiences with arguments, authority, and, presumably, a rhetorical vocabulary for re-addressing the legal issues in the case.

The success of these judicial advocates depends, of course, on the merits of their substantive arguments. Those who criticize Scalia's dissents usually focus on the substantive merits of his reasoning and properly so. After all, if he is illogical, misuses authority, misreads the record, or otherwise compromises the integrity of his analysis, then the other justices rightly rejected his reasoning. But Justice Scalia is highly intelligent, resourceful, and experienced. Even his critics concede these attributes. However, successful arguments depend on more than substantive merit. They also depend on an advocate's credibility and the emotions he or she invokes, both of which are substantially affected by the advocate's writing style.

While the affective or emotive aspects of Scalia's dissents have received considerable attention, this attention usually focuses on revealing or objectionable word choices or phrases – that is, his diction.[40] Even while decrying his aggressive tone and vocabulary as unnecessarily personal and sometimes cruel, commentators still devote most of their analysis to the substantive merits of his arguments. They ignore or insufficiently analyze the other rhetorical forces at play in his dissents.

Greco-Roman Focus on Forensic Style

As the preceding chapters show, rhetorical analysis of forensic style dates to the time of Aristotle. In its Aristotelian sense, rhetoric, including rhetorical style, is the 'faculty [power] of discovering in the particular case what are the available means of persuasion.'[41]

Basing their work on close observation of successful advocates, Aristotle, Cicero and Quintilian examined stylistic strategies in exhaustive detail. In doing so, they emphasized practical, experience-based methods for achieving rhetorical success. As Quintilian observed:

> [I]t is on [style] that teachers of rhetoric concentrate their attention, since it cannot possibly be acquired without the assistance of the rules of art: it is this which is the *chief object of our study*, the goal of all our exercises and all our efforts at imitation, and it is to this that we devote the energies of a lifetime; it is this that makes one orator surpass his rivals, this that makes one style of speaking preferable to another.[42]

As has already been noted, they connected style to all three modes of persuasion: arguments based on logic, arguments based on emotion, and arguments based on the advocate's character or credibility.[43] According to them, successful advocacy depends on a careful mix of all three modes, each complementing the others. In their view, the logical integrity of an argument will be seriously damaged if advocates lack credibility or fail to control the emotional cross-currents of the case. Good advocates employ all three modes simultaneously. Bad advocates forget to.

As the following analysis shows, Justice Scalia falls midway between the two. He is an intelligent, resourceful, but frequently heavy-handed, stylist.[44] He supports his arguments using a full complement of rhetorical tools. He carefully exploits various organizational strategies and relies heavily on all the classically-recommended rhetorical devices: metaphor, simile, antithesis, irony, hyperbole, and rhetorical question. But occasional stylistic miscalculations cause him to damage his own arguments.

More importantly, he frequently damages his *ethos* with inexplicable lapses of rhetorical judgment. In the process he creates a peevish, disagreeable judicial *persona* who is simultaneously indifferent and hostile to the emotional cross-currents of the case. His unconcealed disdain for those who disagree with him makes him seem arrogant. He questions his colleagues' motives and the Court's procedures in intemperate ways, thereby contributing still further to an unflattering picture of himself. All of this combines to further damage his legal arguments.

UNITED STATES V. VIRGINIA: THE MAJORITY OPINION

The target of Justice Scalia's dissent is the majority opinion, which addressed two questions. First, the majority asked whether 'Virginia's exclusion of women from the educational opportunities provided by VMI' denies women the equal protection of the laws guaranteed by the Fourteenth Amendment.[45] Second, it asked whether 'VMI's 'unique' situation – as Virginia's sole single-sex public institution of higher education – offends the Constitution's equal protection principle ...'[46]

Relying on its previous decisions in *J.E.B. v. Alabama ex rel. T.B.*[47] and *Mississippi University for Women v. Hogan*,[48] the Court required '[p]arties who seek to defend gender-based government action [to] demonstrate an *'exceedingly persuasive justification'* for that action.'[49] This justification must show 'that the [challenged] classification serves 'important governmental objectives and that the discriminatory means employed' are 'substantially related to the achievement of those objectives.'[50] While noting that inherent differences between the sexes may justify sex classifications in some cases, the Court added that 'such classifications may not be used ... to create or perpetuate the legal, social, and economic inferiority of women.'[51]

The Court rejected both of the State of Virginia's justifications for VMI's male-only admission policy. The state had asserted: (1) that 'single-sex education provides important educational benefits' and 'contributes to diversity of educational approaches;' and (2) that the unique VMI method of character development and leadership training' – the school's 'adversative' approach – would have to be modified were VMI to admit women.[52] After examining VMI's past and recent history, the Court found that VMI was not created or maintained to promote 'diversifying ... educational opportunities within the Commonwealth.'[53]

As for the State of Virginia's second argument – 'that VMI's adversative method of training provides educational benefits that cannot be made available, unmodified, to women'[54] – the Court noted that similar rationales had been offered in the past to deny women educational opportunities in law, medicine, law enforcement, and federal military academies.[55] The Court concluded that some women are as able as men to meet the challenge of VMI's 'adversative' educational method, and that VMI's goal of producing 'citizen-soldier[s]' is 'great enough to accommodate women.'[56]

The Court also rejected the state's remedial plan, finding that Virginia 'chose not to eliminate, but to leave untouched, VMI's exclusionary policy' and, instead, 'proposed a separate program, different in kind from VMI and unequal in tangible and intangible facilities,' thereby failing to meet its obligation to 'eliminate [so far as possible] the discriminatory effects of the past' and to 'bar like discrimination in the future.'[57]

At great length, the Court criticized the state's proposal to establish Virginia Women's Institute for Leadership (VWIL), a four-year, state-sponsored undergraduate program located at Mary Baldwin College, a private liberal arts school for women.[58] It found that 'VWIL's student body, faculty, course offerings, and facilities hardly match VMI's. Nor can the VWIL graduate anticipate the benefits associated with VMI's 157-year history, the school's prestige, and its influential alumni network.'[59] The Court concluded that 'Virginia's remedy affords no cure at all for the opportunities and advantages withheld from women who want a VMI education and can make the grade,' and that 'the Commonwealth has shown no 'exceedingly persuasive justification' for withholding from women qualified for the experience premier training of the kind VMI affords.'[60]

JUSTICE SCALIA'S DISSENT

In dissent, Justice Scalia asserts that there are numerous flaws in the Court's decision. According to him, the Court mistakenly removed decisions regarding the educational process from the democratic process, 'inscrib[ed]' them into the U.S. Constitution,[61] and rejected a 'long tradition of open, widespread, and unchallenged use [of male-only admissions to VMI] that dates back to the beginning of the Republic.'[62] He further claims that the Court 'contradict[ed]'[63] and abandoned the previously employed intermediate scrutiny standard in sex-classification case[64] and applied instead an 'amorphous 'exceedingly persuasive justification'[65] standard that 'amounts to (at least) strict scrutiny.'[66]

As for the state's argument that VMI's male-only policy supports the state's interest in promoting educational diversity, Justice Scalia asserts that the record contained a 'substantial body of contemporary scholarship and research [that] supports the proposition that, although males and females have significant areas of developmental overlap, they also have differing developmental needs that are deep-seated.'[67] He adds that VMI, like all other self-interested and autonomous colleges in Virginia, unavoidably contributes to the diversity of educational opportunities in the state.[68]

When addressing the state's argument that admitting women to VMI would fundamentally alter its 'adversative' training method, Justice Scalia claims that the Court rejected ample evidence supporting that view.[69] He concludes his criticism by asserting that the state's proposed remedy – establishment of VWIL, a four-year, state-sponsored undergraduate program located at Mary Baldwin College – would adequately solve the problem.[70] He also asserts that concurring Justice Rehnquist wrongly rejected the state's 'diversity' arguments. According to Scalia, VMI's 'adversative' educational method serves an important governmental objective.[71]

Having criticized the reasoning of both the majority opinion and the concurrence, Scalia devotes the last few pages of his dissent to speculating about the consequences of the Court's decision. He is convinced that it 'ensures that single-sex public education is functionally dead,'[72] because no single-sex public institution will be able to provide the Court's 'exceedingly persuasive justification.'[73] Not only that, but '[t]he potential of today's decision for widespread disruption of existing institutions lies in its application to private single-sex education.'[74] He also suggests that the Court's majority was unprincipled in ignoring the Court's own precedents and in self-righteously imposing 'its own favored social and economic dispositions nationwide.'[75]

While this summary of the logical grounds (or *logos*) of Justice Scalia's dissent identifies his main arguments, it falls far short of capturing the tone and spirit of that dissent. Scalia's main arguments are hardly novel – judicial encroachment on democratic processes, failure to honor traditional practices, inexplicable and unclear shifts in the standard of review, and refusal to properly weigh the evidentiary record. All are commonplace criticisms frequently levied by Court critics. What is novel, or at least distinctive, are the rhetorical strategies that Justice Scalia employs to make his points.

A. Pathos, Organizational Strategy and Style

Even a casual examination of Justice Scalia's dissent reveals that he feels passionately about the case. His opening lines excoriate the Court for a multitude of errors. By beginning in this highly emotional fashion, Scalia is following a well-established rhetorical practice approved of by Aristotle, Cicero, and Quintilian, all of whom carefully documented the most effective modes of legal argument. As was seen in Chapter Three, they divided legal arguments into five parts: introduction (*exordium*), statement of the case (*narratio*), argument summary (*partitio*), proof of the case (*confirmatio*) and conclusion (*peroratio*).[76] Each part has a specific rhetorical function to fulfill.

– Exordium

According to Aristotle the purpose of the *exordium*, or introduction, is to make the 'audience receptive.'[77] He and the other rhetoricians knew that logic alone is not enough to make audiences receptive. Good advocates must also ensure that their audiences are emotionally engaged and they must do so at the beginning of their arguments. Cicero, for example, stressed that it is 'essential that [the *exordium*] should have the power of being able to exert ... influence in stirring the minds of the audience ... [because it has] a very great effect in persuading and arousing emotion ...'[78] Like many other rhetoricians, Cicero was convinced that 'men decide far more problems by hate, or love, or lust, or rage, or sorrow, or joy, or hope, or fear, or illusion, or some other inward emotion, than by reality, or authority, or any legal standard, or judicial precedent, or statute.'[79]

Quintilian too thought that the *exordium* exercised a 'valuable influence in winning the judge [or audience] to regard us with favor.'[80] As he noted, 'emotional appeals are concerned with moving the audience and, although they may be employed throughout the case, [they] are most effective at the beginning and end.'[81]

Justice Scalia certainly recognizes the importance of a strong and emotional opening. With the aggrieved cadences of his opening paragraph he attempts to stir up emotions and a sense of outrage in his audience:

> Today the Court *shuts down* an institution that has served the people of the Commonwealth of Virginia with pride and distinction for over a century and a half. To achieve that desired result, *it rejects* (contrary to our established practice) *the factual findings ... sweeps aside the precedents* of this Court, and *ignores the history* of our people. *As to facts:* It explicitly *rejects* the finding that there exist 'gender-based developmental differences' supporting Virginia's restriction of the 'adversative' method to only a men's institution, and the finding that the all-male

composition of the Virginia Military Institute (VMI) is essential to that institution's character. *As to precedent:* It drastically revises our established standards for reviewing sex-based classifications. And *as to history*: It counts for nothing the long tradition, enduring down to the present, of men's military colleges supported by both States and the Federal Government.[82]

With this introduction, Justice Scalia identifies his main argumentative themes in language designed to touch readers emotionally. Couching his argument in absolute terms, he claims that the Court's decision will 'shut down' a venerable institution, that it 'rejects' findings, 'sweeps aside' precedents, and 'counts for nothing' the long tradition of men's military colleges. These particular verb choices suggest that Justice Scalia is writing as an emotionally invested advocate – not as an objective, disinterested Justice of the U.S. Supreme Court. The magnitude of Justice Scalia's emotional interest in this case becomes even clearer when the *VMI* opening is compared with those in some of his other dissents. In those cases his language is very low-key, technical and disinterested because he is not trying to create an emotional response.[83]

– Partitio

Not only does the opening paragraph help set the emotional tone of the dissent, it also concisely identifies Scalia's main reasons for dissenting. This, too, follows a classically-approved practice called *partitio*. As was shown in Chapter Three, the purpose of the *partitio* is to 'set ... forth, briefly and completely, the points we intend to discuss.'[84] More than that, however, the *partitio* is designed, according to Quintilian:

> [to add] to the lucidity and grace of our speech. For it not only makes our arguments clearer by *isolating the points from the crowd in which they would otherwise be lost* and placing them before the eyes of the judge [or audience], but relieves his attention by assigning a definite limit to certain parts of our speech, just as our fatigue upon a journey is relieved by reading the distances on the milestones which we pass.[85]

That is, although good advocates must keep the audience's needs in mind at every stage of their argument, they must be especially mindful of how they begin. An audience's emotional receptivity to an argument is affected not only by the advocate's word choice, but also by the complexity and duration of the argument.

A properly constructed *partitio* reassures the audience that the forthcoming arguments will be easy to understand and of a manageable length. Scalia's opening paragraph meets the classical criteria of making the scope of his arguments clear from the outset and attempting favorably to dispose the audience to those arguments. To do so, he simply identifies his three main lines of argument – arguments based on facts, arguments based on precedent, and arguments based on history.[86]

– Parallel Structure

In his *exordium*, Scalia relies heavily on still another classically-approved rhetorical device: parallel structure. As was previously explained, classical rhetoricians thought parallelism, or *similitudo*, was especially suitable for arousing the audience's emotions and maintaining its interest.

Parallelism, like other rhetorical devices, helps make arguments felt as well as understood. Its purpose is 'to attract the attention of the audience and ... not allow it to flag, rousing it from time to time.'[87] For classical rhetoricians, sentence-level stylistic techniques are rarely employed for purposes of mere embellishment. Instead, they are carefully chosen to clarify or vivify an argument. According to Quintilian, one way to emphasize an argument is to begin or end sentences with the same word. Like other rhetoricians discussing style, he gives detailed instructions. He suggests that for maximum effect 'a number of clauses may begin with the same word *for the sake of force* and emphasis,' or that they 'may end with the same words.'[88]

For the 'sake of force,' Scalia itemizes his main arguments using a number of 'as to' phrases. He claims the Court is wrong '[a]s to facts,' '[a]s to precedent,' and 'as to history.'[89] His substantive points are that the Court rejected well-documented evidence (facts), revised well-established standards of review (precedent), and ignored time-honored traditions (history).[90] The conjunctive 'as to' phrases achieve their emotional force by accretion, each one adding to Justice Scalia's indictment of the majority opinion. The parallel phrases help him sustain emotional momentum and have the added virtue of acting as coherence devices that help unify his argument and make it more comprehensible.

The 'as to' phrases in Scalia's *exordium* adhere very closely to the *Rhetorica ad Herennium's* suggestions regarding 'detailed parallels':

> A Comparison [can] be used for vividness, and be set forth in the form of a detailed parallel ... This Comparison, by embellishing both terms, bringing into relation by a method of *parallel description* ... set[s] the subject vividly before the eyes of all. Moreover the Comparison is presented in the form of a *detailed parallel* because, once the similitude has been set up, all like elements are related.[91]

In sum, Scalia's vocabulary, sentence structures, and organizational strategies place his opening paragraph firmly within the classical tradition of *exordia*. It not only provides readers with a clear picture of the forthcoming substantive arguments, but also sets the emotional tone for those arguments.

When this paragraph is contrasted with the comparatively colorless opening paragraph of the majority opinion, the emotional content of Justice Scalia's opening paragraph comes into even sharper relief. Justice Ginsburg's opening paragraph consists of three simple, dry, declarative sentences, none of them particularly memorable:

> Virginia's public institutions of higher learning include an incomparable military college, Virginia Military Institute (VMI). The United States maintains that the Constitution's equal protection guarantee precludes Virginia from reserving exclusively to men the unique educational opportunities VMI affords. We agree.[92]

Justice Ginsburg's business-like opening is a scrupulously 'neutral, detached, objective, and impersonal' statement of the Court's decision.[93] It contains none of the rhetorical flourishes or distinction of Scalia's opening. It makes no attempt to engage the reader's emotions. It is not an '*exordium*' in the classical sense.

– Peroration

Important as the *exordium* is in rhetorical theory, classical rhetoricians thought the conclusion, or *peroratio*, was even more important. Coming as it does at the end of the trial, it gives advocates their last chance to make an emotional appeal. Aristotle thought it should 'put the audience into the right state of emotion' and should 'make the audience feel the right emotions – pity, indignation, anger, hatred, envy, emulation, antagonism.'[94] Quintilian agreed and observed that '[t]he peroration is the most important part of forensic pleading, and in the main consists of appeals to the emotions.'[95] He too emphasized that '[t]he peroration provides freer opportunities for exciting the passions of jealousy, hatred or anger.'[96] Quintilian insisted that the opening *exordium* and the closing *peroratio* must be carefully coordinated:

> [I]n our opening any preliminary appeal to the compassion of the judge [or audience] must be made sparingly and with restraint, while in the peroration we may give full rein to our emotions, place fictitious speeches in the mouths of our characters, *call the dead to life*, and produce the wife or children of the accused in court, practices which are less usual in *exordia*.[97]

As Justice Scalia completes his dissent, his peroration follows the classical pattern. It is even more emotional than his *exordium*. He does not quite 'call the dead to life,' but he does claim that VMI's 'attachment to such old-fashioned concepts as 'manly honor' has made it a target for those who want to abolish public single-sex education.[98] To illustrate what will be lost by that abolition, he invokes VMI's 'The Code of a Gentleman':

> Without a strict observance of the fundamental Code of Honor, no man, no matter how 'polished,' can be considered a *gentleman*. The honor of a *gentleman* demands the inviolability of his word, and the incorruptibility of his principles. He is the descendant of the *knight*, the *crusader*; he is the defender of the defenseless and the champion of justice ... or he is not a *Gentleman*.[99]

He further illustrates his point by quoting the Code's list of 'gentlemanly' virtues, many of which describe how gentlemen should behave toward women. As 'descendants'of knights and crusaders, gentlemen do not gossip about their girlfriends, visit them when they are drunk, call out to them in the street, discuss their 'merits or demerits,' or 'lay a finger' on them.[100] By invoking the image of knights errant and religious crusaders, Scalia is obviously playing on readers' emotions.[101] He wants them to become indignant over the pending destruction of an institution that instills a sense of 'manly honor.'[102]

By relying on classical emotion-generating techniques, Justice Scalia has strengthened his opening and closing paragraphs. In doing so, he employs all three modes of persuasion, but especially *pathos*. While, from a rhetorical perspective, the *exordium* and *peroratio* contribute greatly to the emotional impact of his dissent, they are but two of the many locations where he uses classically-approved rhetorical strategies to reinforce his arguments.

– Forensic Style

Attentive as he is to matters of organization, Scalia devotes even more attention to sentence-level rhetorical techniques. Like his classical predecessors, he knows that style is critical to his success. As was seen in Chapters Five and Six, classical rhetoricians valued stylistic virtuosity as much or more than any other skill. Beginning with Aristotle they emphasized that knowing which arguments to make was not sufficient. The manner of making them was equally important.[103]

Quintilian insisted that 'oratory in which there is no guile fights by sheer weight and impetus alone.'[104] By 'guile,' Quintilian meant an advocate's use of all available stylistic resources. He also observed that 'although it may seem that proof is infinitesimally affected by the figures employed, none the less [sic] those same figures lend credibility to our arguments and steal their way secretly into the minds of the judges.'[105] As the following analysis demonstrates, no single rhetorical figure or device accounts for the rhetorical impact of Justice Scalia's dissent. Instead, these devices have a cumulative effect. By increments they 'steal their way secretly' into the audience's mind and affect its response to his arguments.

– Metaphors and Similes

From a classical perspective, one of the most important stylistic devices was the well-chosen metaphor.[106] Recognizing that all language is inherently figurative, classical rhetoricians regarded metaphors, similes, and other figurative devices as both figures of thought and figures of speech.[107] Regarding metaphors, Aristotle observed that 'we may start from the principle that we all take a natural pleasure in learning easily; so, since words stand for things, those words are most pleasing that give us *fresh knowledge* ... Accordingly, it is *metaphor* that is in the highest degree *instructive* and *pleasing*.'[108] Both Cicero and Quintilian also recognized that metaphors, and to a lesser degree similes, emotionally engage readers even while instructing them.[109] As Quintilian put it 'rhetorical ornament[s] contribute not a little to the furtherance of our case ... For when our audience find[s] it a pleasure to listen, their attention and their readiness to believe what they hear are both alike increased.'[110]

In his dissent, Justice Scalia repeatedly uses metaphors, similes, and other rhetorical devices to reinforce and clarify his arguments. For example, when criticizing the Court's conclusion that an autonomous university like VMI could not contribute to Virginia's state-wide diversity goals, Scalia observes that '[i]f it were impossible for individual human beings (or groups of human beings) to act autonomously in effective pursuit of a common goal, the game of soccer would not exist.'[111] As for Justice

Rehnquist's demand for more evidence that VMI contributes to state-wide educational diversity, Scalia says that his demand 'is rather like making crucial to the lawfulness of the United States Army record 'evidence' that its purpose is to do battle.'[112] The physicality and quasi-martial tone of Scalia's soccer and army comparisons subtly reinforce his argument that VMI's all-male military environment makes substantial 'diversity contributions' to the state.[113]

These particular examples also illustrate the condescending, mocking tone that Scalia uses throughout his dissent. Elsewhere, he uses a variety of metaphors and similes to accuse the Court of cheating ('load[ing] the dice'),[114] child's play ('Supreme Court peek-a-boo'),[115] amateurism ('do-it-yourself ... factfinding'),[116] bait-and-switch tactics ('ad-hocery'),[117] and criminal activity ('politics-smuggled-into-law').[118] Although these and other rhetorical figures contribute somewhat to Scalia's substantive arguments, they are more important for the way they incrementally, and almost unnoticeably, increase the emotional intensity of his arguments. They help keep readers emotionally engaged.

– Parallelism

Although Scalia favors metaphors and similes, he also uses other, less noticeable, devices. Parallelism, for instance, which played such an important part in his *exordium*, frequently appears when Justice Scalia wants to increase the emotional impact of his argument.

He uses it to emphasize the Court's erroneous conclusion that the State of Virginia did not provide an 'exceedingly persuasive justification' for VMI's male-only admission policy.[119] Relying on a series of parallel predicate phrases, he claims the Court's conclusion 'can only be achieved ... if there are some women *interested in attending* VMI, *capable of undertaking* its activities, and *able to meet* its physical demands.'[120] Each of these phrases isolates a substantive point for separate consideration while simultaneously increasing the emotional impact of the sentence as a whole.

Elsewhere, he asserts that if VMI tailors its educational objectives to meet the Court's requirements, it will always be vulnerable to an Equal Protection violation 'no matter' what it does:

> [I]f it restricts to men even one means by which it pursues that objective – *no matter how* few women are interested in pursuing the objective by that means, *no matter how* much the single-sex program will have to be changed if both sexes are admitted, and *no matter how* beneficial that program has theretofore been to its participants.[121]

The parallel 'no matter how' phrases punctuate and gradually increase the emotional impact of the sentence by itemizing each of Justice Scalia's substantive points. He uses the phrasal cadences produced by parallelism to intensify and provide coherence to his arguments.

– Antithesis

As was pointed out earlier, classical rhetoricians saw strong connections between parallelism and another syntactical device: antithesis. Aristotle was especially fond of antithesis as a method for making arguments *felt*, as well as understood, stating that:

> When the style is ... antithetical, in each of the two members ... an opposite is balanced by an opposite ... 'By nature citizens, by law bereft of their city'. ... This kind of style is pleasing, because things are best known by opposition, and are all the better known when the opposites are put side by side; and is pleasing also because of its resemblance to logic – for the method of refutation ... is the juxtaposition of contrary conclusions.[122]

Aristotle, like other rhetoricians, thought that juxtaposing contrasting ideas brought them into sharper relief, thereby making them more comprehensible.[123] Not only that, antithesis brings with it an aesthetic pleasure that redounds to the credit of the advocate. Aristotle also valued antithesis for its concision: '[T]he more concise and antithetical the saying, the better it pleases, for the reason that, by the contrast, one learns the more, and, by the conciseness, learns with the greater speed.'[124]

At critical junctures in his dissent, Scalia employs antithesis, often in parallel form, for rhetorical effect. When criticizing Justice Rehnquist's concurrence, for example, he uses antithesis to assert that Rehnquist's concurrence 'finds VMI unconstitutional on a basis that is *more moderate* than the Court's but only at the expense of being even *more implausible*.'[125] With parallel phrases, Scalia grudgingly concedes that Rehnquist's concurrence is 'more moderate' than the majority opinion, but then immediately withdraws that concession by claiming it is 'more implausible.'[126] With one phrase he offers a compliment, with the other he takes it back.

Elsewhere, he uses antithesis to repeat his accusation that the Court applies its Equal Protection standards inconsistently: 'The only hope for state-assisted single-sex private schools is that the Court will not apply in the future the principles of law it has applied today. That is a substantial hope, I am *happy* and *ashamed* to say.'[127] That is, he is happy that the Court will not apply the legal principles, but ashamed at the Court's inconsistency. The antithetical elements in both these examples sharply juxtapose Scalia's substantive points with the concision and wit that classical rhetoricians considered persuasive.

– Rhetorical Questions

One of Justice Scalia's favorite figurative devices is the rhetorical question. Here, too, he uses a stylistic device favored by classical rhetoricians like Quintilian, who thought that rhetorical questions 'serve to increase the force and cogency of proof.'[128] Quintilian listed and then subdivided rhetorical questions into several categories: those that emphasize a point, those that criticize a person, those that embarrass others, those that reflect indignation, and those that express wonder.[129] Rhetorical questions are linked to and support emotional arguments. They are also designed to provoke thought. More than half of Quintilian's list is devoted to emotion-inducing questions that 'embarrass,' 'reflect indignation,' and 'express wonder.'[130]

As part of Justice Scalia's on-going criticism of the Court's decision, he regularly asks rhetorical questions that 'reflect [his] indignation.' He also uses them to embarrass his adversaries. For example, he links patriotism to his criticism of the Court's failure to understand that VMI's educational 'mission' is the same as all other colleges.[131] He asks '[w]hich of [the other colleges] would the Old Dominion continue to fund if they did not aim to create individuals 'imbued with love of learning, etc.,' right down to being ready 'to defend their country in time of national peril'?[132] The implication is that the Court is acting unpatriotically. Elsewhere, he uses a rhetorical question to criticize Justice Rehnquist for failing to see that VMI's 'mission' is related to the State of Virginia's diversity goals: 'What other purpose would the Commonwealth have?'[133]

Near the end of his dissent, Justice Scalia uses a pair of rhetorical questions to criticize the Court's inconsistency when applying legal principles: 'After all, did not the Court today abandon the principles of law it has applied in our earlier sex-classification cases? And does not the Court positively invite private colleges to rely upon our ad-hocery by assuring them this [case] is 'unique'?[134] While Scalia's 'ad-hocery' coinage may unnecessarily call attention to itself, it also reflects his indignation at the Court's failure to follow its own legal principles. As with his other rhetorical ploys, Justice Scalia's rhetorical questions help him maintain a high level of emotional intensity. By asking these questions in a tone of mock-confusion, he provokes thought while simultaneously rebuking the Court for its unsettling inconsistency.

As he links the emotional cross-currents of the case with the logical content of his arguments, Justice Scalia demonstrates considerable stylistic sophistication. He uses a variety of rhetorical techniques to attract and maintain his readers' attention and to engage their emotions. In doing so, he does not rely solely on those transparently provocative words and phrases that attract so much public attention. Instead, for the most part, he uses subtle, but classically endorsed, rhetorical strategies.

To create a sympathetic climate for his arguments, he deliberately modulates the emotional content of his opening (*exordium*) and closing paragraphs (*peroratio*). He places metaphors and similes at critical junctures and carefully calibrates their emotional impact. Always alert for a good rhetorical opportunity, he uses a variety of sentence-level devices, including parallelism, antithesis, and rhetorical questions, to control the emotional content of his arguments.

As a result, Scalia's emotional posture changes rapidly. By turns, he is angry, outraged, dismayed, indignant, and ashamed. He concludes in a mood of regret. In short, he plays on the audience's emotions in ways that are recommended by classical rhetoricians from Aristotle to Quintilian. Like any good advocate, he deliberately stirs up emotions in the hope that they will make his audience more receptive to his arguments. In the main, he succeeds, at least on the level of recognizing and exploiting the emotional content of the case.

B. Ethos and Argument

Unfortunately for Justice Scalia, he is less successful in establishing himself as an attractive and trustworthy advocate. As the preceding chapters show, an advocate's *ethos* is just as important to rhetorical success as the other two modes of persuasion. Aristotle insisted that:

> [T]he speaker must not merely see to it that his [argument] ... shall be convincing and persuasive, but he must ... give the right impression of himself ... This is true above all in deliberative speaking ...; for in conducing to persuasion it is highly important that the speaker should evince a certain character, and that the judges should conceive him to be disposed towards them in a certain way ...[135]

Advocates can create a good impression, according to Aristotle, by several means: '[T]here are three things that gain our belief, namely, intelligence, character, and good will.'[136] Aristotle also pointed out that the emotional content of an argument is unavoidably connected to an advocate's *ethos*: '[Y]ou may use each and all of these means [of emotional arguments] ... with a view to making your audience receptive, and withal give an impression of yourself as a good and just man, for good character always commands more attention.'[137]

Like Aristotle, Cicero was convinced that an advocate's *ethos* played a critical part in the success of his arguments. While Cicero agrees with Aristotle that projecting intelligence and good character are important, he focuses on other qualities as well:

> [A]ttributes useful in an advocate are a *mild tone*, a *countenance expressive of modesty, gentle language* ... It is very helpful to display the tokens of *good-nature*, kindness, calmness, *loyalty* and a disposition that is pleasing ... and all the qualities belonging to men who are upright, unassuming and *not* given to *haste, stubbornness, strife or harshness* ...[138]

Cicero repeatedly emphasizes that good advocacy depends on a low-key approach, demonstrating the advocate's good nature, calmness, and loyalty. Elsewhere, he connects these attributes to rhetorical style by observing that 'by means of particular types of thought and diction, and the employment besides of a delivery that is unruffled and eloquent of good-nature, the speaker ... [is] made to appear upright, well-bred and virtuous.'[139]

However, as one of the most successful advocates of his day, Cicero was well aware that advocates must sometimes address audiences 'in quite another way, [which] excites and urges the feelings of the tribunal towards hatred or love, ill-will or well-wishing, fear or hope, desire or aversion.'[140] That is, depending on the audience, advocates may need to abandon the low-key approach in favor of a more aggressive, confrontational stance.

Like the others, Quintilian too sees a close connection between *pathos* and *ethos*. In some senses, '*pathos* and *ethos* are sometimes of the same nature ...'[141] He adds that 'sometimes however they differ, a distinction which is important for the peroration, since *ethos* is *generally employed to calm the storm* aroused by *pathos.*[142] For him, the pacifying power of an advocate's calm good-nature cannot be overstated.

Quintilian also insists that advocates avoid 'the impression that [they] are abusive, malignant, proud or slanderous toward any individual or body of men, especially such as cannot be hurt without exciting the disapproval of the judge [or audience].'[143] Above all, Quintilian regarded rhetoric as the art of a good man speaking:

> Finally *ethos* in all its forms requires the speaker to be a man of good character and courtesy. For it is most important that he should himself possess or be thought to possess those virtues for the possession of which it is his duty, if possible, to commend his client as well, while the excellence of his own character will make his pleading all the more convincing and will be of the utmost service to the cases which he undertakes.[144]

As the foregoing observations illustrate, classical rhetoricians had a finely-honed understanding of how an advocate's character and demeanor affect an audience's response to arguments. Intelligence is important, of course, but other characteristics – good will, modesty, calmness, and loyalty – are more important. Without these qualities an advocate cannot control the emotions triggered by the *pathos* of the case.

Finally, to avoid exciting the disapproval of their audiences, they insist that advocates must not appear abusive, malignant, or hot-tempered. Their advice regarding civility is echoed in VMI's 'The Code of the Gentleman,' which insists that a gentleman '[d]oes not lose his temper; nor exhibit anger, fear, hate, embarrassment, ardor or hilarity *in public.*'[145]

Justice Scalia professedly admires the Code, but seems to have forgotten this particular rule while writing his dissent. Although his dissents take place in a very 'public' forum, he nevertheless 'exhibits' anger, ardor, and hilarity, thereby departing not only from the Greco-Roman standard, but also from VMI's 'Code of the Gentleman.'

Because Justice Scalia miscalculates the negative impact of his rhetorical choices, he damages his *ethos*, and ultimately his legal argument, in several ways. In part this damage arises from an over-artful writing style, hyperbolic legal and factual claims, and ill-advised sarcasm.

– 'Artificial' Words

Of the three, Scalia's over-artful writing style is the easiest to notice. It is also the stylistic feature that attracts the most critical attention.[146] According to classical rhetoricians, word choices, like other aspects of rhetoric, reveal the true character of the advocate. The hallmark of good advocacy was clarity and a good sense of propriety:

> Clearness results above all from *propriety* in the use of words. But *propriety* is capable of more than one interpretation. In its primary sense it means calling things by their right names, and is consequently sometimes to be avoided, for our *language must not be obscene, unseemly, or mean.* Language may be described as *mean* when it is *beneath the dignity of the subject or the rank of the orator.*[147]

Classical rhetoricians admired a simple style and were skeptical of any stylistic mannerism that called attention to itself. Aristotle says that '*[n]aturalness* is persuasive, artifice is just the reverse. People *grow suspicious of an artificial speaker*, and think he has designs upon them.'[148] He was especially suspicious of 'rare words, compound words, and coined words' and insisted that they be 'sparingly used.'[149] Quintilian observed that:

> [T]hose words are best which are least far-fetched and give the impression of simplicity and reality. For those words which are obviously the result of *careful search* and even seem to parade their *self-conscious art*, fail to attain the grace at which they aim and lose all appearance of sincerity ...[150]

Several of Justice Scalia's words and phrases obviously fall in the category of 'artificial.' Some of them are 'beneath the dignity of the subject' and the 'rank of the orator.' Among the more noticeable ones are: 'ad-hocery,'[151] 'do-it-yourself ... factfinding,'[152] and 'Supreme Court peek-a-boo.'[153] These coinages, along with other words and phrases, are obviously the result of 'careful search.' According to both Aristotle and Quintilian this makes audiences suspicious of their author's sincerity.

While Scalia's 'self-conscious' word choices usually call attention to themselves, they do the least damage to his *ethos*. Because they are so obviously biased, readers are forearmed against them. Even so, because so many of Scalia's coinages are also slangy and colloquial, they seem to reflect a certain disdain for the Court's deliberative processes.

Justice Scalia employs a slangy vocabulary throughout his dissent. When criticizing the Court's imprecise and unclear standards of review he asserts, '[w]e have no established criterion for 'intermediate scrutiny' either, but essentially apply it when it seems like a good idea to *load the dice*.'[154] He again uses slang when claiming that 'the Court creates the illusion that government officials ... will have a *clear shot* at justifying some sort of single-sex public education.'[155] Like Scalia's patently 'artificial' words and phrases, these colloquialisms call as much attention to themselves as they do to his arguments and for that reason are rhetorically suspect.[156] Taken as a whole, Scalia's conversational, slangy diction lacks the 'propriety' befitting the dignity of the court. Any lawyer who used such language in a brief or in oral argument would undoubtedly alienate his audience, in part because it appears to be gratuitous and unprofessional.

Justice Scalia, however, is far too skilled a rhetorician to rely solely on such transparently biased phraseology. In fact, many of his word choices convey a bias so subtle that it is likely to escape the audience's notice.

His repeated use of the verb 'enshrine,' with all its religious connotations, falls into this category. At several different points in his dissent, he uses it to mock the Court's decision. First, he claims that the Court '*enshrines* the notion that no substantial educational value is to be served by an all-men's military academy.'[157] He then faults the Court for mistakenly assuming that VMI's 1839 educational policy 'had been *enshrined* and remained *enshrined* ... to keep women in their place.'[158] Finally, he asserts that '[t]he enemies of single-sex education have won; ... their view of the world is *enshrined* in the Constitution.'[159] By relying on the verb's religious connotations, Scalia subtly emphasizes his claim that the wrong ideas have been 'enshrined' but does so in a way that focuses on his ideas, not on his word choices or himself. Had Scalia relied more heavily on subtleties of this sort, his vocabulary would have attracted less attention and fewer suspicions of judicial partisanship. It would also have preserved the proper judicial *ethos*.

– Hyperbole

Justice Scalia also compromises his judicial *ethos* with his noticeable penchant for hyperbole. Although his substantive concerns may be justified, he overstates them in ways that make audiences suspicious.

Both Aristotle and Quintilian think hyperbole, in moderation, is useful. They also think that it provides clear insights into an advocate's character. Aristotle cautiously approved of its use to add liveliness to arguments, but, he noted, '[h]yperboles are characteristic of youngsters; they betray vehemence. And so they are used, above all, by men in an angry passion.'[160] Quintilian too thinks hyperbole is sometimes useful, but he also includes it among the 'causes of the decline of oratory.'[161] He says that misuse of hyperbole arises from a failure to observe a sense of proportion: 'We must therefore be all the more careful to consider how far we may go in exaggerating facts which our audience may refuse to believe.'[162]

Justice Scalia employs hyperbole at several critical junctures in his dissent, the most important being his opening paragraph or *exordium*.[163] In that paragraph, he exaggerates the impact the Court's decision will have, and the processes whereby it reached that decision.[164] Despite Justice Scalia's dire predictions, the Court's decision did not 'shut down' VMI, it did not 'reject' all the lower courts' findings, nor did it 'sweep aside its precedents' or 'ignore history.' Instead, the Court simply reached a result with which Scalia disagreed.

While the hyperbole in Scalia's *exordium* may be rhetorically justifiable as he attempts to engage the interest and emotions of the audience, his use of it elsewhere is less defensible. Frequently, his exaggerations seem to reflect the 'vehemence' and 'anger' that Aristotle and others found damaging to an advocate's *ethos*.[165] For example, at various points in his argument, Scalia accuses the Court of feeling 'free to evaluate everything under the sun by applying one of three tests,'[166] of varying its standard of review 'whenever [it] feel[s] like it,'[167] and of 'destroy [ing] VMI.'[168] Of these three examples, the first two are the most damaging to Scalia's *ethos*. With them, he impugns the very Court processes he and the other justices are sworn to uphold and, in doing so, violates the classical admonition that advocates avoid being 'abusive' or 'slanderous toward any ... body of men ...'[169] To suggest that his colleagues are unprincipled, instead of just mistaken, exceeds the bounds of stylistic and judicial propriety.

– Irony

From the standpoint of *ethos*, the most corrosive rhetorical device Scalia employs is irony. In a variety of ways, he uses irony in ways that reveal not just his disagreements with the Court's decision, but also his contempt for the Court as an institution and the reasoning and motives of his colleagues. Throughout his dissent, Scalia's ironical asides provide a persistently ill-natured running commentary on the workings of the Court.

Classical rhetoricians admired irony as a rhetorical device primarily because of its ability to engage the audience's interest. They thought that by inviting audiences to 'understand something which is the opposite of what is actually said' advocates require them to become active listeners.[170]

However, as Aristotle pointed out, irony frequently 'implies contempt' for its target and therefore it must be used carefully.[171] Moreover, while Aristotle observed that irony 'befit[s] a gentleman,' he warns that, to be most effective, '[t]he jests of the ironical man [should be] at his *own* expense,' not at the expense of others.[172]

Quintilian distinguished several different types of irony, each depending on an advocate's purposes. For example, advocates can pretend to be lost in wonder at the wisdom of others, pretend to own faults they do not have, or pretend to grant to opponents qualities they do not have, etc.[173] Justice Scalia employs these and other types of irony, but does so in such a sarcastic, *ethos*-damaging way that it undermines his arguments.

That said, not all of Scalia's irony has a harsh, *ethos*-damaging tone. Some of it is quite mild and ingratiating. For example, he justifies his dissent by observing that '[s]ince it is entirely clear that the Constitution of the United States – *the old one* – takes no sides in this educational debate, I dissent.'[174] Elsewhere, he feigns confusion about how to answer his own rhetorical question concerning why Virginia should be blamed for treating VMI just as it does other public schools. He says '[t]his is a *great puzzlement*.'[175] He also subtly mocks the Court's perceptions of 'VMI [as] a uniquely prestigious all-male institution, *conceived in chauvinism*, etc.'[176] Tempered in tone and understated, these ironical asides would have little damaging effect on Scalia's *ethos* were it not for the fact that they are coupled with harsher, more intemperate instances in which his irony descends into mere sarcasm.

For example, when accusing the Court of misleadingly describing its previous sex-classification cases, Scalia's sarcasm is patent:

> The *wonderful thing* about these statements is that they are not *actually false* – just as it would not be *actually false* to say that 'our cases have thus far reserved the 'beyond a reasonable doubt' standard of proof for criminal cases,' or that 'we have not equated tort actions, for all purposes to criminal prosecutions.'[177]

He is equally sarcastic elsewhere. When he criticizes the Court's dismissal of the District Court's evidentiary findings, he observes '[h]ow remarkable to criticize the District Court on the ground that its findings rest on the evidence.'[178] Shortly thereafter, he adds that the Court's misguided dismissal of the District Court findings 'makes evident that the parties to this [case] *could have saved themselves a great deal of time, trouble, and expense by omitting a trial*.'[179] As he concludes his dissent, Scalia repeats his accusation that the 'self-righteous Supreme Court' has created an unworkable standard of review while 'acting on its Members' personal view of what would make a 'more perfect Union,' (*a criterion only slightly more restrictive than a 'more perfect world*).[180]

When coupled with Scalia's milder ironical commentary, the unrelenting sarcastic tone of Scalia's criticisms is magnified and, ultimately, counterproductive. As Scalia repeatedly interrupts his substantive criticisms with ironical commentary, the tone of the dissent becomes increasingly sarcastic. This sarcasm, more than any other rhetorical device (except perhaps his name-calling), damages Justice Scalia's *ethos*, and with it, the persuasive impact of his arguments.[181]

Instead of projecting a positive *ethos* by evincing loyalty (to the Court as an institution), calmness (in making his points), goodwill (to his opponents), and a seemly modesty, Justice Scalia projects a negative *ethos* comprising disloyalty (to the Court as an institution), pride (in his own reasoning), intemperance (in his language), and abusiveness (toward his colleagues). In doing so, he ignores or misuses one of the most potent rhetorical tools available to an advocate – his credibility, or *ethos*.

CONCLUSION

In his discussion of 'style' in judicial opinions, Judge Posner of the Seventh Circuit offers several definitions of style, including the following: '[S]tyle' is what is left out by paraphrase.'[182] He adds that:

> Some judicial opinions – those written by the masters – would lose something, and maybe a lot, in being *paraphrased*. But their essential meaning would not be lost. Even the best, the most distinctive, the most eloquent judicial opinion could be rewritten in a very different style and yet convey enough of the meaning of the original to be considered a close substitute for it.[183]

Because Judge Posner focuses primarily on the *logos*, or logic, of an opinion, his point regarding paraphrase is an insightful, but incomplete, definition of rhetorical style. 'Style' in the Greco-Roman sense encompasses more than what is paraphrasable. As Judge Posner observes elsewhere, style also 'establish[es] a mood and perhaps a sense of the writer's personality.'[184]

As the summary near the beginning of this chapter shows, Justice Scalia's arguments are certainly paraphrasable. But a paraphrase cannot duplicate the emotional content of Justice Scalia's arguments, or the 'sense of the writer's personality' that pervades those arguments. For that reason a paraphrase, no matter how complete or exact, is potentially misleading because it eliminates Justice Scalia's polemical 'style.' And, as the foregoing analysis of Scalia's dissent shows, both the emotional impact (*pathos*) and the 'writer's personality' (*ethos*) are as important as logic (*logos*) in making Justice Scalia's arguments successful. They too are part of his 'style.'

To convince those who have not already made up their minds regarding the Virginia Military Institute's male-only admission policy, Justice Scalia must engage their emotions and convince them that he, in Quintilian's phrase, is 'a good man, skilled in speaking.'[185] Unfortunately for his arguments, Justice Scalia's advocacy is only partly successful. While he does succeed in arousing readers' emotions, he repeatedly squanders his emotional capital with gratuitous attacks that compromise his credibility.

While this assessment of Justice Scalia's persuasive abilities is certainly debatable, the 2500-year-old analytical technique whereby it was reached is not. Moreover, given its exhaustive attention to rhetorical detail, this technique can be usefully applied to almost all legal discourse. As the history of legal analysis demonstrates, insights into legal discourse frequently come from unexpected and non-traditional sources, usually bringing with them a deeper understanding of how that discourse succeeds or fails. Analyzing modern legal discourse using the tools created by Greco-Roman rhetoricians adds invaluable perspectives not only on judicial opinions, but on all forms of legal discourse.

Notes

1. Scholarship on the connections between modern and classical rhetorical principles includes: *A Synoptic History of Classical Rhetoric* (James J. Murphy ed. 1983); *A Short History of Writing Instruction* (James J. Murphy ed. 1990); *Learning From the Histories of Rhetoric* (Theresa Enos ed. 1993); Brian Vickers, *In Defence of Rhetoric* (1988); Kathleen E. Welch, *The Contemporary Reception of Classical Rhetoric: Appropriations of Ancient Discourse* (1990); Richard McKeon, *Rhetoric: Essays in Invention and Discovery* (1987).
2. On the subject of 'discovery' and the topics of invention see Richard J. Schoeck, 'The Practical Tradition of Classical Rhetoric,' in *Rhetoric and Praxis: The Contribution of Classical Rhetoric to Practical Reasoning* 28, note 3 (Jean Dietz Moss ed. 1986) ('It is a token of the lastingness of the symbiotic relation between law and rhetoric that in most Anglo-American jurisdictions discovery has meant ... that early stage in the examination of evidence by parties to action at law, or their attorneys ...')
3. American Heritage Dictionary 1494 (4th ed. 2000).
4. Liberal columnist David Broder characterized Scalia's dissent in Grutter v. Bollinger, 123 S. Ct. 2325 (an affirmative action case) as 'sarcastic, dismissive, polemical and smug.' (Washington Post June 29, 2003) and regards its 'patronizing' and 'insulting' tone as just the latest evidence of Scalia's lack of proper judicial temperament. Columnist Maureen O'Dowd characterizes the language in Scalia's dissent in Lawrence v. Texas, 123 S. Ct.2472 (a Texas anti-sodomy case) as 'blustery rants' and 'risibly out-of-date' (New York Times, June 29, 2003). She thinks Scalia is 'blinded by his own bloviation.' See also Alex Kozinski, 'My Pizza with Nino,' 12 Cardozo Law Review 1583, 1586 (1991) ('Scalia's dissents have been labelled "verbal hand grenades" and rightfully so. They are explosive. And, like hand grenades, they throw shrapnel at anyone near the blast without attention to who they are or how they might vote in the next case.')
5. American Heritage Dictionary 11 (4th ed. 2000).
6. PGA Tour, Inc. v. Martin, 532 U.S. 661, 692 (2001) (Scalia, J., dissenting).
7. PGA Tour, Inc. v. Martin, 532 U.S. at 701.
8. PGA Tour, Inc. v. Martin, 532 U.S. at 705 (emphasis added).
9. PGA Tour, Inc. v. Martin, 532 U.S. at 705 (emphasis added).
10. PGA Tour, Inc. v. Martin, 532 U.S. at 705 (emphasis added).
11. United States v. Virginia, 518 U.S. 515, 567 (1996) (Scalia, J., dissenting).
12. United States v. Virginia, 518 U.S. at 567.
13. United States v. Virginia, 518 U.S. at 567.
14. United States v. Virginia, 518 U.S. at 601.

15. United States v. Virginia, 518 U.S. at 567.
16. United States v. Virginia, 518 U.S. at 568.
17. United States v. Virginia, 518 U.S. at 574.
18. United States v. Virginia, 518 U.S. at 569.
19. United States v. Virginia, 518 U.S. at 589, note 5.
20. United States v. Virginia, 518 U.S. at 570.
21. United States v. Virginia, 518 U.S. at 600.
22. United States v. Virginia, 518 U.S. at 571.
23. See Kozinski, 'My Pizza with Nino,' at 1586; Patricia M. Wald, 'The Rhetoric of Results and the Results of Rhetoric: Judicial Writings,' 62 University of Chicago Law Review 1371, 1383 (1995) 'Regular dissenters such as Justice Scalia are particularly prone to stylish stabs.') See also Elizabeth Fajans and Mary R. Falk, 'Shooting from the Lip: United States v. Dickerson, Role [Im]morality, and the Ethics of Legal Rhetoric,' 23 University of Hawaii Law Review 1, 28-29 notes 129, 131 (2000) (asserting that 'Scalia's dissent in Dickerson III is ... hyperbolic' and that 'its assertion of intellectual superiority is offensive').
24. See Joyce J. George, *Judicial Opinion Writing Handbook* 186 (3rd ed. 1993) ('In writing an opinion, the writing judge is involved in a joint venture. The end product is not his opinion alone but rather that of all the members of the panel who form the majority ... Like the trial court decision, it is written by one judge. However, suggested revisions are made by the other participating judges and the opinion is a shared effort.'); Bernard E. Witkin, *Manual on Appellate Court Opinions* 83 (1977) ('In cases of exceptionally fine work, the responsive notes [of other judges] may be very enthusiastic. On the other hand, a Justice may disagree with major details of an opinion, and the result may be considerable revision or sharpening as the opinion goes through draft after draft to accommodate all of the suggestions. The writing judge may make extensive concessions either to keep his majority or to get as close to unanimity as possible') (quoting John P. Frank, *The Marble Palace* 119 (1958); Wald, 'The Rhetoric of Results' at 1377 ('[M]ost judges will compromise their preferred rationale and rhetoric to gain a full concurrence from other members of the panel. In an appellate court composed of strong-minded men and women of different political and personal philosophies, consensus is a formidable constraint on what an opinion writer says and how she says it. Her best lines are often left on the cutting room floor.')
25. Judge Joyce George, former judge of the Ohio Court of Appeals, stresses the need for objectivity. See George, *Judicial Opinion Writing Handbook* at 422 ('The individual technique used by the writer to express the decision made, as well as the reasons for the decision, should be *neutral, detached, objective, and impersonal*' [emphasis added]). In his famous 'Law and Literature' essay, Justice Cardozo calls writing of this kind 'the type magisterial or imperative.'
26. Judge Patricia Wald, former Chief Judge of the U.S. Court of Appeals (D.C. Cir.), makes the point that '[a] dissenter is admitting she has not been able to convince her colleagues ...' Wald, 'The Rhetoric of Results and the Results of Rhetoric' at 1412.
27. Bernard E. Witkin, *Manual on Appellate Court Opinions* 225 (1977).
28. Witkin, *Manual on Appellate Court Opinions* at 226-27.
29. George, *Judicial Opinion Writing Handbook* 224 (3rd ed. 1993).
30. George, *Judicial Opinion Writing Handbook* at 224 (emphasis added).
31. Witkin, *Manual on Appellate Court Opinions* at 226. 'My own view, however, is that most dissents do much more harm than good. They foster resentment on the part of the losing party, they encourage groundless appeals and they introduce an element of uncertainty

where certainty should if possible prevail' (quoting Judge John J. Parker, *Improving Appellate Methods*, 25 New York University Law Review 13 [1950]).

32. Wald, 'The Rhetoric of Results and the Results of Rhetoric' at 1412 ('A dissent speaks to the rest of the court, to courts in other places, to higher courts, to *Congress, to future generations; it brings no hope of present reward or vindication*') (emphasis added).

33. George, *Judicial Opinion Writing Handbook* at 223 ('The dissenter should not attack the majority. The reasons compelling the dissent should be expressed clearly without intemperance, insinuations, or allegations of incompetence.')

34. Witkin, *Manual on Appellate Court Opinions* at 226-27 (quoting Herbert B. Gregory, *Shorter Judicial Opinions*, 34 Virginia Law Review 362, 366 [1948]).

35. George, *Judicial Opinion Writing Handbook* at 223.

36. Wald, 'The Rhetoric of Results and the Results of Rhetoric' at 1413 ('A dissent is liberating. No other judge need agree or even be consulted. Exuberant (or excess) prose is unconstrained.')

37. Richard A. Posner, 'Judges' Writing Styles (And Do They Matter?),' 62 University of Chicago Law Review 1421, 1436 (1995) ('A [judicial] writing has an implied author (a "voice" in a sense that goes beyond signature) as well as an actual author. The implied author is the author whose character and values we infer from the writing itself, as distinct from the character and values that we might infer from a personal acquaintanceship with the author or from a good biography of him.'

38. See George, *Judicial Opinion Writing Handbook* at 421. See also Witkin, *Manual on Appellate Court Opinions* at 233 ('Some commentators have therefore cautioned against taking the position of *an advocate* in an attack on the majority opinion or its authors' [emphasis added]).

39. See Wald, 'The Rhetoric of Results and the Results of Rhetoric' at 1412 ('A dissent speaks to the rest of the court, to courts in other places, to higher courts, to Congress, to future generations ...')

40. One exception to this general approach appears in Fajans and Falk, 'Shooting from the Lip: United States v. Dickerson, Role [Im]morality, and the Ethics of Legal Rhetoric,' 23 University of Hawaii Law Review 1, 28-29 notes 129 and 131 (2000). The authors analyze the rhetoric of the Court's opinion as well as some of Justice Scalia's dissent.

41. Aristotle, *Rhetoric* at 7.

42. 3 Quintilian, *Institutio Oratoria* 185 (emphasis added).

43. Classical rhetoricians created these divisions for purposes of analysis and discussion, but did not consider *logos, pathos*, and *ethos* as completely separable from one another. Each part is connected to and helps define the others. Aristotle, *Rhetoric* at 8. For an extended discussion of the part *ethos* plays in modern legal discourse see Chapter Four. See also 1 Quintilian, at 397 ('There are ... three aims which the orator must always have in view; he must instruct, move and charm his hearers.')

44. United States v. Virginia, 518 U.S. 515, 567 (1996) (Scalia, J., dissenting).

45. United States v. Virginia, 518 U.S. at 530 (citation omitted).

46. United States v. Virginia, 518 U.S. at 530-31 (citation omitted).

47. J.E.B. v. Alabama *ex rel.* T.B., 511 U.S. 127 (1994).

48. Mississippi Univ. for Women v. Hogan, 458 U.S. 718 (1982).

49. United States v. Virginia, 518 U.S. at 531 (emphasis added).

50. United States v. Virginia, 518 U.S. at 533.

51. United States v. Virginia, 518 U.S. at 534 (citation omitted).

52. United States v. Virginia, 518 U.S. at 535.

53. United States v. Virginia, 518 U.S. at 535.

54. United States v. Virginia, 518 U.S. at 540.
55. United States v. Virginia, 518 U.S. at 543-45.
56. United States v. Virginia, 518 U.S. at 545.
57. United States v. Virginia, 518 U.S. at 547 (citation omitted).
58. United States v. Virginia, 518 U.S. at 526-27.
59. United States v. Virginia, 518 U.S. at 551.
60. United States v. Virginia, 518 U.S. at 555-56.
61. United States v. Virginia, 518 U.S. at 567.
62. United States v. Virginia, 518 U.S. at 568 (citation omitted).
63. United States v. Virginia, 518 U.S. at 572.
64. United States v. Virginia, 518 U.S. at 574.
65. United States v. Virginia, 518 U.S. at 573.
66. United States v. Virginia, 518 U.S. at 579.
67. United States v. Virginia, 518 U.S. at 576 (citation omitted).
68. United States v. Virginia, 518 U.S. at 584.
69. United States v. Virginia, 518 U.S. at 585.
70. United States v. Virginia, 518 U.S. at 590-91.
71. United States v. Virginia, 518 U.S. at 592-93.
72. United States v. Virginia, 518 U.S. at 596.
73. United States v. Virginia, 518 U.S. at 597.
74. United States v. Virginia, 518 U.S. at 598.
75. United States v. Virginia, 518 U.S. at 601.
76. For a detailed discussion of the topic of arrangement in legal discourse see Chapter Three.
77. Aristotle, *Rhetoric* at 223-24.
78. 3 Cicero, *De Oratore* at 435.
79. 3 Cicero, *De Oratore* at 325.
80. 2 Quintilian, *Institutio Oratoria* at 19.
81. 3 Quintilian, *Institutio Oratoria* at 181 (emphasis added).
82. United States v. Virginia, 518 U.S. at 566 (Emphasis added).
83. For examples of Justice Scalia's dissents that employ low-key, non-emotional opening paragraphs, see Ornelas v. United States, 517 U.S. 690, 700 (1996) (Scalia, J., dissenting) (a standard of review case); and Saratoga Fishing Co. v. J.M. Martinac and Co., 520 U.S. 875, 885-86 (1997) (Scalia, J., dissenting) (a products liability case). But see Romer v. Evans, 517 U.S. 620, 636 (1996) (Scalia, J., dissenting) (an Equal Protection case) (Justice Scalia opens his dissent with 'The Court has mistaken a Kulturkampf for a fit of spite'); and J.E.B. v. Alabama ex rel. T.B., 511 U.S. 127, 156-57 (1994) (Scalia, J., dissenting) (an Equal Protection case) (where Justice Scalia opens with 'Today's opinion is an inspiring demonstration of how thoroughly up-to-date and right-thinking we Justices are in matters pertaining to the sexes (or as the Court would have it, the genders), and how sternly we disapprove the male chauvinist attitudes of our predecessors.')
84. *Rhetorica ad Herennium* at 31.
85. 2 Quintilian, *Institutio Oratoria* at 149 (Emphasis added).
86. United States v. Virginia, 518 U.S. at 566.
87. 3 Quintilian *Institutio Oratoria* at 461.
88. 3 Quintilian *Institutio Oratoria* at 463 (emphasis added).
89. United States v. Virginia, 518 U.S. at 566.
90. United States v. Virginia, 518 U.S. at 566.
91. *Rhetorica ad Herennium* at 381 and 383 (emphasis added).
92. United States v. Virginia, 518 U.S. at 519.

93. See George, *Judicial Opinion Writing Handbook* at 422.
94. Aristotle, *Rhetoric* at 240.
95. 2 Quintilian, *Institutio Oratoria* at 417.
96. 2 Quintilian, *Institutio Oratoria* at 391.
97. 2 Quintilian, *Institutio Oratoria* at 21 (first emphasis added).
98. United States v. Virginia, 518 U.S. at 601 (1996) (Scalia, J., dissenting).
99. United States v. Virginia, 518 U.S. at 602 (emphasis added).
100. United States v. Virginia, 518 U.S. at 602-03.
101. United States v. Virginia, 518 U.S. at 603. Justice Scalia relies on the emotion-charged figure of the knight errant in another dissent as well. In Romer v. Evans, 517 U.S. 620, 652 (1996) (Scalia, J., dissenting) (an Equal Protection case), Scalia maintains that '[w]hen the Court takes sides in the culture wars, it tends to be with the knights rather than the villains – and more specifically with the Templars, reflecting the views and values of the lawyer class from which the Court's Members are drawn.'
102. United States v. Virginia, 518 U.S. at 603. Rhetorically speaking, Justice Ginsburg attempts a bit more with her *peroratio* than she did with her *exordium*. Her opening makes an emotional appeal based on an ever-evolving sense of constitutional rights. Her opinion closes as follows:

    A prime part of the history of our Constitution, historian Richard Morris recounted, is the story of the extension of constitutional rights and protections to people once ignored or excluded. VMI's story continued as our comprehension of 'We the People' expanded. There is no reason to believe that the admission of women capable of all the activities required of VMI cadets would destroy the Institute rather than enhance its capacity to serve the 'more perfect Union'(citations and footnotes omitted).

    However, even this example is tepid when compared with Justice Scalia's command of the forceful climatic paragraph. In the recent case of PGA Tour, Inc. v. Martin, 532 U.S. 661, 705 (2001) (Scalia, J., dissenting), he concludes his dissent, from the majority opinion allowing disabled golfer Casey Martin to use a golf cart during tournaments, with the following paragraph:

    Complaints about this case are not 'properly directed to Congress.' They are properly directed to this Court's *Kafkaesque* determination that professional sports organizations, and the fields they rent for their exhibitions, are 'places of public accommodation' to the competing athletes, and the athletes themselves 'customers' of the organization that pays them; its *Alice in Wonderland* determination that there are such things as judicially determinable 'essential' and 'nonessential' rules of a made-up game; and its *Animal Farm* determination that fairness and the ADA means that everyone gets to play by individualized rules which will assure that no one's lack of ability (or at least no one's lack of ability so pronounced that it amounts to a disability) will be a handicap. The year was 2001, and 'everybody was finally equal' (emphasis added).

103. Aristotle, *Rhetoric* at 182.
104. 3 Quintilian, *Institutio Oratoria* at 359 (emphasis added).
105. 3 Quintilian, *Institutio Oratoria* at 359 (first and last emphases added).
106. For a fuller discussion of metaphors in legal argument see Chapter Five.
107. Metaphors function in the same way as examples do in inductive proofs. See Aristotle, *Rhetoric* at 147-49; 1 Cicero, *De Inventione* at 89 and 91; and 2 Quintilian, *Institutio Oratoria* at 275-76.
108. Aristotle, *Rhetoric* at 206 (emphasis added).

109. 3 Cicero, *De Oratore*, at 125 (Readers respond favorably to metaphors because their 'thoughts are led to something else and yet without going astray, which is a very great pleasure.')
110. 3 Quintilian, *Institutio Oratoria* at 213.
111. United States v. Virginia, 518 U.S. 515, 584 (1996).
112. United States v. Virginia at 593.
113. Justice Scalia's penchant for highly kinetic metaphors can be seen in other dissents as well. For example, in Lee v. Weisman, 505 U.S. 577, 632 (1992) (Scalia, J., dissenting) (an Establishment Clause case), he accuses the majority of destroying a long-standing tradition of non-sectarian prayer at graduation ceremonies using '[a]s its instrument of destruction, the bulldozer of its social engineering, [with which] the Court invents a boundless, and boundlessly manipulable, test of psychological coercion.'
114. United States v. Virginia, 518 U.S. at 568.
115. United States v. Virginia, 518 U.S. at 574.
116. United States v. Virginia, 518 U.S. at 589, note 5.
117. United States v. Virginia, 518 U.S. at 600.
118. United States v. Virginia, 518 U.S. at 569.
119. United States v. Virginia, 518 U.S. at 572.
120. United States v. Virginia, 518 U.S. at 572.
121. United States v. Virginia, 518 U.S. at 587 (emphasis added).
122. Aristotle, *Rhetoric* at 204-05 (emphasis added).
123. See 2 Cicero, *Topica* 413, 415; 3 Quintilian, *Institutio Oratoria* at 325 and 439, 441; *Rhetorica ad Herennium* at 381and 383.
124. Aristotle, *Rhetoric* at 214.
125. United States v. Virginia, 518 U.S. at 592 (emphasis added).
126. United States v. Virginia, 518 U.S. at 592.
127. United States v. Virginia, 518 U.S. at 600 (emphasis added).
128. 3 Quintilian, *Institutio Oratoria* at 377.
129. 3 Quintilian, *Institutio Oratoria* at 379 and 381.
130. 3 Quintilian, *Institutio Oratoria* at 379 and 381.
131. United States v. Virginia, 518 U.S. at 587.
132. United States v. Virginia, 518 U.S. at 587.
133. United States v. Virginia, 518 U.S. at 592.
134. United States v. Virginia, 518 U.S. at 600.
135. Aristotle, *Rhetoric* at 91 (emphasis added).
136. Aristotle, *Rhetoric* at 92 (emphasis added).
137. Aristotle, *Rhetoric* at 223-24 (emphasis added). For modern recognition of this point, see Chapter Four. See also Posner, 'Judges' Writing Styles (And Do They Matter?), 62 University of Chicago Law Review 1421-1436 ('The creation of the implied author corresponds to the ethical appeal in classical rhetoric – that is, to the devices by which a speaker tries to convince his audience that he is the kind of person who is worthy of belief.')
138. 3 Cicero, *De Oratore*, at 327, 329 (emphasis added).
139. 3 Cicero, *De Oratore*, at 329 (emphasis added).
140. 3 Cicero, *De Oratore*, at 331.
141. 2 Quintilian, *Institutio Oratoria* at 423.
142. 2 Quintilian, *Institutio Oratoria* at 423 (second emphasis added).
143. 2 Quintilian, *Institutio Oratoria* at 11 (emphasis added).
144. 2 Quintilian, *Institutio Oratoria* at 427.

145. United States v. Virginia, 518 U.S. at 602 (1996).
146. See Fajans and Falk, 'Shooting from the Lip: United States v. Dickerson, Role [Im]morality, and the Ethics of Legal Rhetoric,' 23 University of Hawaii Law Review 1, note 33.
147. 3 Quintilian, *Institutio Oratoria* at 197.
148. Aristotle, *Rhetoric* at 186 (emphasis added).
149. Aristotle, *Rhetoric* at 186. Cicero also recommended that new coinages be sparingly used, 4 Cicero, *De Oratore* at 161.
150. 3 Quintilian, *Institutio Oratoria* at 189 (emphasis added).
151. United States v. Virginia, 518 U.S. at 600.
152. United States v. Virginia, 518 U.S. at 589 note 5.
153. United States v. Virginia, 518 U.S. at 574.
154. United States v. Virginia, 518 U.S. at 568 (emphasis added).
155. United States v. Virginia, 518 U.S. at 596 (emphasis added).
156. Justice Scalia's penchant for 'artificial' coinages and slangy phrasings is evident in other dissents as well. See, e.g., Lee v. Weisman, 505 U.S. 577, 631-32 (1992) (Scalia, J., dissenting) ('In holding that the Establishment Clause prohibits invocations and benedictions at public school graduation ceremonies, the Court – with *nary a mention* that it is doing so – lays waste a tradition that is as old as public school graduation ceremonies ...' [emphasis added]). Elsewhere in his Weisman dissent, Scalia asserts that the majority opinion is based on a 'psycho-journey' which results in a 'psycho-coercion' test. Weisman, 505 U.S. at 643-44.
157. United States v. Virginia, 518 U.S. at 567 (emphasis added).
158. United States v. Virginia, 518 U.S. at 581 (second emphasis added).
159. United States v. Virginia, 518 U.S. at 597 (emphasis added).
160. Aristotle, *Rhetoric* at 216 (emphasis added).
161. 3 Quintilian, *Institutio Oratoria* at 345.
162. 3 Quintilian, *Institutio Oratoria* at 343.
163. Scalia writes:

> Today the Court shuts down an institution that has served the people of the Commonwealth of Virginia with pride and distinction for over a century and a half. To achieve that desired result, it rejects (contrary to our established practice) the factual findings ... *sweeps aside the precedents* of the Court, and *ignores the history* of our people. *As to facts*: It explicitly rejects the finding that there exist 'gender-based developmental differences' supporting Virginia's restriction of the 'adversative' method to only a men's institution, and the finding that the all-male composition of the Virginia Military Institute (VMI) is essential to that institution's character. *As to precedent*: It drastically revises our established standards for reviewing sex-based classifications. And, as to history: It counts for nothing the long tradition, enduring down to the present, of men's military colleges supported by both States and the Federal Government.

United States v. Virginia, 518 U.S. at 566 (emphasis added).
164. United States v. Virginia, 518 U.S. at 566.
165. Aristotle, *Rhetoric* at 216.
166. United States v. Virginia, 518 U.S. at 567.
167. United States v. Virginia, 518 U.S. at 568.
168. United States v. Virginia, 518 U.S. at 599.
169. 2 Quintilian, *Institutio Oratoria* at 11.
170. 3 Quintilian, *Institutio Oratoria* at 401.

171. Aristotle, *Rhetoric* at 98.
172. Aristotle, *Rhetoric* at 240.
173. 3 Quintilian, *Institutio Oratoria* at 401, 403.
174. United States v. Virginia, 518 U.S. at 567 (emphasis added).
175. United States v. Virginia, 518 U.S. at 595 (emphasis added).
176. United States v. Virginia, 518 U.S. at 600 (emphasis added).
177. United States v. Virginia, 518 U.S. at 574 (emphasis added).
178. United States v. Virginia, 518 U.S. at 585 (emphasis added).
179. United States v. Virginia, 518 U.S. at 585(emphasis added).
180. United States v. Virginia, 518 U.S. at 601 (emphasis added) (citations omitted). *Cf.* Lee v. Weisman, 505 U.S. 577, 644 (1992) (Scalia, J., dissenting) (an Establishment Clause case) ('*Another happy aspect* of the case is that it is *only a jurisprudential disaster* and not a practical one'). (emphasis added).
181. In the PGA Tour v. Martin case, Scalia's self-indulgent sarcasm is displayed at great length:

> It has been rendered the solemn duty of the Supreme Court of the United States, laid upon it by Congress in pursuance of the Federal Government's power '[t]o regulate Commerce with foreign Nations, and among the several States,' to decide What is Golf. I am sure that the Framers of the Constitution, aware of the 1447 edict of King James II of Scotland prohibiting golf because it interfered with the practice of archery, fully expected that sooner or later the paths of golf and government, the law and the links, would once again cross, and that the judges of this August Court would some day have to wrestle with that age-old jurisprudential question, for which their years of study in the law have so well prepared them: Is someone riding around a golf course from shot to shot really a golfer.

PGA Tour v. Martin, 532 U.S. 661, 700 (2001) (Scalia, J., dissenting).
182. Posner, 'Judges' Writing Style' at 1422.
183. Posner, 'Judges' Writing Style' at 1423.
184. Posner, 'Judges' Writing Style' at 1422.
185. 4 Quintilian, *Institutio Oratoria* at 355.

Bibliography

Primary Sources

Anonymous, *Rhetorica ad Herennium* (H. Caplan trans. 1954).
Aristotle, *The Rhetoric of Aristotle* (Lane Cooper trans. 1932).
Aristotle, *The Art of Rhetoric* (H.C. Lawson-Tancred trans. 1991).
Aristotle, *Aristotle's Poetics: A Translation and Commentary for Students of Literature* Leon Golden trans. 1968).
Aristotle, *Aristotle's Prior and Posterior Analytics* (W.D. Ross trans. 1957).
Marcus Tullius Cicero, *Brutus* (G.L. Hendrickson trans. 2001 ed.); *De Inventione* (H.M. Hubbell trans. 1949); *De Optimo Genere Oratorum* (H.M. Hubbell trans. 1949); *Orator* (H.M. Hubbell trans. 1939); *De Partitione Oratoria* (H. Rackham trans. 1921); *Topica* (H.M. Hubbell trans. 1949); *De Oratore* (E.W. Sutton and H. Rackham trans. 1942).
Marcus Fabius Quintilianus, *Institutio Oratoria* (H.E. Butler trans. 1954).

Secondary Sources on Rhetoric and Ancient History

Adams, John Quincy, *Lectures on Rhetoric and Oratory* (Russell & Russell, Inc. 1962 ed.; 1810).
Aldisert, Ruggero J., *Logic for Lawyers: A Guide to Clear Legal Thinking* (1989).
Barfield, Owen, *Poetic Diction: A Study in Meaning* (1964).
Berlin, James A., *Writing Instruction in Nineteenth-Century American Colleges* (1984).
Burke, Kenneth, *Counterstatement* (1953).
Burton, Steven J., *An Introduction to Law and Legal Reasoning* (2nd ed. 1995).
Campbell, George, *The Philosophy of Rhetoric* (Lloyd F. Bitzer ed. 1963).
Corbett, Edward P.J., *Classical Rhetoric for the Modern Student* (2nd ed. 1971).
Crook, J. A., *Legal Advocacy in the Roman World* (1995); *Law and Life of Rome* (1967).
Enos, Richard L., *The Literate Mode of Cicero's Legal Rhetoric* (1988).
Enos, Theresa, ed., *Learning from the Histories of Rhetoric* (1993).
Frier, Bruce W., *The Rise of the Roman Jurists: Studies in Cicero's* Pro Caecina (1985).
Horner, Winifred Bryan, *Rhetoric in the Classical Tradition* (1988).
Jolowicz, H.F. and Barry Nicholas, *Historical Introduction to the Study of Roman Law* (1972).
Kennedy, George A., *The Art of Rhetoric in the Roman World* (1972); *Classical Rhetoric and its Christian and Secular Tradition from Ancient to Modern Times* (1980); *A New History of Classical Rhetoric* (1994).
Martin, Thomas R., *Ancient Greece: From Prehistoric to Hellenistic Times* (2000).
McCall, Jr., March H., *Ancient Rhetorical Theories of Simile and Comparison* (1969).

McKeon, Richard, *Rhetoric: Essays in Invention and Discovery* (Mark Backman ed. 1987).

Mellinkoff, David, *The Language of the Law* (1963).

Murphy, James ed., *A Synoptic History of Classical Rhetoric* (1983).

Perelman, Chaim, *The Idea of Justice and the Problem of Argument* (John Petrie trans. 1963).

Chaim Perelman and L. Olbrechts-Tyteca, *The New Rhetoric: A Treatise on Argumentation* (John Wilkinson and Purcell Weaver trans. 1969).

Posner, Richard A., *Law and Literature: A Misunderstood Relation* (1988).

Russell, David R., *Writing in the Academic Disciplines* (1991).

Vickers, Brian, *In Defence of Rhetoric* (1988).

Watson, Alan, *The Spirit of Roman Law* (1995).

Welch, Kathleen E., *The Contemporary Reception of Classical Rhetoric: Appropriations of Ancient Discourse* (1990).

White, James B., *The Legal Imagination: Studies in the Nature of Legal Thought and Expression* (1973).

Winterowd, W. Ross, *A Teacher's Introduction to Composition in the Rhetorical Tradition* (1994).

Secondary Sources on Legal Writing

Armstrong, Stephen V. and Timothy P. Terrell, *Thinking Like a Writer: A Lawyer's Guide to Effective Writing and Editing* (1992).

Board of Student Advisers, Harvard Law School, *Introduction to Advocacy* (7th ed. 2002).

Bosmajian, Haig, *Metaphor and Reason in Judicial Opinions* (1992).

Calleros, Charles R., *Legal Method and Writing* (3rd ed. 1998).

Charrow, Veda et al., *Clear and Effective Legal Writing* (3rd ed. 2001).

Cooper, Frank E., *Writing in Law Practice* (2nd ed. 1963).

Edwards, Linda, *Legal Writing: Process, Analysis, and Organization* (3rd ed. 2002)

Garner, Bryan A., *Legal Writing in Plain English* (2001).

Gilmer, Jr., Wesley, *Legal Research, Writing and Advocacy* (1987).

George, Joyce J., *Judicial Opinion Writing Handbook* (3rd ed. 1993).

Huhn, Wilson, *The Five Types of Argument* (2002).

Neumann, Jr. and Richard K., *Legal Reasoning and Legal Writing: Structure, Strategy and Style* (4th ed. 2001).

Oates, Laurel Currie and Anne Enquist, *Just Briefs* (2003).

Peck, Girvan G., *Writing Persuasive Briefs* (1984).

Porter, Karen K. et al., *Introduction to Legal Writing and Oral Advocacy* (1989).

Rambo, Teresa J. Reid and Leanne J. Pflaum, *Legal Writing by Design: A Guide to Great Briefs and Memos* (2001).

Ray, Mary Barnard and Barbara J. Cox, *Beyond the Basics: A Text for Advanced Legal Writing* (1991).

Re, Edward D., *Brief Writing and Oral Argument* (6th ed. 1987).

Schultz, Nancy L. and Louis J. Sirico, Jr., *Legal Writing and Other Lawyering Skills* (3rd ed. 1998).
Shapo, Helene S. et al., *Writing and Analysis in the Law* (4th ed. 1999).
Smith, Michael R., *Advanced Legal Writing: Theories and Strategies in Persuasive Writing* (2002).
Smith, Robert B., *The Literate Lawyer: Legal Writing and Oral Advocacy* (1986).
Squires, Lynn L. et al., *Legal Writing in a Nutshell* (2nd ed. 1996).
Statsky, William P. and R. John Wernet, *Case Analysis and Fundamentals of Legal Writing* (3rd ed. 1989).
Weihofen, Henry, *Legal Writing Style* (1961).
Weiner, Frederick B., *Briefing and Arguing Federal Appeals* (1967).
Wellford, Robin S., *Legal Reasoning, Writing, and Persuasive Argument* (2002)
Witkin, Bernard E., *Manual on Appellate Court Opinions* (1977).

Secondary Sources on Trial and Appellate Advocacy

Berry, Carole C., *Effective Appellate Advocacy: Brief Writing and Oral Advocacy* (3rd ed. 2003).
Carlson, Ronald L. and Edward J. Imwinkelried, *Dynamics of Trial Practice: Problems and Materials* (1989).
Dubin, Lawrence A. and Thomas F. Guernsey, *Trial Practice* (1991).
Frederick, David C., *The Art of Oral Advocacy* (2003); *Supreme Court and Appellate Advocacy* (2003).
Hartje, Jeffrey J. and Mark E. Wilson, *Lawyers' Work* (1984).
Mauet, Thomas, *Fundamentals of Trial Techniques* (3rd ed. 1992); *Trial Techniques* (6th ed. 2002).
Rumsey D. Lake, ed., *Master Advocates' Handbook* (1986).
Stark, Steven D., *Writing to Win: The Legal Writer* (1999).

Essays on Rhetoric and Legal Writing

Amsterdam, Anthony G. and Randy Hertz, 'An Analysis of Closing Arguments to a Jury,' 37 New York Law School Law Review 55 (1992).
Backman, Mark, 'Richard McKeon and the Renaissance of Rhetoric,' in *Rhetoric: Essays in Invention and Discovery* (Mark Backman ed. 1987).
Bosmajian, Haig, 'The Judiciary's Use of Metaphors, Metonymies and Other Tropes to Give First Amendment Protection to Students and Teachers,' 15 Journal of Law and Education 443 (1986).
Brosnahan, James J., 'Overview: Basic Principles of Advocacy,' in *Master Advocates' Handbook* (D. Lake Rumsey, ed. 1986).
Burke, Kenneth, 'The Five Master Terms: Their Place in a "Dramatistic" Grammar of Motives,' in *Landmark Essays on Rhetorical Invention in Writing* (Richard Young and Yameng Liu eds. 1994).

Cardozo, Benjamin N., 'Law and Literature' *Selected Writing* 342 (1947).

Connors, Robert J. et al., 'The Revival of Rhetoric in America,' in *Essays in Classical Rhetoric and Modern Discourse* (Robert Connors, Lisa Ede and Andrea Lunsford eds. 1984).

Fajans, Elizabeth and Mary R. Falk, 'Shooting from the Lip: United States v. Dickerson, Role [Im]morality, and the Ethics of Legal Rhetoric,' 23 University of Hawaii Law Review 1 (2000).

Fletcher, George P., 'Fairness and Utility in Tort Theory,' 85 Harvard Law Review 571-73 (1972).

Graves, Richard L., 'Symmetrical Form and the Rhetoric of the Sentence,' in *Essays on Classical Rhetoric and Modern Discourse* (Robert Connors, Lisa Ede and Andrea Lunsford eds. 1984).

S. Michael Halloran, and Merrill D. Whitburn, 'Ciceronian Rhetoric and the Rise of Science: The Plain Style Reconsidered', in *The Rhetorical Tradition and Modern Writing* (James J. Murphy ed. 1982).

Hanley, Robert F., 'Brush Up Your Aristotle,' 12 Litigation 39, No. 2 (Winter 1986).

Henly, Burr, '"Penumbra": The Roots of a Legal Metaphor,' 15 Hastings Constitutional Law Quarterly 82 (1987).

Hill, Forbes I., 'The Rhetoric of Aristotle,' in *A Synoptic History of Classical Rhetoric* (James J. Murphy ed. 1983).

Hill, James C., 'The Importance of Sincerity,' in *Master Advocates' Handbook* (D. Lake Rumsey ed. 1986).

Holmes, Oliver Wendell, 'The Theory of Torts,' 7 American Law Review 652, 654 (1873), reprinted in 44 Harvard Law Review 773 (1931).

Jamar, Steven D., 'Aristotle Teaches Persuasion: The Psychic Connection,' 8 Scribes Journal of Legal Writing 61 (2001-2002).

Johnson, Nan, 'Three Nineteenth-Century Rhetoricians: The Humanist Alternative to Rhetoric as Skills Management,' in *The Rhetorical Tradition and Modern Writing* 106 (James J. Murphy ed. 1982).

Jossen, Robert J., 'Opening Statements,' in *Master Advocates' Handbook* (D. Lake Rumsey ed. 1986); 'Opening Statements: Win it in the Opening,' 10 *The Docket* 1 (1986).

Keating, Karl, 'Winning With Aristotle: The Four Kinds of Arguments' 52 California State Bar Journal 308 (1977).

Kinneavy, James L., 'Translating Theory into Practice in Teaching Composition: A Historical View and a Contemporary View,' in *Essays on Classical Rhetoric and Modern Discourse* (Robert J. Connors et al. eds. 1984).

Kozinski, Alex, 'My Pizza with Nino,' 12 Cardozo Law Review 1583 (1991).

Lanni, Adriann, 'Precedent and Legal Reasoning in Athenian Courts: A Noble Lie?' 43 American Journal of Legal History 27 (1999).

Lloyd-Jones, Richard, 'Using the History of Rhetoric,' in *Learning from the Histories of Rhetoric: Essays in Honor of Winifred Bryan Horner* 20 (Theresa Enos ed. 1993).

Maio, Dennis Peter '*Politeia* and Adjudication in Fourth-Century B.C. Athens,' 28 American Journal of Jurisprudence 16 (1983).

Miller, Susan, 'Classical Practice and Contemporary Basics,' in *The Rhetorical Tradition and Modern Writing* (James J. Murphy ed. 1982).

Miller, Thomas P., 'Reinventing Rhetorical Traditions,' in *Learning from the Histories of Rhetoric: Essays in Honor of Winifred Bryan Horner* (Theresa Enos ed. 1993).

Moss, Jean Dietz, 'Prologomenon: The Revival of Practical Reasoning,' in *Rhetoric and Praxis: The Contribution of Classical Rhetoric to Practical Reasoning* (Jean Dietz Moss ed. 1986).

Murphy, James J., 'Roman Writing Instruction as Described by Quintilian,' in *A Short History of Writing Instruction from Ancient Greece to Twentieth-Century America* (James J. Murphy ed. 1990).

Murray, Edward L., 'The Phenomenon of the Metaphor: Some Theoretical Considerations,' 2 Duquesne Studies in Phenomenological Psychology 288 (A. Giorgi, C. Fischer and E. Murray, eds. 1975).

Murray, James E., 'Understanding Law as Metaphor,' 34 Journal of Legal Education 714 (1984).

Ochs, Donovan J., 'Cicero's Rhetorical Theory,' in *A Synoptic History of Classical Rhetoric* (James J. Murphy ed. 1983).

Perlman, Peter, 'Jury Selection,' *Master Advocates' Handbook* (D. Lake Rumsey, ed. 1986).

Posner, Richard A., 'Judges' Writing Styles (And Do They Matter?),' 62 University of Chicago Law Review 1421 (1995).

Schoeck, Richard J., 'Lawyers and Rhetoric in Sixteenth-Century England,' in *Renaissance Eloquence: Studies in the Theory and Practice of Renaissance Rhetoric* (James J. Murphy ed. 1983); 'The Practical Tradition of Classical Rhetoric,' in *Rhetoric and Praxis: The Contribution of Classical Rhetoric to Practical Reasoning* (Jean Dietz Moss ed. 1986).

Speiser, Stuart M., 'Closing Argument,' *Master Advocates' Handbook* at 236.

Vero, J.P., 'Nine Secrets for Living with Judges,' 17 Litigation 18 (1991).

Wald, Patricia M., 'The Rhetoric of Results and the Results of Rhetoric: Judicial Writings,' 62 University of Chicago Law Review 1371 (1995).

Winter, Steven L., 'Transcendental Nonsense, Metaphoric Reasoning and the Cognitive Stakes for Law,' 137 University of Pennsylvania Law Review 1105 (1989); 'Death is the Mother of Metaphor,' 105 Harvard Law Review 745 (1992).

Woods, Marjorie Curry, 'The Teaching of Writing in Medieval Europe,' in *A Short History of Writing Instruction from Ancient Greece to Twentieth-Century America* (James J. Murphy ed. 1990).

Dictionaries and Reference Books

American Heritage Dictionary (4th ed. 2000).

Cassell's New Compact Latin Dictionary (D.P. Simpson ed. 1971).

Princeton Encyclopedia of Poetry and Poetics (Alex Preminger ed. 1965).

Webster's Third New International Dictionary (1981).

Index

Printed in Great Britain
by Amazon